Mobile Commerce Application Development

Lei-da Chen
Creighton University, USA

Gordon Skelton
Jackson State University, USA

CYBERTECH PUBLISHING
Hershey • London • Melbourne • Singapore

Acquisitions Editor: Renée Davies
Development Editor: Kristin Roth
Senior Managing Editor: Amanda Appicello
Managing Editor: Jennifer Neidig
Copy Editor: Jennifer Young
Typesetter: Cindy Consonery
Cover Design: Lisa Tosheff
Printed at: Yurchak Printing Inc.

Published in the United States of America by
CyberTech Publishing (an imprint of Idea Group Inc.)
701 E. Chocolate Avenue
Hershey PA 17033
Tel: 717-533-8845
Fax: 717-533-8661
E-mail: cust@idea-group.com
Web site: http://www.cybertech-pub.com

and in the United Kingdom by
CyberTech Publishing (an imprint of Idea Group Inc.)
3 Henrietta Street
Covent Garden
London WC2E 8LU
Tel: 44 20 7240 0856
Fax: 44 20 7379 3313
Web site: http://www.eurospan.co.uk

Library of Congress Cataloging-in-Publication Data

Chen, Lei-da, 1973-
Mobile commerce application development / Lei-da Chen and Gordon W. Skelton.
p. cm.
Summary: "This book provides in-depth coverage of the various tools and techniques for developing wireless and mobile applications"--Provided by publisher.
Includes bibliographical references and index.
ISBN 1-59140-806-7 (hardcover) -- ISBN 1-59140-602-1 (soft cover) -- ISBN 1-59140-603-X (ebook)
1. Mobile commerce. 2. Wireless communication systems. 3. Mobile communication systems. I. Skelton, Gordon W. II. Title.
HF5548.34.C46 2005
006.7--dc22

2005004521

British Cataloguing in Publication Data
A Cataloguing in Publication record for this book is available from the British Library.

All work contributed to this book is new, previously-unpublished material. The views expressed in this book are those of the authors, but not necessarily of the publisher.

Mobile Commerce Application Development

Table of Contents

Preface .... **vii**

Acknowledgments .... **xi**

Chapter I.
Introduction to M-Business Applications: Value Proposition, Applications, Technologies, and Challenges **1**

Introduction *1*
Value Proposition *2*
M-Business Applications *3*
M-Business Technologies *13*
M-Business vs. E-Business Applications *15*
Challenges in M-Business *17*
Conclusion *18*
Discussion Questions *19*
References *19*

Chapter II.
Wireless Application Protocol (WAP) **22**

Introduction *22*
WAP Architecture *25*
Software Development Kits (SDKs) and Emulators *29*
Summary *34*
Discussion Questions *34*

Chapter III.
Wireless Markup Language (WML) 36
Introduction *36*
WML Elements *37*
XML Header *37*
Decks and Cards *38*
Navigation *42*
Summary *62*
Exercises *63*

Chapter IV.
WMLScript 65
Introduction *65*
WMLScript Functions *66*

Chapter V.
WMLScript Standard Libraries 85
Introduction *85*
Integrating WMLScript Libraries with WML and
WMLScript Functions *86*
Summary *117*
Exercises *118*

Chapter VI.
XHTML Basic 119
Introduction to XHTML *119*
XHTML Basic *120*
Summary *134*
Exercises *135*

Chapter VII.
Dynamic Wireless Application Development I: Developing
Wireless Applications Using ColdFusion 136
Introduction *136*
Building the Database *138*
Creating an ODBC Connection *140*
Creating the SAS Heading *141*
Creating the Customer Search Feature *142*
Managing State Using Cookies *159*
Interacting with E-Mail Service *162*

Creating a Feature to Report Travel Expenses *164*
Building a Shopping Cart *170*
Session Variables *172*
Confirming Orders *176*
Viewing the Shopping Cart *179*
Developing SAS for Mobile Handsets *181*
Summary *191*
Project *192*

Chapter VIII.
Dynamic Wireless Application Development II: Developing ASP .NET Mobile Web Applications Using Visual Studio .NET 193
Introduction *193*
Parking Finder Application *194*
Building the Application *197*
Summary *226*
Project *226*

Chapter IX.
Mobile Application Development I: Developing Mobile Applications Using Microsoft Embedded Visual Tools 228
Introduction *228*
Desktop Pocket PC Emulation *229*
Mobile vs. Wireless Applications *229*
Creating an eVB Application *230*
Naming Controls *231*
Order Placement System (OPs) *247*
Creating a WinSock Internet Connection *260*
Creating Menus *262*
Creating Setup Files *267*
Summary *268*
Project *269*

Chapter X.
Mobile Application Development II: Developing Smart Device Applications Using Visual Studio .NET 270
Introduction *270*
Order Placement System *271*
Starting a New Visual Studio .NET Smart Device Application *272*
Creating the Forms *273*

Installing the SQL Server CE Database on the Emulator *276*
Creating the New Orders Form *280*
Adding Menus *303*
Summary *304*
Project *305*

Glossary **308**

About the Authors **314**

Index **316**

Preface

The explosive growth in the demand for mobile and wireless products and services, from both businesses and consumers in the recent years, indicates that mobile commerce is starting to take off. As more and more companies begin to realize the compelling value offered by mobile and wireless technologies and start to explore mobile business opportunities, IT professionals need to understand the business and technical issues related to mobile commerce application development. *Mobile Commerce Application Development* introduces you to the various technologies and techniques that are widely used for developing m-commerce applications today. The book is designed to provide readers with an appreciation for the use of wireless and mobile technologies in achieving business objectives and changing the way business strategies are being implemented, an understanding of the various technologies used in m-business, and technical skills for developing and deploying wireless and mobile commerce systems.

In this book, mobile commerce application development techniques are introduced within the context of their applications. Readers learn to use these techniques by developing business applications. This approach is highly successful and widely used in information technology training. Readers with any systems development background will be able to quickly grasp the technologies and techniques discussed in this book.

This book is organized in 10 chapters as follow.

Chapter I provides a high level overview of the value proposition, applications and technologies relevant to mobile commerce. The chapter discusses the drivers behind the growth of mobile commerce and explains how mobile and wireless technologies offer compelling values to businesses. The chapter presents a technology-independent and application-oriented impact/value framework for m-business applications. The framework includes twelve business opportunities enabled by mobile and wireless technologies. The chapter also provides readers with an in-depth discussion of the various technologies that support Wireless Personal Networks, Wireless Local Area Networks, and Wireless Wide Area Networks. The chapter concludes with a discussion on the challenges companies will encounter when they conduct mobile business.

Chapter II examines the Wireless Application Protocol (WAP). The history and current status of WAP are presented. In order to understand the layers of the protocol, the architecture is illustrated, along with a thorough discussion of each layer. WAP provides the necessary support for using wireless Internet applications.

In addition to the discussion of the WAP, software development kits (SDKs), which allow the user to develop applications, are examined. Each toolkit presented in the chapter is readily available.

Chapter III discusses the Wireless Markup Language (WML) and takes the reader through the syntax of the language. Examples are provides that illustrate the creation of wireless Internet applications that use various elements of the WML.

Chapter IV illustrates how the WMLScript is used to enhance WML documents similar to the ones created in Chapter III. Both the use of WMLScript functions and their relationship to WML documents are studied. The chapter discusses the data types supported by the scripting language. The creation of variables and the operators they use are presented in the chapter. Decision-making, flow control, and iteration in WMLScript functions are illustrated and how they are used in the creation of useful applications.

The WMLScript Standard Libraries are examined in detail in Chapter V. Each major function contained in the standard libraries is discussed, along with an example of how the function can be accessed and the results of using that function. The use of examples is presented to aid the reader in understanding how the standard libraries can be employed in creating applications.

XHTML Basic allows the user to create applications that are compliant with WAP without the use of WML. The advantage of using XHTML Basic is discussed in this chapter. The creation of applications is illustrated throughout the chapter. Integration of WML documents and WMLScript functions with XHTML is discussed, along with the presentation of appropriate code examples. The use of Cascading Style Sheets and XHTML Basic is examined.

Chapter VII through Chapter X focuses on the technologies and techniques for developing two categories of mobile commerce applications: wireless and mobile applications. Wireless applications are designed to function when the mobile device is connected to networks (e.g., the Internet) or other devices wirelessly. Mobile applications, on the other hand, may or may not involve wireless communication with networks or other devices. Mobile applications can function without a network connection. The differences between wireless and mobile applications require developers to use different technologies and techniques when developing these applications.

Chapter VII discusses the techniques for developing dynamic wireless applications using Macromedia ColdFusion, a server-side Web application development tool. The chapter illustrates the use of ColdFusion through the example of a mobile sales force automation system. The system operates on both personal digital assistants and mobile handsets. Topics discussed in this chapter include ColdFusion Markup Language (CFML), Web-based database programming, state management in the Web environment (form variable, URL variable, cookie, and session variable), e-mail service, application-level security, Wireless Telephony Application Interface (WTAI), and shopping cart application.

Chapter VIII discusses the techniques for developing dynamic wireless applications using Microsoft Visual Studio .NET, an integrated development environment. In the recent years, the .NET framework has gained increasing popularity among developers due to its versatility and ease of use. Wireless applications can be developed using the ASP.NET Mobile Web Application tool in Visual Studio .NET. This chapter illustrates the use of this tool through an example of a parking finder application. Relevant topics discussed in this chapter include ASP.NET, Visual Basic .NET, and Web-based database programming (OleDbDataAdapter, OleDbDataCommand, and OleDbDataReader objects).

Chapter IX discusses the techniques for developing mobile applications using Microsoft's Embedded Visual Tool. This chapter uses a series of examples to illustrate the use of Embedded Visual Basic for developing mobile applications. While Embedded Visual Tool has some limitations compared to more sophisticated development tools such as Visual Studio .NET, it is a free software that can be downloaded from the Web. It proves to be an excellent learning tool for new programmers. Relevant topics discussed in this chapter include Embedded Visual Basic variable, control structures (e.g., sequence, choice, and repetition), array, file control, HTTP WinSock control, and menu-driven graphic user interface design.

Chapter X discusses the techniques for developing mobile applications using Microsoft's Visual Studio .NET. Smart Device Application tool was introduced in Visual Studio .NET 2003, and it was designed to enable developers to develop and deploy mobile applications for Pocket PC or Windows CE platforms quickly. This chapter illustrates the use of the Smart Device Application tool through the example of an order placement system. Relevant topics discussed in this chapter include Visual Basic .NET, SQL Server CE, and database programming (SQLCeConnection, SQLCeCommand, and SQLCeDataReader objects).

We believe that this book makes a major contribution in the diffusion and education of mobile commerce application development technologies and techniques. The book is designed to appeal to a broad audience base including IT professionals, corporate managers, and university students. Throughout the book, our objective has been to keep the material practical. For IT professionals and corporate managers, this book will help them understand the wide array of development technologies for wireless and mobile applications. By following the hands on application building exercises in this book, readers will acquire technical skills that can be readily applied to work. Currently, a growing number of universities are starting to offer courses in the mobile commerce area in response to market demands. The material in this book is well suited for a course in mobile commerce application development. Both authors have extensive experience in higher education, and the material in this book has been tested in both undergraduate and graduate IT and mobile commerce courses. The hands-on application building approach used in this book was well received by students from a wide range of IT background.

Acknowledgments

I wish to acknowledge my mentors Dr. Mark Gillenson and Dr. Ravi Nath for their guidance and support. I wish to thank my wonderful colleagues at Creighton University, in particular, Dr. Cindy Corritore, Dr. Robert Marble, Dr. Robert Moorman, Dr. Vasant Raval, and Dr. Deborah Wells, for their friendship, support, and many intellectually stimulating conversations. I also wish to thank Ken Dalley, Kerri Lawless, and Michele Zuerlein for their contribution to this book.

I want to especially thank Yien-Wah for her constant support and giving me the inspiration for this book. Finally, I want to thank my parents and my sister who have given me encouragement and love throughout my life.

Lei-da Chen

First, I want to thank my wife, Janet, for again allowing me to be involved with writing a book on wireless application development. Her support and understanding has made the effort worthwhile. I owe you a vacation!

Secondly, I want to thank Dr. Mahmoud Manzoul, Dr. Robert Whalin, Dr. Bill Blair, and Angie Jackson for their confidence in me and their help in my current endeavors. I also want to thank Dee Dee Sessums and Frank Ezelle for all of the support and help that they have given me over the years and for their true friendship.

Finally, I want to especially thank all of my students at Jackson State who have inspired me with their dedication to learning and their keen interest in computer engineering. Their commitment has given me inspiration to reach for higher goals.

Gordon Skelton

Chapter I

Introduction to M-Business Applications: Value Proposition, Applications, Technologies, and Challenges

In this chapter, you will:

- Learn about the drivers behind the growth of m-business
- Learn about the value proposition of m-business
- Learn about the major categories of m-business applications
- Learn about the technologies that enable m-business
- Learn about the m-business challenges companies are facing today

Introduction

Leung and Antypas (2001) defined mobile business (m-business) as both "content delivery (notification and reporting) and transactions (purchasing and data entry) on mobile devices". Another term often used for m-business is "wireless e-commerce", as such business activities often leverage wireless and Internet technologies. While still in its infant stage, m-business is destined to have a much larger footprint in the future. If projections hold true, revenues from m-business will grow to $200 billion worldwide by 2004, and the number of U.S. m-business users will grow to 29 million (Kelly, 2001). The major factors that drive the growth of m-business include:

- Mobile devices such as Internet-enabled handsets, personal digital assistants (PDA), and portable computers are gaining popularity among business and consumer users.
- The wireless infrastructure and support are constantly being upgraded by vendors in order to provide seamless and affordable access. Advances in mobile and wireless technologies are making anywhere, anytime computing a reality.
- Companies want to remove delays and inefficiencies from traditional business processes and explore new business opportunities by allowing employees and consumers to access critical business information from anywhere at anytime.

Value Proposition

Before investing in a mobile project, an organization needs to identify the business drivers behind the project and demonstrate how m-business solutions will help solve existing problems, capitalize new opportunities, or create a competitive edge. Therefore, it is imperative for organizations to understand the value produced by m-business. Evidence has shown that m-business offers organizations the benefits of new channels to reach customers, cost reduction, increased customer satisfaction and revenues, and reduced cycle time by redesigning workflows.

Balasubramanian, Peterson, and Jarvenpaa (2002) conclude that the reason m-business offers values unattainable by conventional business practices is because mobile technologies relax spatial and/or temporal constraints of activities. For example, with mobile technologies, a field worker can check and reply e-mails at any time. Without the right mobile technologies, the activity can only be performed at a location where a computer and a network connection are present. In the same vein, Chen and Nath (2003) believe that the value of m-business is a function of the user's immediacy of information needs and user mobility. As the user's immediacy of information needs and/or mobility increase, the value of m-business solutions that can address the user's needs increases (see Figure 1). At one extreme, we have a traveling stock trader whose ability to access real time market information and transact on the go is crucial. M-business applications that can offer the trader these capabilities will prove to be very valuable. On the other hand, when there is no pressing need for information and the receiver of information is mostly stationary, m-business offers minimal value.

The value can be further enhanced by m-business applications that demonstrate high levels of personalization and context-awareness. Timely information or services based on the user's location and interests are offered by these applications, which can help organizations to better target the right customer and seize business opportunities at the right time. However, the two crucial components of these applications, location identification technologies and database marketing techniques, have provoked a great deal of controversy in the recent years due to consumers' privacy concerns.

M-Business Applications

The number of m-business applications is on the rise. Generally, these applications can be categorized into these four categories: business-to-consumer (B2C), business-to-business (B2B), business-to-employee (B2E), and consumer-to-consumer (C2C). M-business creates an effective B2C market by utilizing the intimate nature of mobile devices and communication channels. Examples of these applications include mobile banking, stock trading, retailing,

Figure 1. Value proposition of m-business (Adapted from Chen & Nath, 2004)

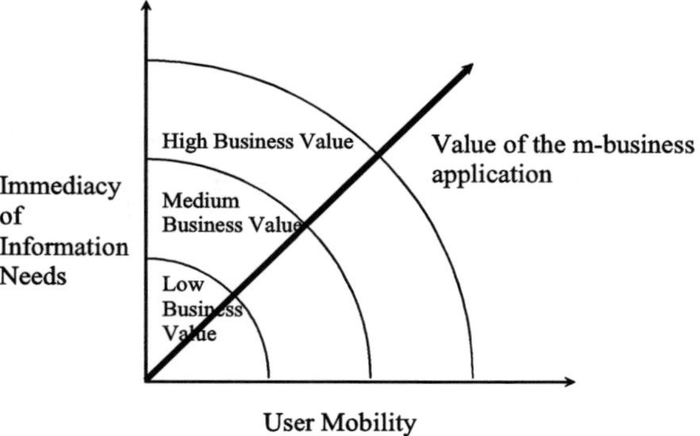

content delivery, and concierge services. While many of the lessons learned from B2C e-commerce pervade, new business opportunities can be found in m-business. As Paul May (2001) suggested in his book, *Mobile Commerce*, early experience in B2C m-commerce had taught us the following three lessons:

- Successful mobile commerce services depend on the value perceptions of consumer groups.
- Mobile commerce is most suited for accommodating consumers' impulse buying.
- The relevance of an offer to the user's current position (e.g., location, time and mission) will take precedence over price.

B2B and B2E m-business will likely generate the most revenue as we have seen in the e-commerce arena. Mobile applications for asset and personnel management, collaboration, inventory management, supply chain management, and corporate data access are increasingly seen in organizations today. C2C m-business embodies personal communication applications such as wireless voice communication, short message services, buddy lists, peer-to-peer file sharing, and mobile games.

M-business applications can be found in a wide array of industries ranging from healthcare to transportation. A meaningful categorization of these applications will be helpful to managers in identifying new m-business opportunities. We have developed a technology-independent and application-oriented impact/value framework for m-business applications that will help readers sort through existing m-business applications (See Table 1). The model posits that m-business applications are likely to dramatically compress the time required for accessing information and completing business processes, allow individuals and organizations to overcome geographic limitations by making information accessible from anywhere at anytime, help restructure relationships between the provider and the recipient of the information, and proactively seize business opportunities by providing location-specific services. These impacts will result in increased efficiency in operation, improved effectiveness in decision making, and innovative business processes that generate competitive advantage. Each cell in the framework represents a unique business opportunity enabled by m-business. The forthcoming sections briefly discuss each m-business opportunity and representative applications that take advantage of these opportunities.

Table 1. A framework for m-business applications

		Value		
		Efficiency	**Effectiveness**	**Innovation**
Impact	**Time**	Reduce Business Process Cycle Time	Reduce Information Float	Enhance Service Quality
	Mobility	Capture Information Electronically Anytime-Anywhere	Access Critical Information Anytime-Anywhere	React to Problems and Opportunities Anytime-Anywhere
	Relationship	Enhance Connectivity and Communication	Increase Collaboration	Increase Information Transparency to Improve Supply Chain
	Location Leverage	Track and Surveillance	Alert and m-Marketing Campaigns	Localize

Reduce Business Process Cycle Time

These applications allow a task's critical information to be delivered to the user wirelessly when requested, resulting in a significant business process cycle-time reduction. For example, at Embassy Suites hotels, maintenance and housekeeping crews are equipped with mobile text messaging devices. Using a silent page, the front desk can inform the crew the location and nature of the repair without physically locating them (McGarvey, 2002b). Also, at the Las Vegas Four Seasons, customer food orders are wirelessly transmitted from the poolside to the kitchen (Terry, 2002). Yet another example where wireless systems have significantly enhanced efficiency involves Johns Hopkins Hospital where pharmacists use a wireless system for accessing critical information on clinical interventions, medication errors, adverse drug reactions, and prescription cost comparisons (Keane, 2002). Cost savings of over $1,000 a day, per pharmacist, have been reported as the system allows each pharmacist to perform an average of six more interventions a day.

Reduce Information Float

Getting the right information to the right persons at the right time has always been one of the top concerns of businesses. Wireless systems reduce information float by delivering needed and relevant information to field decision-makers so that time-sensitive business decisions can be made on the spot. For example, at Carlson hotels, managers use Pocket PCs to access all the information they need to manage the properties in real-time. The wireless system compiles information from the hotel's various information systems and delivers it to the manager. This information ranges from how many minutes it takes room service to fill an order to the night's occupancy level. Equipped with such critical information, managers can quickly spot any problems or opportunities at their hotel and react to them (McGarvey, 2002b).

Enhance Service Quality

The wireless technology allows organizations to bring their services to where their customers are, hence a higher level of customer convenience and service quality can be achieved. For example, the Sheraton hotel in New Jersey is experimenting with a new wireless check-in technology in order to reduce the waiting time for guests during check-in and check-out (McGarvey, 2002b). Employees carrying wireless devices will be able to check guests in the lobby, parking area, meeting rooms, and any other hotel facilities. The system also allows a key to be issued at the time of check-in from a portable imprint device. This application offers the hotel guests a real and visible convenience. Industry analysts also predict a 25 percent annual growth rate for the sales of wireless point-of-sale (POS) terminals in the next few years.

Capture Information Electronically Anytime-Anywhere

Paper-based business processes often result in data reentry, repetitive tasks, increase in errors, and waste of human and natural resources. M-business applications allow data capture anywhere in the field and the ability to interact with the company headquarters in resolving problems and answering client questions. For example, consider the operating efficiencies achieved by many utility companies by virtue of employing wireless systems for maintenance inspectors. With a wireless infrastructure, maintenance inspectors can send in the repair request by checking a few boxes on the screens of their hand-held devices. A work request is automatically generated and dispatched to the repair technician. The new and improved process saves time, reduces errors, and leads to a quicker and more proactive maintenance approach (Kuchinskas, 2002). It is reported that due to these advantages, most utility companies expect to recuperate their costs on the mobile systems within 6 to 18 months.

Access Critical Information Anytime-Anywhere

M-business allows users to have access to critical information from anywhere at anytime resulting in greater abilities to seize business opportunities. Target opportunities of this type can be found in situations where a large portion of the workforce is geographically dispersed and highly mobile, and where rapid access to information creates competitive advantages and business opportunities. Producer Lloyds Insurance Company specializes in crop insurance. Since September 2001, it has equipped its field agents with laptops and a host of mobile devices to provide remote access to the company's Policy Administration & Services System (PASS) and Online Policy Update System (OPUS). This remote access has dramatically mobilized the field agents, which is a critical success factor for the insurance industry. This system allows the agents to get instant quotes, create policies in-the-field, prepare various insurance forms, and determine claim status. Such services effectively improve the agents' chance of closing a deal which would otherwise slip away. Some insurance companies project a 17 to 21 percent increase in annual revenue due to the implementation of such systems (Rachel, 2001).

React to Problems and Opportunities Anytime-Anywhere

Besides allowing user access to critical information from anywhere at anytime, some wireless systems let users react to the information. These innovative systems have changed the way businesses operate and the way employees work. Opportunities abound where resolving problems quickly and onsite avoids significant loss and shut down of operations, and where constantly changing conditions require close monitoring and quick reaction. A number of software companies offer wireless network management tools so that network managers can react to problems from any location (Yokomizo, 2002). These wireless network management tools are designed to remotely solve some of the most common problems that bring down corporate networks. The cost savings, convenience, and quick resolution to network problems these tools offer have enticed both large and small companies without an onsite IT crew.

Enhance Connectivity

It is well known that meaningful improvements in customer-firm communication result in enhanced customer loyalty. Wireless access allows customers to receive value-added services when they need them. Consequently, as the customer's dependence on the service increases, so does the cost of switching to another company. Gartner Group estimates that the percentage of North American banks that offer wireless services will increase from the current 5 percent to 29 percent by 2003. A number of banks, such as Citibank and Juniper Bank, send their customers alerts on balance level, bill payments, and check clearances. As customers get more and more comfortable with wireless security, many banks plan to offer wireless bill payments so that customers can act on the alerts (Fox, 2002). Brokerage firms like Fidelity Investments offer their customers stock quote alerts.

Opportunities for revenue-enhancement can also be found in situations where consumer awareness can be translated into sales. Marketers are seeking opportunities to convert cellular phones into an efficient advertising channel. In Europe, businesses are experimenting with sending short message to consumers' wireless devices to promote their products and services. Survey shows that most consumers in Europe and U.S. are willing to receive relevant advertisements via wireless communication (McDonough, 2002). In addition, businesses are using permission-based marketing to target the most receptive group of consumers without alienating them, while some companies, such as BTcellnet, are exploring consumers' reactions to non-opt-in advertisements. Marketers for companies like 20th Century Fox and Pepsi are using mobile games to entice consumers. Mobile games that can be easily played on the small screens of mobile devices increase interaction levels between business and consumer (Rendon, 2002a).

Increase Collaboration

Wireless systems are restructuring and improving relationships within organizations and between business partners. Information can be synchronized centrally and shared with every employee and business partner. Such systems result in more effective business processes. As Paul May indicated in his book, *Mobile commerce*, wireless collaboration tools will be especially useful in "outdoor" sectors such as architecture, construction, and engineering (ACE) projects (2001). Historically, the construction industry has struggled with the lack of coordination among many subcontractors collaborating on a project. When the right information and building materials are not in the right hands at the right time, it affects the builder's bottom line by wasting time and materials. A family of new mobile project management tools enables contractors to track project workflow and share information with subcontractors. With vital project information readily available via mobile devices, contractors and subcontractors can collaborate in an effective fashion. As a result, human errors are prevented and cost savings are significant (McGarvey, 2002a).

Increase Information Transparency to Improved Supply Chain

High levels of information transparency in the supply chain can be achieved with wireless systems. In some cases, supply chain parties gain timely information about orders and shipments. In other cases, the supply chain is totally revolutionized by new wireless technologies. The new wireless supply chain software allows business customers to access information regarding order status and inventory level, and also to execute transactions using a wide array of handheld devises (Nelson, 2000). This will soon become common practice in supply chain management enabling suppliers to build closer relationships with their customers. The Massachusetts Institute of Technology Auto ID Field Center is developing a globally standardized and low-cost radio frequency identification (RFID) technology. The new RFID has the potential to replace the Universal Product Code (UPC) on products as it can wirelessly provide all retail supply chain parties with real-time information about the location of a product. The RFID will improve the accuracy and speed of inventory management, and most importantly, it will significantly increase the information transparency between the retailer and the manufacturer. The right amount of the product can be supplied to the right place at the right time, thus reducing a retailer's loss in revenues resulting from out-of-stock products (Rendon, 2002b).

Track and Surveillance

By leveraging the location information, organizations that manage mobile assets are achieving unprecedented efficiency. These opportunities are abound in situations where the management of mobile assets is crucial to the success of the business. For example, in the trucking industry truck drivers depend on the global positioning systems (GPS) to determine the best route. These GPS-based systems also provide the driver with information pertaining to the nearest restaurant, gas station, or a rest area. Furthermore, fleet managers at the headquarters can dispatch the mobile workforce more efficiently and react to any changes in the shipment since they know exactly where the shipment/truck is at any given moment. Consequently, customers can get a highly accurate status report of their shipments and can be informed of any schedule changes due to unexpected heavy traffic or severe weather conditions. Overall, such wireless systems lead to efficient operations, better utilization of mobile workforce, and higher customer satisfaction (Stevens, 2001). Similar applications can be developed to track any mobile personnel and assets, control inventory, and manage supply chain.

Alert and M-Marketing Campaigns

For the U.S. Army, it is important to get real-time weather alerts to the field as weather conditions significantly impact the performance of weapon systems and personnel. Newly developed hand-held devices enable soldiers in the field to access real-time weather alerts and evaluate the effects of the weather on the mission. The vendor is also considering the possibility of combining this technology with the GPS systems so that the information can be automatically retrieved for the location of the mission (Sauter & Torres, 2002). The same can be done for businesses where location information is crucial. The nationwide implementation of the E911 Act will provide businesses and carriers with a new dimension of customer data—real-time location data. This capability will allow marketers to push relevant alerts and advertisements to the consumer when he or she is at a certain location. Businesses are seeking opportunities to leverage the location data to provide their customers with more targeted advertisements and enhanced services. Alert systems and m-marketing campaigns based on the customer's location are promising applications. Imagine getting an alert on your mobile phone that you have a prescription to pick up when you drive within a one-mile radius of the pharmacy. One day, a consumer may get a reminder on a mobile device that his or her car is due for an oil change and that there is an auto service shop 500 feet away that is running an oil change special. Experience gained by retailers suggests that location-based m-marketing campaigns are most effective for promoting last minute offers and attracting impulse buys.

M-Business in Practice

Offering Mobile and Wireless Solutions to Small to Medium Enterprises in the Service Industry

Founded in 2001, Codex Corporation is quickly establishing itself as a leading provider of wireless and mobile solutions and ancillary data services. The company headquarters in Maple Grove, Minnesota, 17 miles northwest of Minneapolis. In 2003, the company expanded its operation by opening the Codex Engineering and Support Center (CESC) in Clarion, Iowa. Originally founded to develop wireless and mobile sales force and field service automation solutions for small to medium enterprises, Codex Corporation now offers a wide range of products and services including mobile device provisioning and management services, application and data hosting, data backup services, consulting services, and training and education.

Codex's products help business manage, share, and synchronize mission-critical data throughout the workforce via mobile and wireless computing technologies. The company's two flagship business solutions, OnSite© and FastTrack©, are receiving increasing popularity among small to medium enterprises.

OnSite is a comprehensive platform designed for sales and service organizations to streamline critical business processes, and improve information collection and sharing throughout the organization. Built upon the Microsoft® .NET framework, OnSite supports desktop PCs and handheld devices under a single platform. The OnSite desktop system supports the entire business process from inventory management to customer sales and relationship management. Linked to and synchronized with the desktop system, OnSite Mobile enables the field salespeople to use their Pocket PC devices to submit orders via mobile order forms, access account histories, manage inventory, and capture electronic signatures.

FastTrack is designed to improve the efficiency and effectiveness of auto retail sales forces. It allows salespeople to access the most up-to-date inventory information during sales interactions and provide highly personalized services to each customer. The mobile solution enables salespeople to search new and used car inventories, capture customer information, and e-mail car buyers detailed vehicle specs, including images anywhere on the lot from a Pocket PC. Its My Showroom feature adds a highly personalized touch to the car shopping experience by allowing salespeople to save any number of vehicles to a customer profile and e-mail detailed specs on every vehicle to the customer with few simple clicks.

To educate Codex Corporation's target customers about the benefits mobile technologies can bring to their businesses, Codex offers a risk-free Pilot Program that allows companies to evaluate the mobile solutions before purchasing. Codex also provides extensive training programs to ensure that customers are achieving the maximum benefits offered by the solutions after deployment.

A profitable, emerging leader in the wireless industry, Codex Corporation has made impressive progress. Kenneth Dally Jr., president and CEO of Codex, attributes the company's success to doing whatever it takes to satisfy the customer. The company is currently expanding its product lines to healthcare and law enforcement.

Codex is currently developing two solutions for healthcare and law enforcement. The company's healthcare solution, FocalPoint© is a customer care system that collects accurate, timely, and detailed information about every patient, tracks employee performance, and analyzes all of the collected data to pinpoint strengths and weaknesses of the healthcare provider, as well as to personalize every customers' visit to the hospital or clinic. All of the information is made available to nurses, team leaders, and administrators in real-time via Pocket PCs to track departmental and organizational performance, identify high and low-performing employees, and ensure the unique needs and preferences of every patient are always met.

The company's law enforcement solution is designed for jail and prison systems to electronically document hourly cell checks, and every inmate activity, such as medical requests and dosages given. The law enforcement solution uses passive RFID chips on jail cells to enable jailers to wirelessly document their rounds as required by law. Among the benefits of the law enforcement solution is its ability to use RFID technology to eliminate common paper-based processes that are highly repetitive and time consuming. Through RFID, a jailer can automatically document the cell number, the inmate, the current state of the inmate, and the time of the cell check. The system is also effective against preventing potential litigation against the jail or prison system by improving the documentation of an inmate's incarceration, which can save jail and prison systems thousands of dollars per year in legal fees.

Discussion Questions:

1. Given Codex Corporation's expertise in providing wireless and mobile solutions to small to medium enterprises in the service industry, what future projects will allow the company to build on its existing expertise and complement its existing product lines?

Localize

Opportunities for localizing information on the fly can be found in situations where consumers in different geographic regions have significantly different needs; and where business opportunities may arise as location changes. Businesses have realized that consumers in different geographic areas respond to different product advertisements. Vert, a technology company, has found a way to integrate electronic billboards on top of taxicabs with the GPS system to create a more powerful promotional tool. Based on the location of the taxicab detected by the GPS system, the central server will wirelessly transmit electronic advertisements to be displayed on the top of the taxicab. The type of advertisements displayed depends on the information the company has about the area. This tool allows marketers to better target their customers (Schibsted, 2001).

M-Business Technologies

Wireless technology refers to the hardware and software that allows transmission of information between devices without using physical connections. The successful delivery of m-business applications relies on the reliability and availability of wireless network technologies. Today's wireless network solutions include Wireless Personal Area Networks (WPANs), Wireless Local Area Networks (WLANs), and Wireless Wide Area Networks (WWANs). Each of these wireless network solutions serves its unique purpose and embodies an array of attendant technologies. With a wide range of mobile devices and multiple technical platforms coexisting, it is important to put all these in perspective. Table 2 summaries the attendant technologies for different types of wireless networks.

Within personal areas (e.g., an office and an automobile), traditional wireless communication technology such as infrared can be found in devices ranging from remote controls to PDAs. One of this area's most promising new technologies is Bluetooth. Bluetooth is a global standard for wireless connectivity that was quickly adopted by many device manufacturers. It uses short-range radio technology to connect small devices, such as laptops, PDAs, mice, and other peripheral devices, to each other and other networks. The technology has the potential to replace the cables that connect digital devices and offers users a higher level of freedom within their personal areas. The Bluetooth technology was especially designed for making ad hoc interactions between different devices in a heterogeneous computing environment easy. Its relatively high data transfer speed and extremely low power consumption have made it the ideal technology for many business situations.

Analogous to a traditional wired local area network (LAN), many organizations have adopted the Wi-Fi (e.g., IEEE802.11b) technology to provide wireless access to users within a local geographical area (e.g., a building, campus, airport, coffee shop, and hotel). According to a recent study, the market penetration of WLAN in the U.S. has reached 10 percent, and users have credited WLAN with attainment of convenience, flexibility, mobility, time saving, and productivity gains (Cisco Systems, 2001).

WLAN technologies allow both peer-to-peer communications between devices and point-to-multipoint communications through access points that cover a radius of 50-100 meters. The most widely adopted Wi-Fi standard today, IEEE802.11b, transmits data at the 2.4 GHz spectrum at a speed of 11 Mbps using direct sequence spread spectrum (DSSS). Recently, IEEE802.11a and

Table 2. Wireless networks and their attendant technologies

Wireless Networks	Attendant Technologies
WPANs	Line-of-sight infrared, radio frequency (RF), and Bluetooth.
WLANs	Spread spectrum technology (802.11b), Orthogonal Frequency Division Multiplexing (802.11a and 802.11g), Infrared, and narrowband technology.
WWANs	Analog cellular networks, digital cellular systems and Personal Communications System (PCS), Cellular Digital Packet Data (CDPD), Code Division Multiple Access (CDMA), Time Division Multiple Access (TDMA), Global System for Mobile Communications (GSM), General Packet Radio Service (GPRS), Enhanced Data Rates for GSM Evolution (EDGE), CDMA2000, W-CDMA, and satellites.

IEEE802.11g have become commercially available. In contrast to IEEE802.11b, both IEEE802.11a and IEEE802.11g use orthogonal frequency division multiplexing (OFDM) and transmit data at the speed of 54 Mbps.

Today's WLAN technology still has its weaknesses. A recent investigation by *Businessweek* (Green, Rosenbush, Crockett, & Holmes, 2003) found that the challenges faced by Wi-Fi technology included unclear standards, spotty security, limited range, hidden costs, and lack of inter-operability. In addition to technical difficulties, it is still too early for organizations to determine the real return on investment (ROI) of WLAN and many organizations are seeing little usage of WLAN after its implementation.

Wireless wide area networks (WWAN) allow users to communicate and access resources within a wide geographical area such as a city, a region, an entire country, or even around the world. This achieved through the use of cellular networks and satellites. Throughout the history of wireless communications, several generations of cellular network technologies were developed, and different regions have adopted different, and sometimes incompatible, technology standards. While WWAN offers users unprecedented freedom and many m-business opportunities, in many regions, the absence of new generation cellular networks (2.5G or 3G) with high data transmission rates has impeded the growth of m-business. Furthermore, the incompatible regionally adopted technology standards have limited the globalization of m-business applications. Nevertheless, today, many innovative m-business applications are capable of providing value such as wireless banking, wireless stock trading, remote monitoring, and location-based wireless services.

WWAN technologies can be categorized by generation. Early generations of cellular networks were designed primarily for voice communication using circuit switching. Introduced in 1978, the first-generation (1G) cellular wireless networks were analog networks called Advanced Mobile Phone Systems (AMPS). Compared to newer generations of cellular technologies, AMPS networks were inefficient in the use of limited wireless spectrum and supported limited encryption and advanced services (Agrawal, Chari, & Sankar, 2003). These limitations prompted the development of the second-generation (2G) cellular wireless networks. The basic 2G technologies include Time Division Multiple Access (TDMA), Code Division Multiple Access (CDMA), and Global System for Mobile Communications (GSM). These technologies are widely used around the world today. GSM was adopted by most Asian and European countries, while CDMA, the building block for the 2.5G and third-generation (3G) networks, was adopted in the U.S. Although a huge improvement over the 1G technologies, 2G cellular networks are voice-centric and circuit-switching. The data transmission rate of 2G networks was limited to 14.4kbps.

As the need for wireless data communication increased, newer generations of cellular technologies were designed to make data communication more efficient. 2.5G technologies, such as General Packet Radio Service (GPRS), CDMA 2000 1x, and Enhanced Data Rates for GSM Evolution (EDGE), offer data transmission rates of up to 384kbps. The 3G wireless networks offer broadband, packet-based transmission of multimedia data at a rate of up to 2Mbps for stationary users. The two most popular 3G cellular technologies are Wideband CDMA (W-CDMA) and CDMA 2000 3x.

Besides terrestrial cellular networks, satellites also provide support for WWAN. They are especially useful in remote locations where cellular services are sparse. Satellites are also crucial components of the global positioning system (GPS). Widely used in commercial devices today, GPS uses satellites to track the latitude, longitude, and altitude of a person or object using a technique called triangulation. While it is highly accurate, it is expensive to operate and does not work well indoor.

M-Business vs. E-Business Applications

M-business applications are different from e-business applications in many aspects; therefore, developing m-business applications requires a different set of tools, techniques, and strategies. Most e-business applications cannot be readily transferred to the mobile platforms. When a company attempts to replicate their e-business success by simply moving its Web applications to a wireless environment, the environment often fails to provide the support the applications need to be successful or usable. To successfully move a Web application to a wireless environment, the scope of the application must be redefined, the user interface must be redesigned, and its network and processing requirements must be reassessed. To do this, developers need to start by understanding the differences between e-business and m-business applications.

Singhal, Alvinen, Bridgman, Bevis, Suryanarayana, Chan, Mauney, and Hild (2001) pointed out that m-business applications differed from e-business applications in three areas: device, network, and user. Table 3 summarizes some of these differences outlined by Singhal et al. (2001). The differences require developers to think creatively about how to deliver the benefits of m-business applications to users while addressing the constraints of client devices and wireless networks. At the same time, developers must also recognize the unique opportunities m-business applications present. For example, the personal nature of client devices (e.g., handsets and PDAs) allows applications to be more personalized and targeted; location identification technologies have created many new and exciting opportunities to provide context-based products and services; wireless networks make it possible to deliver timely information to users anytime anywhere.

The key to successful m-business applications is to have a good understanding of the values of m-business application and realistic expectations. Phatak (2001) suggested that the four steps to implement the right wireless applications for a company are:

1. Select an application where the return from providing mobile access will be high.
2. Throughout the development process, focus on the unique characteristics of mobile devices.
3. Select a development and integration partner with experience in both mobile and enterprise systems.
4. Keep in mind that handheld devices will become an even more compelling platform in the near future as the 3G technologies provide higher bandwidths and significant performance improvements.

Table 3. Differences between e-business applications and m-business applications

	E-Business Applications	M-Business Applications
Device	Monitor resolutions range from 640x480 to 1600x1200.	Screen sizes range from 4 lines of text and 12 characters per line to 120x160 and displays 11 lines of text.
	Monitor displays hundreds to millions of colors.	Vast majority of handset displays are gray-scale or support limited number of colors.
	Keyboard and mouse are the primary input devices.	Input methods (keypad and stylus) are laborious to use.
	Client devices have capable CPU and considerable memory.	Client devices have little processing power and memory.
Network	Network speeds range from 28.8KB per second to more than 1MB per second.	Data speeds range from less than 100 bits per second to 28.8KB per second.
	Networks are stable.	More latency, less connection stability and less predictable availability are expected from networks.
User	The user is likely to be computer literate.	The user may not necessarily have any desktop computing experience.
	The user may spend extended periods of time "surfing the net".	The user expects to complete the task within a few minutes.
		The user tends to be engaged in other activities at the same time.

Challenges in M-Business

As Patrick Brans pointed out in his book, *Mobilize Your Enterprise*, companies that do not consider mobilizing will be at a serious disadvantage in today's fast-paced business environment. Nevertheless, many obstacles that hinder the adoption of m-business still exist. These obstacles mainly include high costs of wireless mobile Internet access, concerns over privacy and security, device limitations, and the lack of global standards for wireless communication. Consumers and businesses have not embraced m-business as enthusiastically as previously predicted. As a result, the actual adoption of m-business has been much slower, especially in the U.S. and Europe. Based on the current adoption data, one source suggests that m-commerce will only account for 1.2 percent of total carrier revenues in 2006 (Luna, 2002). Many have also attributed much of the slow adoption to the slowdown in the U.S. and global economy in the recent years.

Still in its infancy, m-business needs to address many of the challenges that lie ahead. To better illustrate these challenges, Tarasewich, Nickerson, and Warkentin (2002) identified three dimensions of m-business issues: technical, application, and global issues. Managers as well as developers must take these issues into consideration while designing m-business solutions.

In order for m-business to continue to grow, technical issues such as device limitations, usability, standardization, and integration of different wireless technologies must be addressed. The m-business field is governed by a chaotic array of platforms, devices, and standards. Each device class differs tremendously from other classes in terms of screen resolution and button functions. Developing business applications for such a diverse group of client devices proves to be extremely difficult. Furthermore, the small screens of mobile devices and their limited input capabilities have created many design challenges. The miniaturization of mobile devices has resulted in many devices with screens that are too small to display any meaningful data. The limited data entry capabilities of mobile devices have also made m-business applications clumsy and hard to use. In addition, most devices are only useful in bandwidth-limited applications due to the low bandwidth and unreliability of wireless data services today.

Among the application-related issues, the most daunting challenges are identifying killer applications, maintaining data integrity, ensuring data security, and attending to legal and privacy issues. While most of the Internet security threats and privacy issues pervade m-business applications, m-business applications introduce new risks due to its mobility and communication medium, and managers and developers must be sensitive to these attributes when designing m-business solutions.

Global issues raise the question of what impact social, legal, and cultural characteristics of different nations will have on the globalization of m-business. Issues such as the lack of global standards, the disparity in wireless technology adoption, and global access-pricing variations must be addressed.

Conclusion

This book introduces readers to the exciting world of m-business application development. This topic is both important and timely in today's business environment. According to the hype cycle of new technologies (Coyle, 2001), m-business went through the stages of initial implementation, peak of inflated expectations, and trough of disillusionment during the last few years. As business managers and technologists begin to better grasp the potentials and limitations of wireless and mobile technologies, we are entering the stage of enlightenment, which will ultimately lead m-business to the plateau of productivity. A deep understanding of the business implications, applications, and technologies of m-business will help an organization stay competitive in the future. This chapter provides a high level overview of the value proposition, applications and technologies relevant to m-business. The subsequent chapters will delve into the techniques used in developing real-world m-business applications.

Discussion Questions

1. Define what is m-business. Identify a problem at work that can be solved using m-business applications. Describe the benefits of m-business applications to businesses and consumers.
2. Identify the major differences between e-business and m-business applications. How can a developer address the constraints and unique features of mobile client devices during the development process?
3. Discuss the impact of Wi-Fi technology on businesses and consumers. What are the disadvantages of wireless LANs compared to wired LANs?
4. Outline the obstacles for m-business adoption. Discuss which obstacle will prove to be the most difficult to overcome.

References

Agrawal, M., Chari, K., & Sankar, R. (2003). Demystifying wireless technologies: Navigating through the wireless technology maze. *Communications of the AIS*, *12*, 166-182.

Balasubramanian, S., Peterson, R.A., & Jarvenpaa, S.L. (2002). Exploring the implications of m-commerce for markets and marketing. *Journal of the Academy of Marketing Science, 30*(4), 348-361.

Chen, L.D. & Nath, R. (2004). A framework for mobile business applications. *International Journal of Mobile Communications*, *2*(4).

Cisco Systems. (2001) Wireless LAN benefit study. NOP World-Technology, *http://newsroom.cisco.com/dlls/tln/WLAN_study.pdf*

Coyle, F.P. (2001). *Wireless Web: A manager's guide.* NJ: Addison-Wesley.

Fox, L. (2002). Wireless banking's next wave. *Mbusiness*, March, 33-34.

Green, H., Rosenbush, S., Crockett, R.O., & Holmes, S. (2003). Wi-Fi means business. *Businessweek*, 86-92.

Keane, B. (2002). Lowering health care costs out-of-the-box. *Wireless Business & Technology*, *2*(2), 36-38.

Kelly, S. (2001). M-commerce slower than expected. *Communications News*, *38*(7), 10.

Kuchinskas, S. (2002). Wireless helps utilities go with the flow. *Mbusiness*, February, 27-28.

Leung, K. & Antypas, J. (2001). Improving returns on m-commerce investments. *Journal of Business Strategy*, *22*(5), 12-16.

Luna, L. (2002). The m-commerce m-plosion: Is there still hope? *Telephony*, October 14, 48-54.

May, P. (2001). *Mobile commerce: Opportunities, applications, and technologies of wireless business*. Cambridge, UK: Cambridge University Press.

McDonough, B. (2002). BT Cellnet tests the waters for mobile ads. *Mbusiness*, February, 39-40.

McGarvey, R. (2002a). Building the wireless way. *Mbusiness*, February, 41-43.

McGarvey, R. (2002b). Hospitality checks out wireless. *Mbusiness*, March, 18-23.

Nelson, M.G. (2000). Real-time wireless access to supplier information. *Informationweeks.com*, October 2, 151.

Phatak, A. (2001). Implement the right WAP applications for your company. *Wireless Business & Technology*, October, 34-39.

Rachel, K. (2001). Mobilizing the insurance industry. *Wireless Business & Technology, 1*(9), 62-64.

Rendon, J. (2002a). Mobile game ad play. *Mbusiness*, February, 43-44.

Rendon, J. (2002b). The supply chain's RFID gambit. *Mbusiness*, March, 43-45.

Sauter, D. & Torres, M. (2002). Mobile weather technology for the army. *Wireless Business & Technology*, *2*(2), 58-62.

Schibsted, E. (2001). The sizzle. *Business2.com*, April 17, 56.

Singhal, S., Alvinen, J., Bridgman, T., Bevis, D., Suryanarayana, L., Chan, J., Mauney, D., & Hild, S. (2001). *The wireless application protocol: Writing applications for the mobile Internet.* New York: ACM Press.

Stevens, M.G. (2001). What has 18 wheels and no wires? *Wireless Business & Technology*, *1*(9), 52-55.

Tarasewich, P., Nickerson, R.C., & Warkentin, M. (2002). Issues in mobile e-commerce. *Communications of the AIS*, *8*, 41-64.

Terry, L. (2002). Wireless checks into hotels. *Wireless Business & Technology*, *2*(2), 30-33.

Yokomizo, S. (2002). Dial 'r' for remote administration. *Mbusiness*, February, 31-32.

Chapter II

Wireless Application Protocol (WAP)

In this chapter, you will:

- Learn about the purpose and history of the Wireless Application Protocol (WAP)
- Examine the WAP Architecture
- Discuss some of the available Software Development Kits (SDKs) that support applications developed under the WAP
- Observe the steps required to install Nokia's WAP SDK, and Openwave's Mobile Internet Tool Kit (NITK)

Introduction

In this chapter, you are introduced to the Wireless Application Protocol (WAP), which was designed to support the development of applications over cellular networks in order to provide communication and data services for a variety of users. In addition to the protocol we will go through the process of installing both the Nokia Mobile Internet Toolkit, 4.0, and the Openwave SDK 6.2.2. These toolkits are used through out the chapter of this book where WML, WMLScript, WMLScript Standard Libraries, and XHTML Basic are discussed.

WAP - The Wireless Application Protocol

In 1997 Ericsson, Motorola and Nokia, along with Unwired Planet, now Openwave, formed an organization, WAP Forum Ltd. The desire was to support the development of wireless data services that were carrier independent. The result of that endeavor was the creation of the first version of the Wireless Application Protocol. Version 1.X of the Protocol evolved over a period of time, adding functionality to support the evolving wireless community and newer mobile devices. The latest version of WAP, 2.0, was released in August 2001. Version 2.0, backward compatible with the earlier versions of WAP, provided the following enhancements:

- Added support for standard Internet communication protocols: IP, TCP, HTTP
- Continued development of WAP support over emerging higher speed telecommunication technologies
- Provided application environment that includes support for PDAs, pagers, mobile phones, and other wireless devices
- Address unique characteristics of wireless devices: small screens, limited memory, limited user interfaces, limited battery-life
- Minimized processing power requirements, optimized network resources
- Incorporated flexibility in support of different manufacturers and their device uniqueness.

In 2002, the Open Mobile Alliance and the WAP Forum merged to the form the Open Mobile Alliance (OMA). The OMA, www.openmobileilliance.org, established a set of goals that would serve as a direction for their work. The goals, as taken from their Web site are:

- Deliver high quality, open technical specifications based upon market requirements that drive modularity, extensibility, and consistency amongst enablers to reduce industry implementation efforts.
- Ensure OMA service enabler specifications provide interoperability across different devices, geographies, service providers, operators, and networks; facilitate interoperability of the resulting product implementations.

- Be the catalyst for the consolidation of standards activity within the mobile data service industry; working in conjunction with other existing standards organizations and industry to improve interoperability and decrease operational costs for all involved.
- Provide value and benefits to members in OMA from all parts of the value chain including content and service providers, information technology providers, mobile operators, and wireless vendors such that they elect to actively participate in the organization. (www.openmobilealliance.org)

The Open Mobile Alliance is only an advisory group, not a regulatory agency; therefore, its pronouncements are treated only as recommendations. For this reason, there exists a variety of different implementation of microbrowsers supporting different versions of WML.

WAP - History and Future

As the cellular phone system took root and grew, it was logical that users would eventually want to have access to the same data they enjoy on their desktop PCs. In response to this demand a communications protocol needed to be developed. As with all protocol work, the process was evolutionary with numerous steps occurring before a workable model was created.

The growth of mobile wireless Internet applications is not necessarily dependent upon WAP and WML. Other competing models challenge the future acceptance of WML. Various languages, like J2ME, XHTML Basic, and WML. Microsoft Mobile Internet Toolkit, designed for integration with Microsoft's .Net Framework, can be used to build wireless mobile Internet applications. The toolkit is capable of producing systems of supporting either HTML or WML based applications. Microsoft's FrontPage, used for the creation of Web pages, is capable of producing WML documents from HTML documents. With modification to the basic HTML documents one can then have the Web page available for viewing PDAs and PocketPCs, as well as WAP-enabled cell phones.

WAP Architecture

Constructed of six layers, the WAP architecture provides a variety of services that support the wireless transmission of text. Figure 1 illustrates the structure of the Wireless Application Protocol. Here you can see the how the various layers are implemented. Because WAP is a layered protocol, the process of transmitting a message from a wireless device to the WAP server and back requires that the message pass down though the layers, across the physical carrier, and then back up the protocol stack to where the WAP server can then place the message on to the Internet. The reverse occurs when a message is sent by the WAP server to the wireless device.

To understand the WAP, Table 1 provides a brief description of each of the layers of the protocol stack. Each of the layers is described in detail in the following sections.

Figure 1. Wireless application protocol stack

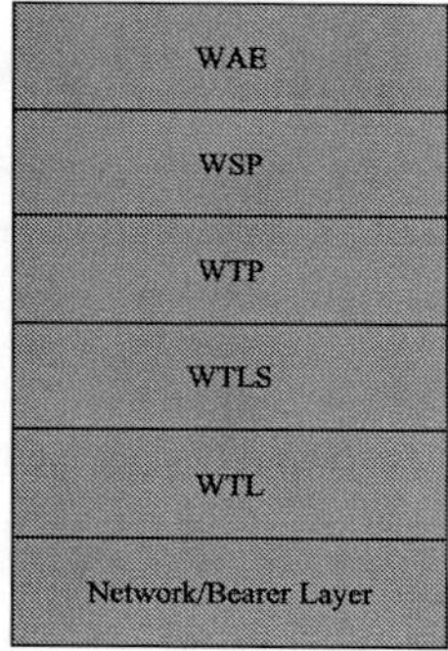

Table 1. WAP architecture

Layer/Abbreviation	Description
Application Layer Wireless Application Environment (WAE)	Environment for development of mobile services and applications; WML and WMLScript reside in this layer
Session Layer Wireless Session Protocol (WSP)	Provides methods for exchange of content between wireless device and application server, relationship of wireless device and network is client/server
Transaction Layer Wireless Transaction Protocol (WTP)	Provides support for various transaction types; reliability based on type of transaction
Security Layer Wireless Transport Layer Security (WTLS)	Provides authentication, privacy, and secure connection, implementation is optional
Transport Layer Wireless Transport Layer	Interface between upper layers and Network Layer; detection and correction supported; used Wireless Datagram Protocol (WDP)
Network Layer	Referred to as the Bearer Layer; physical connectivity of network and wireless devices

Application Layer: WAE

Of primary concern to the developer, the WAE supports the implementation of the Wireless Markup Language (WML) and its related scripting language, WMLScript. The WAE provides two user agents, resident on the client side, the WAE user agent and Wireless Telephone Applications user agent (WTA). The WAE user agent includes the microbrowser and text messaging. The WTA supports the integration of telephone with WML/WMLScript applications.

Session Layer: WSP

The WSP provides the necessary interface between the WAE and the application server for the exchange of services. Two different types of services are supported by WSP:

- *Connection-oriented service:* Uses the Wireless Transaction Protocol (WTP) to ensure reliable message exchange between a server and a wireless device. This service provides for automatic suspension and recover whenever a connection is lost as in handoffs between cells in a cellular network
- *Connectionless service:* Uses the Wireless Datagram Services (WDS) protocol to provide message transmissions but does not guarantee reliable delivery. Message transmission under the connectionless protocol is similar to that used for forms of paging.

Transaction Layer: WTP

The WTP supports wireless message transaction for both secure and nonsecure message exchange. In unreliable messages, WTP lies on top of the User Datagram Protocol (WDP), a protocol of the Internet Protocol (IP). Three different types of transactions are supported under WTP:

- Nonreliable, one-way requests,
- Reliable, one-way requests, and
- Reliable, two-way request-reply.

The transaction layer is optimized for use with a low bandwidth environment.

Security Layer: WTLS

Under the WTLS there are four different secure services provided:

- Data integrity: Makes certain that data exchanged between wireless device and server is not altered.
- Privacy: Public and private keys are used to protect information being transmitted. Encryption is also supported.
- Authentication: Users have to be authorized to access resources and sites.
- Denial-of-service (DoS) protection: Aids in the prevention of numerous and unverified messages (denial-of-service attacks) that may overwhelm communication services.

Transport Layer: WTL

The Wireless Datagram Protocol (WDP), used at this layer, provides an interface between the upper layers of the WAP protocol stack and the Network Layer. The WDP also provides for error detection and correction.

Network Layer

Also known as the Bearer Layer, the physical network layer supports the wireless network. Various networks and bearer technologies are implemented by wireless service providers to implement the network layer.

Basic WAP Transactions

A WAP-based application appears to the user to operate in much the same manner as a HTML-based application. However, WAP required some additional components in order to accommodate communication between the wireless device and the Internet. Figure 2 illustrates the WAP transaction process.

Figure 2. WAP transaction model

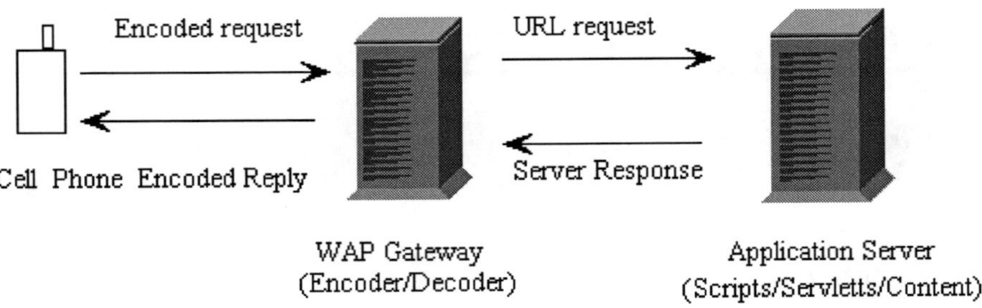

WAP is a binary encoded protocol; therefore, the transaction received at the wireless device must be encoded. The following is a list of the steps that occur when a request is received at the WAP gateway from the wireless device and in turn sends a response to that device.

- The WAP gateway translates the WAP request into conventional HTML
- The Gateway sends the request forward to the Internet
- A Web server processes the URL
- If request is CGI then it is processed as normal and the contents are returned
- The Web server adds an HTTP header and returns the message to the WAP Gateway
- The WAP Gateway compiles the WML into the required binary from
- The Gateway then sends WML back to wireless device
- The wireless mobile device receives the WML document by means of the WAP protocol
- The microbrowser on the wireless device processes the WML document and displays the document, the reply, on the device's screen

When a message is sent from or to a wireless device, the message must pass through a WAP gateway where it is transformed from a WML document to a HTML document or visa versa. The HTML document is then forwarded to the proper Application Server where the request is fulfilled. The resulting data is sent back to the WAP gateway where it is encoded and returned to the wireless device. Figure 2 gives a basic overview of this process. Note that the wireless device will first communicate with the cellular or paging network and then that cellular network will communicate with a wired network in order to send the message to the WAP gate. Those components are not illustrated in this diagram.

Software Development Kits (SDKs) and Emulators

A number of different companies have produced and released SDKs and device emulators that support the development and testing of WML documents and WMLScript applications. Additional languages, for example, J2ME, XHTML Basic, HTML, are included in some of these toolkits.

When developing wireless mobile Internet applications it is strongly recommended that you employ as many emulators as possible to test your wireless applications before they are deployed. Table 2 provides a limited list of SDKs and emulators that can be used to develop or test wireless mobile Internet applications. Some of these products require purchasing them while others merely require the user to register with the company.

In this textbook, we will using Nokia's Mobile Internet Toolkit (NMIT 4.0) and the Openwave Mobile SDK 6.2.2. NMIT provides you with templates for the creation of WML, WMLScript, and XHTML documents, to name a few. The

Table 2. SDKs and emulators

Openwave	Openwave Mobile SDK 6.2.2	developer.openwave.com
Yospace	Smartphone Emulator – Developer Edition 3.0, supports 15 different handsets in one emulator package	www.yospace.com
Nokia	Nokia Mobile Internet Toolkit 4.0	www.forum.nokia.com
Motorola	WAP SDKs	http://idenphones.motorola.com/iden/developer/developer_tools.jsp

Openwave Mobile SDK, is a more general emulator that will be used in various chapters to test and view mobile Internet applications. Because these are the tools of choice, the next two sections examine these two tools.

Nokia Mobile Internet Toolkit 4.0

The Nokia Mobile Internet Toolkit (NMIT) 4.0 is the latest software development kit (SDK) from Nokia that supports development of mobile Internet applications. The SDK is composed of both development tools and a browser that can be used to view various forms of Web sites. NMIT supports XHTML, MMS, WAP, WML, and WAP push messages from either the Internet or from files on a local computer.

The toolkit can be downloaded from www.forum.nokia.com.

In addition to the toolkit, Nokia also provides a Nokia Browser Simulator that can be used to view your applications and a Nokia WAP Gateway Simulator. The Gateway Simulator allows you to test interaction with a WAP gateway without having a live WAP gateway installed.

The NMIT provides a means for compiling WMLScript functions. This capability is quite helpful since some microbrowsers require that WMLScript functions be compiled. For this reason, it is quite helpful to employ the NMIT to develop your applications. You can then use additional emulators to view and test your applications. Such is the case in the chapters on WML, WMLScript, and XHTML Basic. The examples in that portion of this text were developed by using the NMIT and then they were viewed with the Openwave Mobile SDK, discussed in the next section.

The installation process for the Nokia toolkit is quite straightforward. The only issue to be concerned about is the fact that you will have to register as a developer with Nokia. During the installation process you will be asked to agree to the software license, determine where the application files are to be located, and what file types will be associated with the toolkit. You will want to respond to the WML, WMLScript, WBMP, and XHTML extensions at a minimum. The purpose of these file extensions is discussed in the following chapters.

Once the SDK has been installed then you will be able to access the package either by locating the toolkit or from a shortcut on the desktop.

Once you start NMIT and choose new under file you will be presented with the screen in Figure 3.

Figure 3. NMIT initial screen for new WAP application

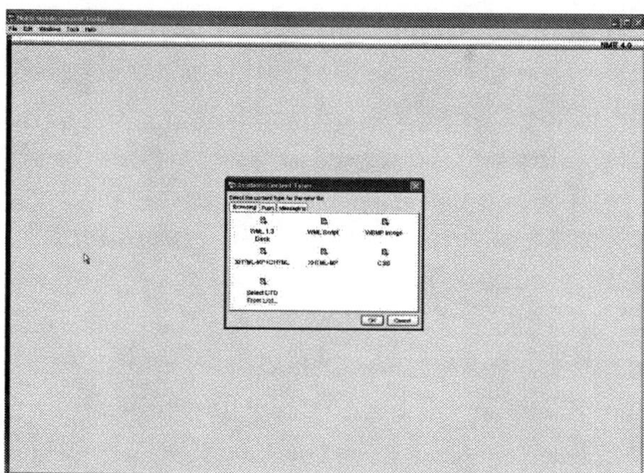

Figure 4. WML initial template

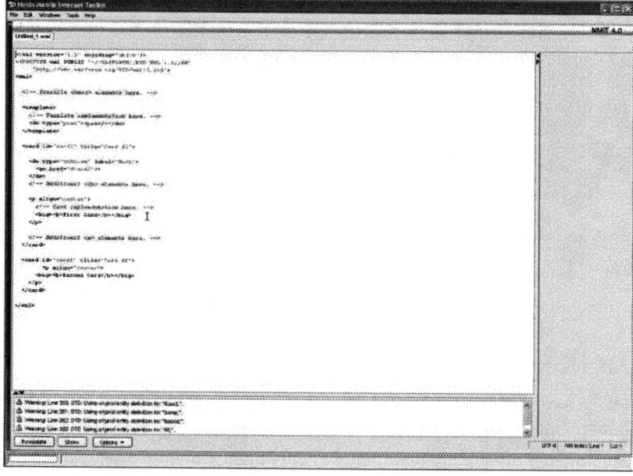

At this point you choose the type of application you want to develop. In Figure 4, the Wireless Markup Language, examined in Chapter 3, was chosen. The screen in Figure 4 presents a template for the development of a WML document.

Openwave Mobile SDK 6.2.2

The Openwave Mobile SDK provides an emulator that can be used to test WML, WMLScript and XHMTL documents and scripts. The toolkit can be downloaded from the following URL:

http://developer.openwave.com/dvl/tools_and_sdk/

There are two different versions of the toolkit, a WAP version and a HTML version. In order to access WMLScript functions, you will need to install the HTML version, then the WAP plug-in. A comprehensive set of tools, documentation, and examples can be downloaded in one package. At the time of writing this text, the latest version of the SDK is version 1.5. Download that package. The SDK version 1.5 contains:

Openwave Phone Simulator 6.2.2. Main Package
Openwave Phone Simulator 6.2.2 WAP Simulator Plug-in
Openwave MMS SDK
Openwave Location Studio SDK
Openwave WAP Push Library.

These tools will be included, along with additional documentation and examples in a single compressed file, OpenwaveMobileSDK.zip. One the file is downloaded you can extract its contents by using a software program like WinZip. You will need to install the following files, Openwave_SDK_622.exe and Openwave_SDK_622wap.exe in this order. The first contains the Openwave Phone Simulator. The second file is a plug-in that allows you to develop applications that include WML and WMLScript for WAP based applications.

To install the toolkit you will first need to register with Openwave as a developer. The registration form will be displayed the first time you attempt to download the toolkit. Once you have properly registered with Openwave, you will be able to download the application. The file, Openwave_SDK_622.exe, will need to be saved in a location that you can easily locate. It is suggested that you use a folder named Openwave, located on your C drive. Once the file has been downloaded, locate the directory you stored the downloaded files.

By default, these two files will be placed in the following folder:

Base Folder (the one you chose, in this example, Openwave)
OpenwaveMobileSDK
client

Sdk

the files will be located in this folder

Simply double click on the file name you want to install.

Once the basic toolkit has been installed, then you will want to install the WAP plug-in. Note: If you attempt to install this first you will receive a notice that you must install the base package prior to installing the add-in.

One of the weaknesses with the Mobile SDK 6.2.2 is that it does not support the integration of XHTML Basic, WML, and WMLScript functions. This weakness is discussed further in Chapter 6. An example is given on how to resolve this restriction when developing such applications. To make certain that you choose the right version of the SDK, you should click on the Openwave SDK 6.2.2 WAP icon placed on your desktop by the installation program.

When you start the Openwave SDK 6.2.2, you will be presented with the following screen, see Figure 5.

This simulator can then be used to access documents you have created and saved on your PC. To access a file you simply go to File on the toolbar and then choose the Open and you will be able to browse to the proper file stored on your computer.

Figure 5. Openwave SDK 6.2.2 phone simulator

Summary

The Wireless Application Protocol (WAP) was developed in order to provide mobile users access to Internet-based applications. The first version of WAP was released in the late 1990s. The latest version of WAP is 2.0, however, many cell phones still only support version 1.3.

The WAP is a layered protocol containing six layers:

- WAE: Wireless Application Layer
- WSP: Wireless Session Protocol
- WTP: Wireless Transaction Protocol
- WTLS: Wireless Transport Layer Security
- WTL: Wireless Transport Layer
- Network Layer

A WAP Gateway is required in order to decode and encode messages sent from a WAP-enabled wireless device to application servers on the Internet.

Various companies have developed simulators and toolkits to aid you in the development of WAP-based applications. Two such toolkits are the Nokia Mobile Internet Toolkit (NMIT) 4.0 and the Openwave SDK 6.2.2. Both of these toolkits are available on the Internet for download, installation, and application development.

Discussion Questions

1. The common protocols used for the Internet are the Internet Protocol (IP) and the Hypertext Protocol (HTTP). Compare and contract these two protocols with the Wireless Application Protocol (WAP). What is a protocol? What are the advantages and disadvantages of using a stacked architecture for a protocol?
2. Version 2.0 of the WAP standard identifies XHTML as its markup language. What are the reasons for using XHTML instead of WML as the language for creating wireless Internet applications?

3. What are the issues one should consider in regard to privacy and data security when developing wireless Internet applications using WAP?

Chapter III

Wireless Markup Language (WML)

In this chapter, you will:

- Learn the elements of a WML document
- Learn to format text in a WML document
- Learn navigation control
- Learn how to use tables
- Learn how to employ templates for uniform softkey definition for all keys in a deck
- Learn to define variables and assign values
- Learn how images can be integrated into a WML document

Introduction

Associated with the Wireless Application Protocol is a markup language, similar in concept to Hypertext Markup Language (HTML) used to develop Web pages. This language, Wireless Markup Language (WML), produces an XML document. In order to develop WML documents which can be used successfully for user input-output it is necessary that you understand both structure and syntax. This chapter provides a thorough foundation in WML. That foundation supports work in following chapters.

WML Elements

Each WML document must contain these basic elements:

- Header which indicates the version of XML and the XML document type definition (DTD)
- A deck which is indicated by the <wml> ... </wml> tag pair
- One or more cards indicated by the <card> ... </card> tag pair

Useful programs, of course, require more than these fundamental elements. We will examine the other elements that lead to the development of functional applications.

XML Header

The XML header required for all WML document, often referred to as WML programs or scripts, is, for the most part standardized. Its format is:

```
<?xml version=”1.0"?>
<!DOCTYPE wml PUBLIC “-//OPENWAVE.COM//DTD WML 1.3//EN”
    “http://www.openwave.com/dtd/wml13.dtd”>
```

NOTE: Many of the software development kits (SDKs) use a template-like approach to software development. In using these SDKs they created the XML header for you.

The XML header states that the Version of XML being reference in the program is 1.0 with a WML data type definition. In addition, the name and location of the DTD is included.

Decks and Cards

WML programs contain a single deck and one or more cards. The deck represents the body of your program and is indicated by a beginning <wml> tag and terminates with a </wml> tag. This relationship is comparable to <html> and </html> in an html document.

WML is a very strict document definition. Because the language is case sensitive, an error will be indicated if you fail to comply with its rules. HTML, on the other hand, is less sensitive, therefore, if you are familiar with developing HTML documents you may encounter difficulties at first conforming to WML's requirements.

To illustrate the basics of a WML document, Figure 1 presents a WML document containing one card.

NOTE: Line numbers associated with this program are for illumination purposes only and not included in the source code used in WML documents.

Lines 1 through 3 hold the standard WML document type definition.

Lines 4 and 5 are remarks. Remarks or comments, begin with the <! — and end with —>. Any characters contained within the beginning and ending tags of a comment are ignored when the program is interpreted.

Line 6 contains the beginning WML tag and tells where the WML document begins. All WML program must be enclosed in a single pair of <WML> and </WML> tags.

Figure 1. Introduction to WML program

```
1     <?xml version="1.0"?>
2      <!DOCTYPE wml PUBLIC "-//OPENWAVE.COM//DTD WML 1.3//EN"
3       "http://www.openwave.com/dtd/wml13.dtd">

4    <! - -WML Document - - >
5    <! - - Figure 3.1 - ->
6    <wml>
7    <card id='card1' title='Card 1'>
8     <p>
9       Hello!
10    </p>
11   </card>
12   </wml>
```

Line 7 contains the card declaration. A card is bounded by a <card>...</card> pair of tags. On the card statement, there are two elements, the id element, which gives the card a unique identifier, and the title element, which is used to label the card when it is displayed on the wireless device screen.

Line 8 contains the paragraph beginning tag. Paragraphs are blocks of related text and code.

Line 9 contains literal text that is displayed when the document is accessed.

Line 10 contains the closing paragraph tag </p> matched with the opening <p> tag on line 8.

Line 11 contains the closing card tag </card> matched with the opening <card> tag on line 7.

Line 12 contains the closing document tag </wml> matching the opening <wml> tag on line 6.

Using the a text editor to write this code and the Openwave 6.2.2 emulator, the WML deck is displayed as shown in Figure 2.

The WML document produces the output shown on the screen, "Hello!" along with the title at the top of the screen, "Card 1." You are able to provide both output, as well as, information on the device. The card title is helpful in letting the user known where they are within a program and can aid the developer in testing and debugging.

Figure 2. OpenWave emulator used to display Example 1

Formatting a Document

In WML documents the individual statements, called paragraphs, are distinguished by being enclosed in <p>...</p> tags. Statements can be separated by using the paragraph tags. Paragraph text can be formatted in a number of different ways.

```
<p align=center>
<p align=right>
<p align=left>
```

A hard line return is produced by the <br/> tag. This tag forces the next text to appear on a separate line. To produce blank lines you can include multiple <br/> tags.

```
<p>
Line 1</br></br>
Line 3
</p>
```

Displaying the document illustrates the use of the align statement and the line break tag.

To modify the text appearance, in essence the font and its size, you are using to display the text on your wireless device, you can chose one or more of the following tags.

Table 1.

Tag	Meaning
<b>...</b>	Displays bold text
<big>...</big	Displays large text
<em>...</em>	Displays enhanced text
<i>...</i>	Displays italicized text
<small>...</small>	Displays text in smaller font
<strong>...</strong>	Displays text in strong text
<u>...</u>	Displays text underlined

Figure 3.

```
<wml>
<card id = "Card1" Title="Formatting Text">
<p>
  <b>Bold</b><br/>
  <big>Big</b><br/>
  <em>Emphasized</em></br>
  <i>Italics</i></br>
 <small>Small</small</br>
 <strong>String</strong></br>
<u>Underline</u></br>
<big><b><i><u>BoldItalicUnder</u></i></b></big></br>
</card>
</wml>
```

The WML document in Figure 3 uses each of these different tags to illustrate their use.

Displaying the document in Example 3 results in the following output.

As you can see from Figure 4, WML, though limited in its text formatting ability, does provide a means by which output can be enhanced to improve its visual quality.

NOTE: When combining tags be certain to end the tags in the reverse order in which they are opened, e.g. <b><u>...</b></u> will result in an error being identified.

Figure 4. Formatting text

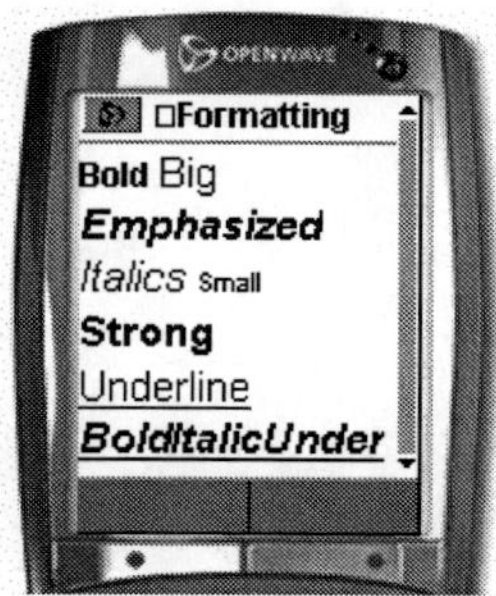

Navigation

To explain further the creation of WML-based projects, the concepts of WML are illustrated through the development of a simple information system. Its design is quite simple. An initial menu is provided that allows the user to choose the region of the United States for which they want to receive information about a particular state. Once you select the region, a list of the states that lie in that region is presented. Finally, the user is able to select a particular state. For that state, the name of the state capital, the population of the capital, and the county in which the capital resides are shown. The user is given an option to return to the menu shown on the prior screen.

Figure 5 presents the basic design for the state capital information system. Each of the boxes represents a separate card in the WML deck.

Each of the sub-cards, for example, the list of states and the individual states, will contain and option allowing the user to return to the previous card. This navigation is necessary to prevent the user from having to restart the program each time they desire to go to another state.

Cards should be designed to compliment the limited screen size of the wireless device, particularly if you are designing a system for use on a cellular phone. A rule of thumb is to limit card size to the size that displayed on two screens. This

Figure 5. Basic state capital information design

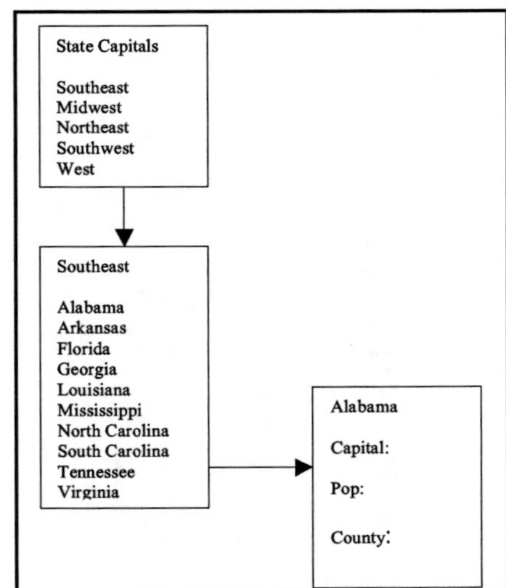

rule will aid in reducing the amount of scrolling required to view the information. If the data extends past the two-screen limit, then additional cards are added to the deck to handle this information.

To begin the implementation, start with the main card. Links to additional cards are added as the program is developed. In this chapter, you are shown different ways in which you can link to cards within the same deck and to cards contained in other decks.

To assure quality and correctness of your programs it is wise to develop your programs in small segments. Test your program after you create each card. Thorough testing throughout the coding phase will greatly enhance the accuracy of your programs and will reduce the amount of time required to find defects.

In our State Capital Information System, we will begin by developing the first screen, which contains the list of regions of the United States. This screen contains a title, "State Capitals" and a list of the geographical regions: Southeast, Northeast, Midwest, Southwest, and West.

First, develop the card that contains this information. Add links once the main card is completed and tested.

The initial program contains one card and multiple paragraphs signified by the <p> ...</p> pairs.

After this card has been created, you can view the output by using an emulator. Execute the program and observe the results on the simulated device. The result should be displayed as shown in Figure 7.

Figure 6. State capital main menu card

```
<?xml version="1.0"?>
 <!DOCTYPE wml PUBLIC "-//OPENWAVE.COM//DTD WML 1.3//EN"
      "http://www.openwave.com/dtd/wml13.dtd">

 <! - - Capital Info Main Screen - - >
<wml>
 <card id='main' title='State Capitals'>
  <p>
    Southeast
  </p>
  <p>
    Midwest
  </p>
  <p>
    Northeast
  </p>
  <p>
    Southwest
  </p>
  <p>
    West
  </p>
 </card>
</wml>
```

Figure 7. State capital main menu

Figure 8. Use of <a> to link two cards together

```
<?xml version="1.0"?>
  <!DOCTYPE wml PUBLIC "-//OPENWAVE.COM//DTD WML 1.3//EN"
      "http://www.openwave.com/dtd/wml13.dtd">

  <! - - Capital Info Main Screen - - >

 <wml>

<card id='main' title='State Capitals'>
   <p>
     <a href='#cardse'>Southeast></a>
   </p>
   <p> Midwest </p>
   <p> Northeast </p>
  <p>  Southwest </p>
  <p>  West    </p>
  </card>

  <card id='cardse' title='Southeast'>
   <p> Alabama        </p>
   <p> Arkansas       </p>
   <p> Florida        </p>
   <p> Georgia        </p>
   <p> Louisiana      </p>
   <p> Mississippi    </p>
   <p> North Carolina </p>
   <p> South Carolina </p>
   <p> Tennessee      </p>
   <p> Virginia       </p>

  </card>
 </wml>
```

Once you have this program working correctly, it is time to add the first link to list of states for a given region. In this case, we will add the Southeast region states, contained in the design presented in Figure 5. This list will be contained in a separate card. We will give that card the title, "Southeast" and an id of "cardse". The following code implements the Southeast list of states.

Links can be added through the use of the <a> … </a> tag pairs. The hypertext reference is included within those tags, along with a description if desired. The description, enclosed in quotation marks, will appear on the device's screen. The link allows the program branch to the location indicated by the link text, in this case, '#cardse'. The use of the pound sign means that the link location is local to the current deck from which it is called.

Note; To make the source code shorter for display purposes in this chapter, single line paragraphs are contained in a single line with <p>...</p> pairs on the same line. It is a common practice to have the <p>...</p> tags appear on their own lines.

Executing this code results in the screen shown in Figure 9.

Due to the limitation of this example, you can only select Southeast to list the states in that region. In a complete example, each of the regions would be linked to a list of the states in that region.

Pressing the button under the checkmark causes the WML document to transfer control to the card identified as 'cardse'. At that point, the following screen, Figure 10. is displayed showing the states in the Southeast Region. You will notice that you must scroll down to see all of the states.

Once the main screen and the list of states for the Southeast have been developed, we can tie the main screen to the Southeast. This requires the development of a link. Two different ways are provided for implementing links. The first way employees an anchor, similar to that used in HTML. The second method uses the <go> statement to cause the browser to branch to either a card in the same deck or to a card in another deck. Use pf the <go> statement is illustrated in the section, Indirect Events, later in this chapter.

Figure 9. Region linked to state list

Figure 10. List of states in Southeast

Table 1 shows the syntax of the <anchor> statement and the meaning of its use for linking to different cards and different decks.

To illustrate the usage of both types of links, the connection between the main card and the region card is created by both methods. First, using the <a>...</a> the link is created by the following statement:

```
<a href="#region" title="Southeast"<Southeast></a>
```

Here the linkage is local to a card in the same deck.

Viewing the WML document in your simulator presents the following output shown in Figures 12 and 12a.

Table 2. Syntax of <a> element used to link to cards

Type of <anchor> link	Syntax
Link to card in same deck	<a href="#card2" title = "Second Card">Second Card</a>
Link to card in another deck on same server	<a href="#card2" title "Second Card">Separate Deck</a>
Link to card in separate deck on different server	<a href=http://www.secondserver.com/wmldeck.wml>Remote Server"</a>

Figure 11. Code containing link to regional state list

```
<?xml version="1.0"?>
   <!DOCTYPE wml PUBLIC "-//OPENWAVE.COM//DTD WML 1.3//EN"
      "http://www.openwave.com/dtd/wml13.dtd">
   <! - - Capital Info Main Screen - - >
   <wml>
   <card id="main" title="State Capitals">
    <p>
      <a href="#cardse">Southeast></a>
    </p>
    <p> Midwest    </p>
    <p> Northeast  </p>
    <p>  Southwest </p>
    <p>  West      </p>
   </card>
   <card id="cardse" title="Southeast">
    <p>  Alabama         </p>
    <p>  Arkansas        </p>
    <p>  Florida         </p>
    <p>  Georgia         </p>
    <p>  Louisiana       </p>
    <p>  Mississippi     </p>
    <p>  North Carolina  </p>
    <p>  South Carolina  </p>
    <p>  Tennessee       </p>
    <p>  Virginia        </p>
   </card>
  </wml>
```

Pressing the button below the softkey indicated by the default check mark causes the program to execute the link and display the state list for the Southeast.

Finally, to complete the state capital program, a final card is added to the deck. That card provides the detailed information about each state's capital: name, population, and county. The code in Figure 13 produces the output shown in Figure 14.

To access the information for Alabama's capital, a second link as added that used the <a>…</a> pair to provide for linking to a separate card in the same

Figure 12. Usage of <a> tag to branch to card in same deck

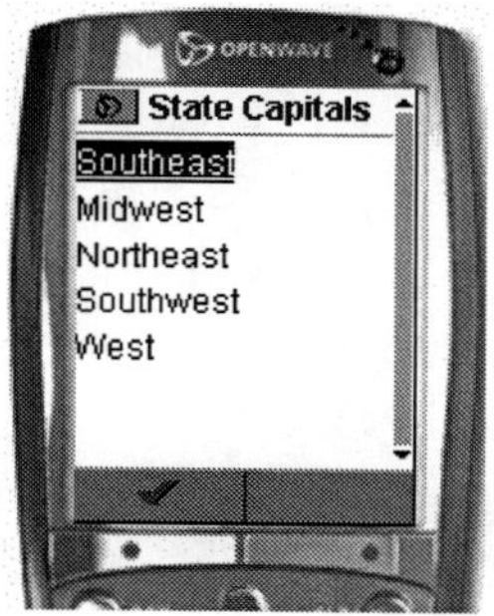

Figure 12a. List of states in Southeast Region

Figure 13. Additional card for displaying Alabama's capital information

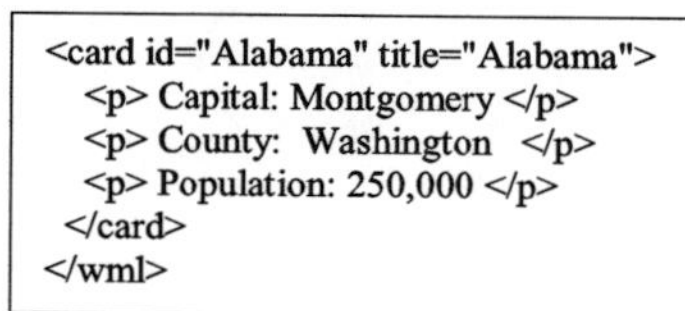

```
<card id="Alabama" title="Alabama">
   <p> Capital: Montgomery </p>
   <p> County:  Washington  </p>
   <p> Population: 250,000 </p>
  </card>
</wml>
```

Figure 14. Alabama state capital information

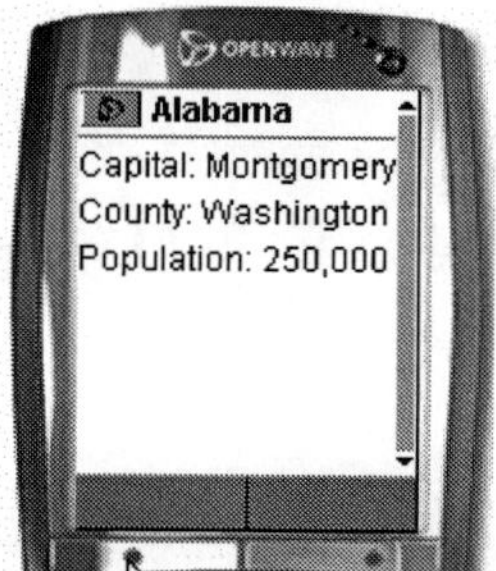

deck that contains the city, county, and population data.

The <anchor> element is similar to the <a> element. The <anchor> supports the same attributes with the exception of the href. The <anchor> element can be combined with the <go> and <prev> to support navigation between cards where the destination is specified. The syntax of the <anchor> use to navigate to a second card is:

```
<anchor> title = “card title”>
        softkeylabel
    <go href= “#cardid”/>
</anchor>
```

Tables

To aid in the organization of data and to assist in the formatting of text displayed on the wireless device one can use tables. A table consists of rows and columns. The declaration of a table provides for the number of columns. Each row, however, is declared individually. The <table> … </table> tag causes a table to be included in a card. On the <table> statement one includes the number of columns the table contains, thus the complete table declaration is:

```
<table columns = “n”>
```

where n represents an integer value for the number of columns you desire.

Once the table is declared then the individual rows are included within the <table>…</table> tags. Each row will contain a <tr> table row tag and a <td> table data tag. A complete single column row statement appears as:

```
<table column=”1”>
      <tr><td>Row 1</td</tr>
   </table>
```

For the purposes of enhancing the state capital program, a table is employed on the individual state card. Here you can format the labels and the data for the capital's name, its population, and county. The source code appears in Figure 15.

The table displays as shown in Figure 16.

As you can see, the use of a table makes the screen well formatted. As always, you have to be careful of the amount of text you are displaying. Spelling out the word "Population" would cause the screen to appear crowded.

Figure 15. Table used to format state capital data

```
<table columns="2".
  <tr>
    <td>Capital</td>
    <td>Jackson</td>
  </tr>
  <tr>
    <td>Population</td>
    <td>250,000</td>
  </tr>
  <tr>
    <td>County</td>
    <td>Hinds</td>
  </tr>
</table>
```

Figure 16. Table used to format output for state capital information

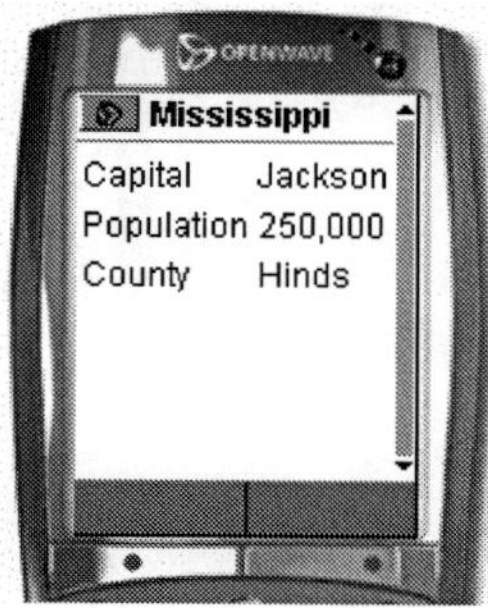

Figure 17. Use of bolding with table data

```
<table columns="2".
    <tr><td><b>Capital</b></td><td>Jackson></td></tr>
    <tr><td><b>Population</b></td><td>250,000</td></tr>
    <tr><td><b>County</b></td><td>Hinds</td></tr>
  </table>
```

Figure 18. Bolding of labels for enhanced data presentation

Figure 19. Use of <b> tag to bold entire table

```
<b>
  <table columns="2".
  <tr><td>Capital</td><td>Jackson></td></tr>
  <tr><td>Pop</td><td>250,000</td></tr>
  <tr><td>County</td><td>Hinds</td></tr>
  </table>
</b>
```

Figure 20. Bolding entire table

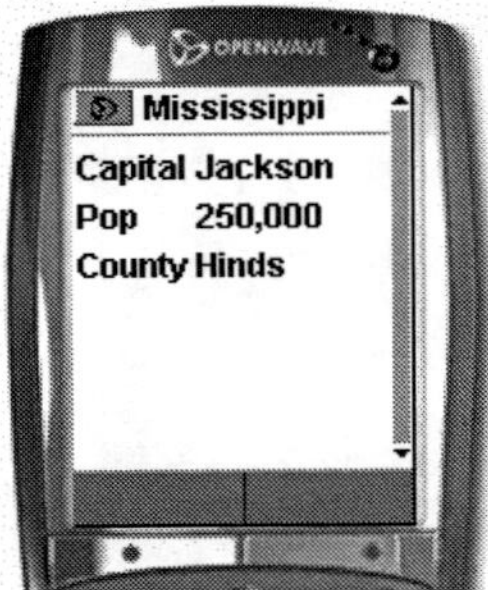

Use of additional tags assists in enhancing the appearance of the text on the screen. The <b>, <i>, <em> are examples of such tags. In the capital example, bolding makes the data easier to recognize on the screen, see Figure 17.

This bolding makes the screen appear as shown in Figure 18.

If you want to apply bolding to the entire table, you place the <b> tag prior to the table declaration, as illustrated in the code segment in Figure 19.

This slight change to the location of the bold tag results in changes to the appearance, see Figure 20.

As you can see in Figure 20, the bolding of the entire table is not as effective as the bolding of the individual labels on the data as seen in Figure 18.

Table cells can be associated with links. Using a table improves the format and appearance of the data while continuing support for links through the use of the <a>...</a> taps. The following example, Figure 21, illustrates the use of a table with links for the different regions. The table contains two columns with align used to aid in formatting. The use of the align="LR" causes the first column to

Figure 21. Using table to format, align and link to

```
<?xml version="1.0"?>
<!DOCTYPE wml PUBLIC "-//OPENWAVE.COM//DTD WML 1.3//EN"
"http://www.openwave.com/dtd/wml13.dtd">

<!-- WML file created by the Openwave SDK -->

<wml>
      <card id="card1" title="Regions">
   <p>
   <table columns = "2" align="LR">
     <tr>
       <td><a href="Southeast.wml">Southeast</a></td>
       <td><a href="Northeast.wml">Northeast</a></td>
     </tr>
     <tr>
       <td><a href="Midwest.wml">Midwest</a></td>
       <td><a href="Southwest.wml">Southwest</a></td>
     </tr>
     <tr>
       <td><a href="West.wml">West</a></td>
     </tr>
   </table>
   </p>
      </card>
</wml>
```

Figure 22. Use of table for alignment and links for regions of United States

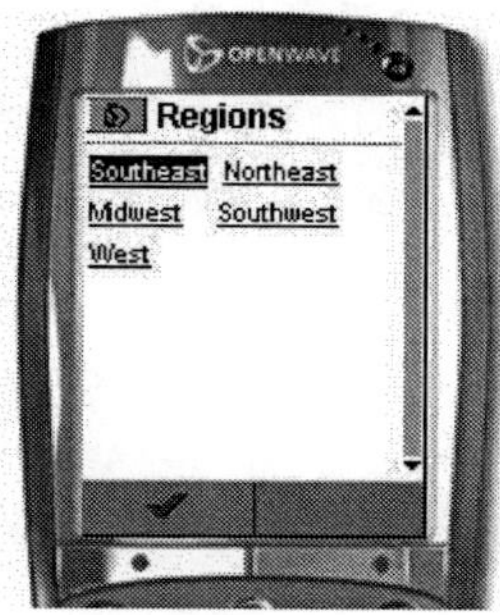

right justified and the 'R' results in the second columns being right justified. This alignment aids in making the information more readable.

Note: In this example, each of the different regions links to a separate WML document on the same server.

Figure 22 presents the results of viewing this WML document on the Openwave simulator.

It is important to realize that when using tables to display columns of data, such as in the above example, you may be required to use the <small> ...</small> tag combination to reduce the font size and thereby, properly display the data in columns.

Using Images

Traditional Web-based systems rely heavily on graphics. WML on the other hand is restricted in its support for images due to the limited characteristics of mobile wireless devices, in particular cell phones. WML only supports the wireless bit map graphics (wmbp) image format. These images are limited in their resolution due to their restricted size.

To include an image in a WML document you have to use the <img> tag. The general syntax of the <img> statement is:

```
<img align="bottom|middle|top" src="filename.wbmp" alt="text" height="value"
hspace="value" localsrc="name"|id" src="path" space="value" width="value"
/>
```

Figure 23. Use of images in WML

```
<?xml version="1.0"?>
<!DOCTYPE wml PUBLIC "-//OPENWAVE.COM//DTD WML 1.3//EN"
"http://www.openwave.com/dtd/wml13.dtd">

<!-- WML file created by the Openwave SDK -->

<wml>
        <card id="ms" title="Mississippi">
      <p>
     <img src="c:\programs_3\logo.wbmp" alt="Missing"/>
   </p>
  </card>
</wml>
```

Figure 24. Logo for state of Mississippi

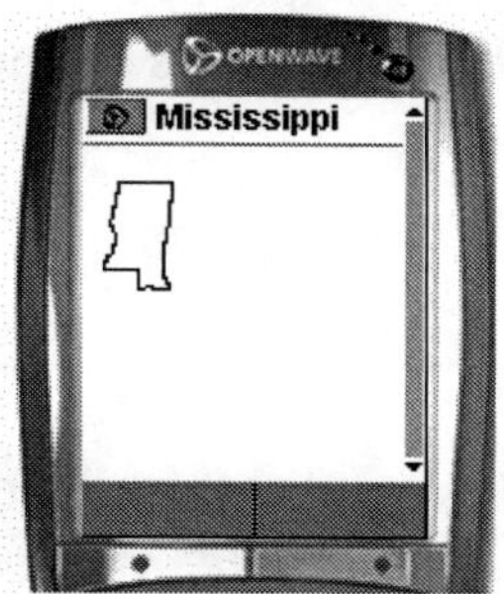

The src (source) indicates the image's location and the alt (alternative) executes if the wbmp file cannot be located. These are the only two elements required for using the <img> tag.

The following code, shown in Figure 23, illustrates the use of an image in a WML document.

Using the simulator to display this document presents the image of the state of Mississippi shown in Figure 24.

The size of the image can be adjusted during the process of creating the .wbmp file.

Events

The <do> element, introduced above when we used it for navigation, contains a number of different actions that can be used to control the flow of a program

Table 3. Events

Action supported by <do> element	Definition
accept	Causes a task to occur, similar to concept of using an enter key
prev	Causes return to previous card in the history stack
help	Presents available help on an action or topic
reset	Resets the wireless device
options	Asks for more operations
delete	Remove an item
unknown	Maps task to any key

and to cause specific events to occur when you enter or leave a card. Events are divided into two primary groupings: 1) events caused by the user and 2) events caused indirectly. Table 3 presents the actions related to the <do> element.

Indirect Events

WML supports three different events that are the result of an indirect action of the user. Moving from one card to another can be used to trigger an event, either from moving to a card or returning to a card already visited during the execution of the program. The <onenterforward> is used to trigger an event whenever a card is visited, except when <prev/> is used to return a card on the browser's history stack.

When revisiting a card you can use the <onenterbackward> element to cause an event to occur. This event is triggered whenever you enter a card via the <prev/> which accesses the last card stored on the browser's history stack.

The <onpick> event occurs as a result of the user choosing from an list of options within a <select> element. Use of the <select> element presented a menu to user, who can then choose one of the options. An example of the <onpick> illustrates the content of the statement and how it relates to the <do> command.

Timer Events

Timer events are ones that occur after a set amount of time. One of the basic ways in which the timer event can be used is the introduction of a "Splash Screen". A splash screen is one that is displayed when a program first runs and provides such information as the name of a company, the name and version of a program, a company logo or other information. The timer event receives a value measured in 10th of a second, that is, if you want to screen to be displayed for 15 seconds you have to enter a value of 150.

```
<card id="cardid" title="card name" ontimer="#next_card"> <timer value =
"###"/>
```

Figure 25. Use of <onevent> to select region

```
<wml>

<card id="menu"?
  <p> <select name="Region">
      <option value="Southeast"
        <onevent type="onpick">
          <go href="#secard" />
        </onevent>
        Southeast
      </option>
</card>
</wml>
```

Figure 26. Use of timer for introductory page

```
<?xml version="1.0"?>
<!DOCTYPE wml PUBLIC "-//OPENWAVE.COM//DTD WML 1.3//EN"
"http://www.openwave.com/dtd/wml13.dtd">
<!-- WML file created by the Openwave SDK -->
<wml>
 <card id="splash" title="Welcome" ontimer="#menu">
     <timer value = "50"/>
   <p>
    WELCOME TO THE STATE CAPITAL PROGRAM
   </p>
  </card>
  <card id="menu" title="MENU">
   <p>
    <a href="northwest.wml">Northeast</a>
   </p>
   <p>
    <a href="southwest.wml">Southeast</a>
   </p>
   <p>
    <a href="midwest.wml">Midwest</a>
   </p>
   <p>
    <a href="southwest.wml">Southwest</a>
   </p>
   <p>
    <a href="west.wml">West</a>
   </p>
  </card>
  </wml>
```

Figure 27. Splash screen displayed for five seconds

Figure 28. Menu displayed after Splash screen

The ontimer="#next_card" contains the id of the card you want the program to branch to after the time limit expressed in the timer value statement where the ### represents a user determined value.

The output from this program is two separate screens. The first screen, Welcome screen, is displayed on the wireless device for five seconds and then the second screen, MENU, is displayed for the user to select what region for which they want information.

Variables

The limitations of WML force the developer to use other scripting languages to manipulate the data and to make decision-making and looping available. WML does support user input. Data input by the user can be used in the program for more advanced purposes than simple display.

Variables are declared in a WML document and assigned a value through the use of the <setvar> command or they can be interactively assigned a value with

Figure 29. Use of <setvar> to assign value to state information

```
<?xml version="1.0"?>
    <!DOCTYPE wml PUBLIC "-//OPENWAVE.COM//DTD WML 1.3//EN"
      "http://www.openwave.com/dtd/wml13.dtd">
  <wml>
  <card id="AL" title="Alabama">

   <onevent type="onenterforward">
     <refresh>
     <setvar name="city" value="Montgomery"/>
     <setvar name="pop" value="201,568"/>
     <setvar name="county" value="Montgomery"/>
     </refresh>
   </onevent>
   <p>
   <b>
   <table columns="2".
         <tr>
           <td><small><b>Capital</b></small></td>
          <td><small>$(city)</small></td>
         </tr>
         <tr>
          <td><small><b>Pop</b></small></td>
          <td><small>$(pop)</small></td>
         </tr>
         <tr>
          <td><small><b>County</b></small></td>
          <td><small>$(county)</small></td>
         </tr>
     </table>
     </b>
    <p>
   </card>
  </wml>
```

user input from the keypad. In extending our state capital program, the values for each state can be assigned to variables and then displayed. Figure 29 illustrates the assignment of values for an individual state. Though this is a primitive example, you can see that by assigning the values in the beginning of

Figure 30. Output of values stored in variables

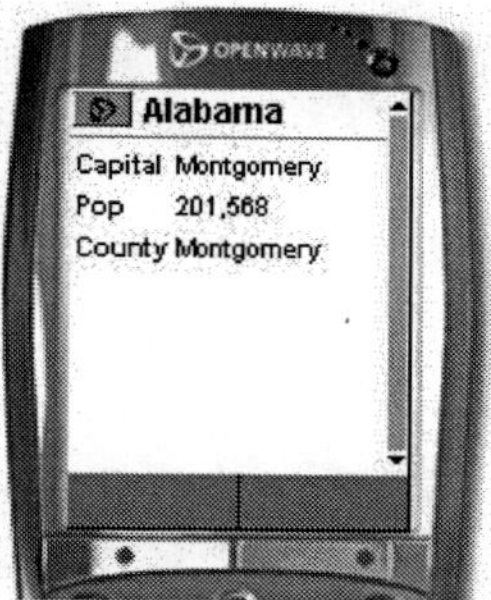

Figure 31. WML document using <input> to assign data to a variable

```
<?xml version="1.0"?>
  <!DOCTYPE wml PUBLIC "-//OPENWAVE.COM//DTD WML 1.3//EN"
     "http://www.openwave.com/dtd/wml13.dtd">

  <! - - Capital Info Main Screen - - >

  <wml>
 <card id="main" title="State Capitals">
  <onevent type="onenterforward">
   <refresh>
    <input name="user" title="Name: "/>
   </refresh>
  </onevent>
     <p>
   <do type="accept" label="Regions"
    <go href="#regions"/>
   </do>
 </card>

<card id="regions" title="Regions">
  <p>
  <small>
  Hello $(user). </br> Please select a region.
  </small>
  <p> <a href="#cardse">Southeast</a> </p>
  <p> Midwest </p>
  <p> Northeast </p>
  <p> Southwest </p>
  <p> West    </p>
  </card>

  <card id="cardse" title="Southeast">
   <p> Alabama  </p>
   <p> Arkansas  </p>
   <p> Florida   </p>
   <p> Georgia   </p>
   <p> Louisiana  </p>
   <p> Mississippi    </p>
   <p> North Carolina </p>
   <p> South Carolina </p>
   <p> Tennessee </p>
   <p> Virginia </p>
  </card>
 </wml>
```

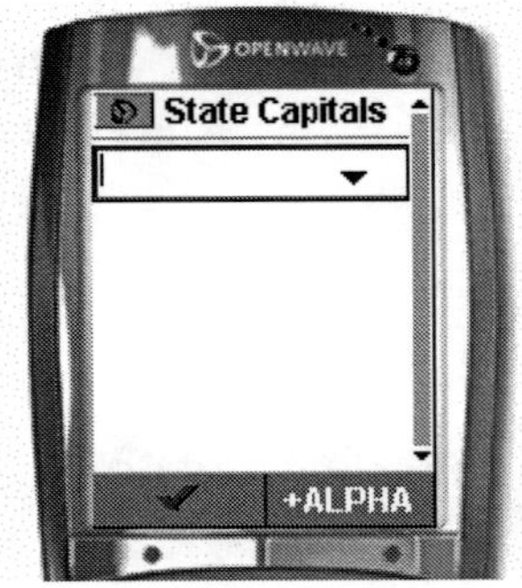

Figure 32. Prompt for user's name

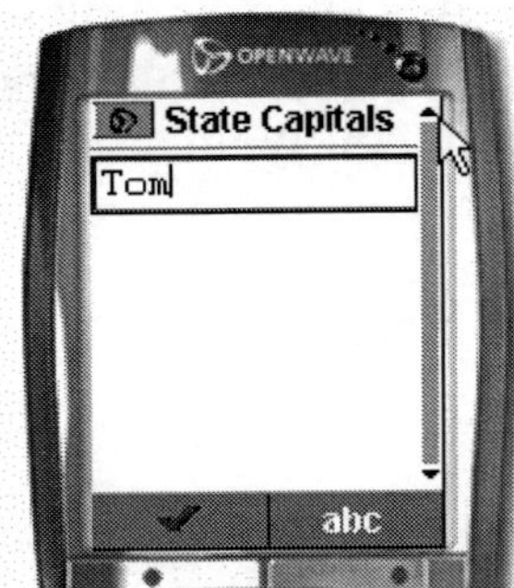

Figure 33. After entering name

Figure 34. Before moving to next card

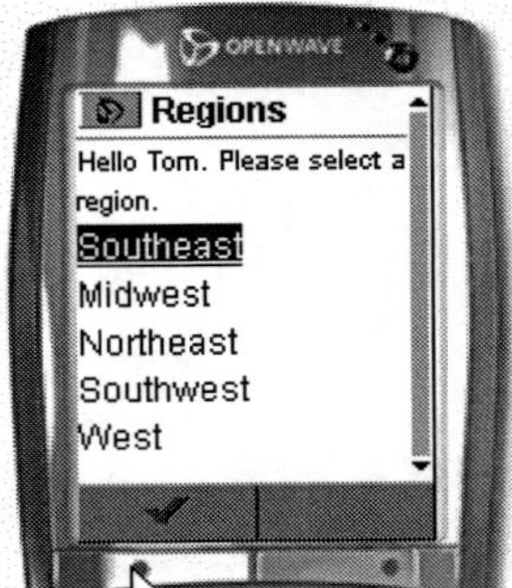

Figure 35. Selection of regions

a program allows one to use the card for more than one state. You simply have to change the values and then display them by the use of the $( ).

Figure 30 shows the out put of the program on the Openwave device emulator.

Now that you understand that you display the value contained in a variable by the use of a dollar sign, $, and having the variable's name enclosed in parentheses, we can advance to the next level where the individual is able to enter a value from the keypad of the wireless device. Example 31 illustrates how the <onenterforward> event can be used in conjunction with the <input> element to prompt the user for input and then use the data input later in the program on another card.

Though the above example set reflects a simple example of the use of variables and input, you can begin to see how input can be quite helpful in developing useful applications.

Table 4. Specifiers for input statement

Specifier	Input
A	Any non-lowercase, non-numeric character (uppercase alphabetic and punctuations)
a	Lowercase alphabetic and punctuations
N	Any numeric character
X	All uppercase characters including +,.,and -.
x	Lowercase alphabetic, numeric, and punctuation characters
M	Any character, browser assumes is uppercased
m	Any character, browser assumes is lowercased
*f	Number of characters allowed by format specifier *f*
nf	Specifiy number of characters for a specific format
\c	Literal character, c, is output, no input allowed

The allowable values accepted in a input statement can be controlled through the use of the format and maxlength attributes.

<inputname="variable name" format="format type" maxlength="integer value" />. The input mask specifiers are outlined in Table 4.

To assist the user when requesting input, you can use the <select> statement. <select> is very helpful in reducing the number of keystrokes required by the user and also restricts input only to acceptable values. Figure 36 shows the use of <select> statement with its associated <option>...</option> tags.

Figure 36. Use of <option> to control data entry

```
<?xml version="1.0"?>
   <!DOCTYPE wml PUBLIC "-//OPENWAVE.COM//DTD WML 1.3//EN"
      "http://www.openwave.com/dtd/wml13.dtd">

  <! - - Capital Info Main Screen - - >

  <wml>

<card id="regions" title="Regions">
  <p>
   <select name="region">
     <option value = "N">North</option>
     <option value = "S">South</option>
     <option value = "W">West</option>
     <option value = "E">East</option>
   </select>
   </p>
  </card>

  </wml>
```

The limitation of using the simple <option> statement is that in WML you have no means by which a value can be used in a decision statement, for example, if ... then. We will examine how decisions can be made in the next chapter where we will examine WMLScript. For now, we have to be satisfied with the limitations of WML and see how we can work around them. Up to now we have been limited to the use of links with the <a>...</a> and <anchor>...</anchor> tags and the <do> statement.

Figure 37. Output of <option> for selecting regions

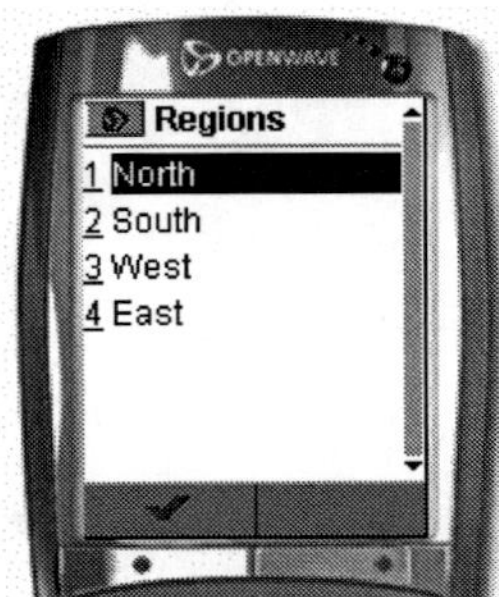

Figure 38. Use of <option onpick> to display capital information

```
<?xml version="1.0"?>
  <!DOCTYPE wml PUBLIC "-//OPENWAVE.COM//DTD WML 1.3//EN"
     "http://www.openwave.com/dtd/wml13.dtd">
 <wml>
 <card id="AL" title="State Capitals">

  <onevent type="onenterforward">
   <refresh>
    <setvar name="capital_city" value="" />
   </refresh>
  </onevent>
  <p>
   Choose State

  <select name="capital">
    <option onpick="#capital_info" value="Lincoln">
      Nebraska
    </option>
    <option onpick="#capital_info" Value="Jackson">
      Mississippi
    </option>
  </select>
  <br/>
  </p>
 </card>

 <card id="capital_info" title="Capital Info">
  <p>
  <small>Capital: $(capital).</small>
  </p>
  <do type="accept" label="Home">
   <prev/>
  </do>
 </card>

 </wml>
```

Figure 39. Use of <optgroup> to aid in selection of region

```
<?xml version="1.0"?>
  <!DOCTYPE wml PUBLIC "-//OPENWAVE.COM//DTD WML 1.3//EN"
     "http://www.openwave.com/dtd/wml13.dtd">
 <wml>
 <card id="home" title="State Capitals"
  <p>

  <select name="region" multiple="true">
    <optgroup title="Regions">
      <option value="Northeast">Northeast</option>
      <option value="Southeast">Southeast</option>
      <option value="Midwest">Midwest</option>
      <option value="Southwest">Southwest</option>
      <option value="West">West</option>
    </optgroup>
  </select>

  <do type="accept" label="Regions">
    <go href="#regions" />
  </do>
 </p>
 </card>

 <card id="regions>
  <p>
   Selected Region: <br/>
   $(region)
  </p>
 </card>

</wml>
```

Figure 40. Region options using <optgroup>

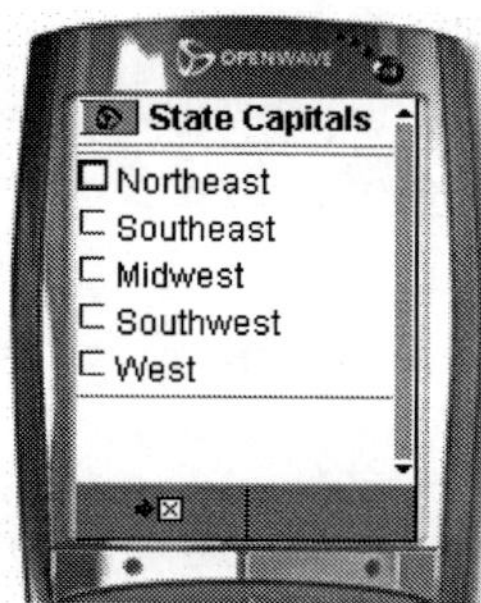

Figure 41. After selecting Southeast

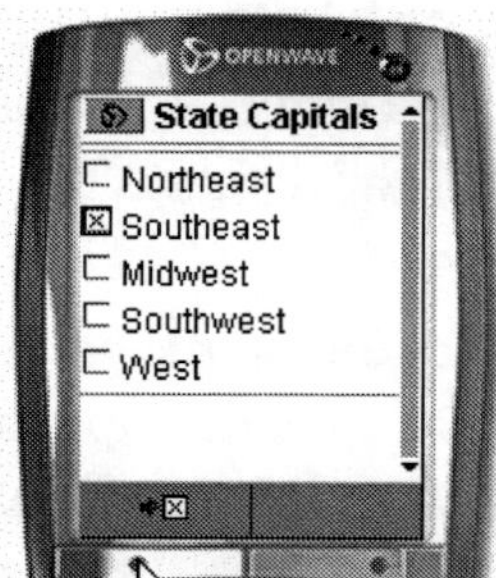

The <option> and the <optgroup> elements can be used to provide for another means of navigation. Figure 36 provides an example where the <option> statement, along with the onpick element, allows the user to chose which link to navigate.

Figure 42. Scroll down to display Regions

Figure 43. Displaying selected region's value

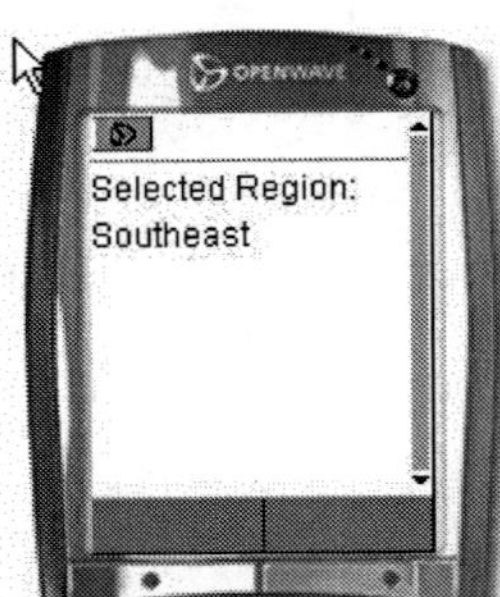

The <optgroup> aids in making user input easier to manage. Grouping of related elements allows you to implement menu-like presentations. The <select> statement, along with the <optgroup> creates a collapsible screen thus aiding in efficient space utilization. Figure 37 illustrates the use of the <optgroup> for the presentation and selection of the desired region from a list of different geographical regions (Figures 38 and 39).

In Figure 40, you see the list of the regions from which you can choose. Once scroll to the desired region you can press the left button and an X appears in the box next to that region (see Figure 41). Continuing to scroll down past the last region, West, and you will then see the "Regions" label appear on the above the left button (Figure 42). Clicking on the left button the program navigates to the next card and displays the name of the selected region, illustrated in Figure 43.

From the above example you can see that the use of the <optgroup> aids in both the appearance and the input of data since it restricts the required user input to only by the scroll buttons and the left button. This limitation is a marked improvement over having the user spell out the name of the desired region.

Summary

In this chapter, you have been introduced to the use of WML documents as means of communicating with the user. WML is a markup language derived from the eXtensible Markup Language (XML). WML is designed to be used on WAP-enabled microbrowsers supported by a variety of devices, which include both cell phones, and other handheld devices.

WML supports the formatting of values and the formatting of output through the use of a variety of methods. Text formatting tags are included which allow for setting the size, the boldness, italicization, and underlining. The use of tables helps in establishing where the text appears on the screen. Paragraph statements are used to tie output into a common unit, which can be formatted as desired.

WML documents are composed of a deck and one or more cards. Through the use of navigation tags, the program can access these cards either programmatically or in response to user input. Individual cards can have both a title, displayed on the top of the device's screen, and a unique identifiers used for navigation.

Images or graphics have a limitation in WML documents. Only those graphic or image files which are of the Wireless Bit Graph format are displayed by the WAP browser. Special software must be used to create these figures and must end in the .wbmp file extension. Only limited images can be displayed.

Navigation between cards in the same deck and between cards in a separate deck are supported through the use of <a> ... </a> tags and the href element and the <anchor>...</anchor> elements with the <go> elements. Further control of navigation is provided by the use of events such as the <onenterforward>, <onenterbackward>, <onpick>, and timer events.

Users are allowed to input values with the <input> statement. The value input can be stored in a variable within the WML document by use of the <setVar> element.

Exercises

1. Write a WML program that displays the following statement on the wireless device:

   "Welcome to WML!"

2. Modify the program in Exercise 1 to include a splash screen that displays a WML graphic of your choice prior to displaying the welcome statement.

3. Create a WML program that uses a table to display information about your movies showing at your local movie theatre. The program will allow you to choose between Children's Movies, Action Movies, Comedies, and Dramas. Once you chose the type of movie, then you will be give a list. Choosing one of the movies will then present a brief summary of the plot.
4. You work for a company that provides software development and technical support to the insurance company. You boss wants you to develop a WML application that provides the user with access to the phone numbers of the support personnel. Develop a WML program that provides the user with the following information:

Tech Support
Sales
Accounting

The following employees are located in these departments, along with their phone numbers:

Tech Support

Bob555-1111
Sally 555-1112

Sales

Mary 555-2221
Lisa555-2222

Accounting

Ed 555-3331

Use a table to aid in formatting the information on the wireless device.

Chapter IV

WMLScript

In this chapter, you will:

- Learn about the use of the WMLScript
- Learn about WMLScript functions
- Learn about data types supported by WMLScript
- Learn how to declare and use variables
- Learn about operators used in WMLScripts
- Learn how to implement decision making, flow control, and iteration
- Learn how to interact with WMLScripts and how to pass arguments to a WMLScript

Introduction

WMLScripts improve the use of WML documents through their ability to support decision-making, arithmetic operations, iteration, and parameter passing. Furthermore, since they are executed on the server, they aid in memory management. Without any additional language support, one can still write reasonably complex wireless mobile Internet applications by using WML documents and WMLScript functions. However, to reduce the amount of work required to create useful applications, a set of standard libraries has been developed that are easily integrated into your WMLScript functions. These standard libraries are discussed in depth in Chapter V.

WMLScript Functions

WMLScript functions are developed by using the WMLScript language. This scripting language is similar to other languages in that the programmer is able to declare variables, control the flow of the execution, perform mathematical operations, make decisions based on relational and Boolean operators, and return a value from the function.

The WMLScript functions can be called from either a WML document or from another WMLScript function. Functions to be accessed from outside of the current WMLScript file are declared as *extern*, otherwise they contain no declaration. WMLScript functions are unable to execute on their own but must be called from either a WML document or another WMLScript function.

Supported Data Types

WMLScript supports a limited number of data types that can be used in your programs. These data types, outlined in Table 1, are the primary ones used in most programming languages, save for the invalid data type used to indicate that a particular value does not correspond with the other acceptable data types.

Variables

A variable in a program represents a storage location in the computer's memory. In that memory location one can store values which can be accessed when needed in the program. WMLScript supports integer, floating point, string, Boolean, and Invalid data types. Each of these data types is described in the following sections.

WMLScript requires that a variable be of one of these data types. It is common in many programming languages to have the type of a variable identified whenever the variable is declared. With WMLScript, there is a slight twist to a variable being declared. First the variable must be declared, then its type is derived from the type of data stored (assigned) to that particular variable. Figure 1 illustrates this principle.

In this example, the variable *var1* is first declared by using the *var* keyword and then giving the variable a name, *var1*. Following that statement, an assignment

Table 1. Data types supported in WMLScript

Data Type	Acceptable Values	Modifiers
Integer	-2,147,483,648 to 2,147,483,647	OX or ox to indicate value is hexadecimal O for octal
Floating Point	1.17549435E-38 to 3.4028235E38	Exponential numbers can be expressed by following a value with E or e
String	Value contained with either single apostrophes or double quotes	
Boolean	True or False	
Invalid	Any value not representing on of the above 4 data types	

Figure 1. Variable declaration and type resolution

```
extern function variable_declaration( ) {

var var1;

var1 = 20;

}
```

statement is use to assign the value, 20, to *var1*. Since 20 is an integer value then *var1* is a variable of type integer and can be used throughout the program to store an integer value.

Comments and Documentation

To assist in program understanding and to provide for internal documentation, comments and documentation are supported in WMLScript by two different formats: single and multi-line comments. The single line comment can also be used to provide comments on the same line as active source code.

```
var variable_one;     // single line comment


/* multi-line comment
     All lines between opening slash asterisk and closing asterisk slash are
ignored during execution
*/
```

During the construction of a program, comments are also very helpful. You can comment-out a series of lines in order to prevent them from being executed. Once you have developed and tested the other code, then the commented-out code can be included and tested.

Operators

WMLScript documents support a variety of operators that allow you to create advanced programs capable of handling such tasks as decision-making, arithmetic operations, and program flow control. The following sections examine the various operators supported in WMLScript functions.

Assignment

WMLScript provides a number of different assignment operators that can be used in your applications. These assignment operators, outlined in Table 2, combine arithmetic operators and the assignment operator. Bitlevel operators can also be combined with the assignment operator to form a shorthand version.

NOTE: The basic assignment operator is the single equal sign, =. The double equal sign, ==, is used as a relational operation for equality.

To assign a value to a variable use the appropriate assignment operator.

Arithmetic

WMLScript supports standard arithmetic operators. The operators are used for addition, multiplication, division, and subtraction. Integer math operators are also provided. The arithmetic operators are listed in Table 3.

Table 2. Assignment operators

Operator	Operation
=	Assign
+=	Add two numbers or concatenate two strings and assign the result
-=	Subtract and assign
*=	Multiply and assign
/=	Divide and assign
Div=	Integer division and assign
%=	Integer division and assign remained
<<=	Assign result of bitwise shift left
>>=	Assign result of bitwise shift right
>>>=	Assign result of bitwise shift right and fill leading bits with zeroes
&=	Assign result of bitwise AND
^=	Assign result of bitwise exclusive OR
!=	Assign result of bitwise OR

Table 3. Arithmetic operators

Operator	Operation
+	Addition
-	Subtraction or unary minus
/	Division (floating-point)
Div	Integer division
%	Modulus operator returns remainder after integer division
*	Multiplication (both integer and floating-point)

Table 4. Preincrement, postincrement, predecrement, postdecrement operators

Name	Operator	Meaning
Preincrement	++a;	A = a + 1;
Postincrement	A++;	A = a; a = a + 1
Predecrement	--a;	A = a – 1;
Postdecrement	a--;	A = a; a = a – 1;

Table 5. Logical operators

Operator	Meaning
&&	And
||	Or
!	Not

In addition to the basic arithmetic operators, WMLScript also supports the use of post- and pre- increment and decrement operators, shown in Table 4.

Logical

Logical operators, as listed in Table 5, can be combined with relational operators, discussed in the following section, to increase the effectiveness of your programs and to perform more complex decision-making. Expressions and logical operators evaluate to a Boolean value of either True or False. To understand their usage, truth tables, shown in Tables 6, 7, and 8 present each of the three logical operators.

Table 6. Truth table for logical operator && (AND)

AND	Value 1	Value 2	Boolean Evaluation
&&	T	T	T
	T	F	F
	F	T	F
	F	F	F

Table 7. Truth table for logical operator || (OR)

OR	Value 1	Value 2	Boolean Evaluation
||	T	T	T
	T	F	T
	F	T	T
	F	F	F

Table 8. Truth table for logical operator ! (NOT)

NOT	Value A	Boolean Evaluation
!	T	F
	F	T

Table 9.

Operator	Meaning
==	Equal
<	Less then
>	Greater than
<=	Less than or equal
>=	Greater than or equal
!=	Not equal

Relational Operators

Relational operators are used to compare two values and determine their relationship to one another. Relational operators are also referred to as comparison operators. The acceptable values for use with a relational operator are constants and variables. You can compare a constant with a variable or you can compare two variables. The result of the comparison is a Boolean value that can then be used to control the execution of a program. Multiple comparison expressions can be combined with logical operators to provide for more complex decision-making and for controlling program execution. Table 9 gives the relational operators supported in WMLScript functions.

Special Operators

WMLScript provides support for a number of special operators which in certain instances appear to be functions, however, by definition they are actually operators.

The special operators are the *isvalid* operator, *conditional* operator, and the *comma* operator. Each of these operators has own special functionality and instance where it is useful.

isvalid Operator

The invalid operator is used to indicate that the value contained in a specific variable is either valid or not valid for that variable type. The operator returns a Boolean value of true if the value is correct for that variable, or false if the value is not valid.

```
isvalid(operator);

var variable_type;
var i = 10;
var_type = typeof(i);

// returns a 0 indicating that the i is an integer
```

The following example shows the use of the isvalid( ) operator.

```
var variableA, variableB, isvalid_result;

variableA = 'a';
variableB = '1/0';
```

```
isvalid_result = isvalid(variableA); // returns True
isvalid_result = isvalid(variableB); // returns False
```

Conditional Operator

The conditional operator uses a rather cryptic syntax to represent an *if then else* statement. This operator is also known as the "implied if". A variable or expression is evaluated and its Boolean value determines which value is returned. If the value evaluates to True then the first value is returned, else the second value is returned. The syntax for the conditional operator is show below.

```
evaluation expression ? variable1 : variable2;

var number1, number2, result;

number1 = 100;
number2 = 50;
result = (number1 <= number2) ? "Number 1 is greater" : "Number 2 is greater"
```

In this instance, the result will contain the literal "Number 2 is greater" since 100 is not less than or equal to 50.

typeof Operator

As expected, the typeof( ) operator is used to return the data type of a variable or constant. The typeof( ) operator returns an integer value representing one of the supported data types under WMLScript, see Table 10.

An example of using this operator reveals both the syntax and the meaning of the operator.

```
var variable_type;
variable_type = typeof(i);
```

Table 10. Integer values representing data type used with typeof( ) operator

Integer value	Data type represented
0	Integer
1	Floating point
2	String
3	Boolean
4	Invalid

Note: Depending on the type of variable i represents, the value assigned to variable_type will be one of the 5 values shown in Table 10. The specific syntax for the *typeof* operator allows for an element to be tested. The value can be either enclosed in parentheses or else without them: variable_type=typeof i;

Decision-Making

Decision-making is supported in WMLScript documents through the use of *if* and *if-else* statements.

If Statements

If statements are used in WMLScript functions to make decisions regarding which portion of the script is executed or what value is assigned to a variable. The basic format of the *if* statement is:

```
if (conditional expression) {
    statement(s);
}
```

The conditional expression is evaluated and if it returns TRUE then the statement(s) contained within the curly braces are executed, else the statements are bypassed.

WMLScript also provides a more advanced version of the *if* statement by providing for the use of the *if-else* construct. The format for this version is:

```
if(conditional expression) {
    statement(s);
}
else
  {
  statement(s);
  }
```

In this form, the conditional expression is evaluated and if it is found to be True then the first set of statements are executed. If the expression evaluates to False, then the set of statements following the else are executed.

Iteration

Iteration or looping, is the process of executing a block of code more than once or until a particular condition is met. In WMLScript iteration is supported by two different constructs—the *while* loop and the *for* loop.

While Statement

The *while* loop is a conditional loop that continues executing until a particular conditional test evaluates to false. The code contained within the curly braces following the *while* statement is executed as a single block.

```
while(conditional expression) {
    statement(s);
}
```

For Statement

The *for* statement is a counting loop that has an initial value for the control variable. The loop continues to be executed until the conditional variable is equal to or greater than the end value.

```
for (var control_variable = initial_value; control_variable conditional state-
ment; control_variable increment)
{
  statement(s);
}
```

In this instance, the control variable is set to a starting value, it is then tested by the conditional statement. If that conditional statement is evaluated as True then the loop is executed and the control variable is incremented by the value of the increment. If the conditional statement evaluates to False, then the *for* loop terminates.

Example

```
for (i = 1; i<10; i++)
{
  statement;
  statement;
}
```

In this example, the control value is *i* is initialized to one. As long as *i* is less than 10, then the two statements are executed and *i* is incremented each time by one, for example, i++.

Break and Continue Statements

The *break* and *continue* statements are used to control the continued execution of a while loop. If a condition exists where you need to terminate a while statement before the conditional expression evaluates to false, you can execute the break statement and the while loop will be terminated and program control will transfer to the next statement in your WMLScript program.

The continue statement works in a similar manner, however, with a different effect. When the continue statement is encountered, the program continues to execute. An if statement could be evaluated which would modify the content of the control variable.

Example

```
var control_var = 0;

while (control_var < 10) {

  if control_var < 10 then
    control_var = control + 1
}
```

Interacting with WMLScripts

WMLScript functions, by themselves, are not executable. They must be accessed from a WML document or from another WMLScript. WMLScripts can be called with or without passing an argument (value) to the function. In addition, functions also contain the ability to return a value after completing execution. To understand these capabilities, examples of using WMLScript functions are demonstrated in the following sections.

Argument Passing

In order to interact with a WMLScript function it is often necessary that one or more values be passed to the function. As we saw in the last chapter, WML documents support the ability to have the user enter values and store them in variable within a WML card.

```
<wml>
 <card title="WMLScript Example">
   <do type="accept" label="Welcome">
      <go href="hello.wmls#hello_func('message')"/>
   </do>
  <p>
     $(message)
  </p>
```

```
</card>
</wml>
```

Following the theme of the state capital information system used in Chapter 4, an example is developed that allows the user to enter a two-digit state code and then the WMLScript function returns the sales tax rate for that particular state. The WML document is used for both user input of the state's two-character abbreviation and to display that state's sales tax rate. Once the user enters the abbreviation she presses the button beneath the softkey labeled "TaxRate". Control is then passed to the WMLScript *tax_rate* and the specific WMLScript function, *main()*. After executing the function, control is returned to the WML document which then displays the result in the second card identified as "rate". The details of the WMLScript program are shown in Figure 2.

NOTE: A related application would extend the information about a particular state to include the state's sales tax rate. (Note: An assumption is made regarding a state's sales tax rate. That assumption is that the sales tax rate is consistent across all political jurisdictions. In reality, many states allow local municipalities to add special sales tax percentages. In our example, this variance is not recognized.)

Figure 2. WMLScript used to return correct sales tax rate for desired state

```
extern function main(state_code) {
  var state_id;
  var tax_rate;


    if (state_code == "AL") {
          tax_rate = "6.5";
          WMLBrowser.setVar("tax_rate",tax_rate);
       }

    if (state_code == "MS") {
          tax_rate = "7.0";
          WMLBrowser.setVar("tax_rate",tax_rate);
       }

    WMLBrowser.go("tax_driver.wml#rate");
}
```

In the WMLScript in Figure 2, you will note that tax rate for only two states is presented. If you want to make this function truly operational, you will have to enter *if* statements for each state and the District of Columbia.

In order to produce the desired sales tax rate result we employ a function from the Standard WMLScript library, WMLBrowser.setVar( ). The setVar function is used to assign a value from within a WMLScript function to a variable in a WML document. The Standard WMLScript Libraries are discussed in detail in Chapter V.

The WML document used to called this WMLScript function is presented in Figure 3.

Figures 4 through 6 show the results of accessing this WML document and its related WMLScript function. The first screen, Figure 4.4 presents the user with a field in which to enter the state abbreviation. Once the value is entered, the key below the label is pressed and the result is displayed in Figure 6. The user is unaware that control is passed to the WMLScript function stored on a WAP server. In that function the result is determined and returned to the wireless device.

Note: If you are using the Openwave SDK 6.2.2 emulator, you must choose the WAP version. Furthermore, both the WML document and the WMLScript file must be compiled. The reference to the WMLScript function will be *filename.wmlsc*. Notice the *c* at the end of the file extension. This *c* indicates that the WMLScript file is compiled.

Pressing the software key under the TR, tax rate retrieval, results in the WMLScript function returns the state sales tax rate, see Figure 6.

Building on the tax rate program, the following example expands the usefulness of the application by providing the user with the capability of employing the sales tax rate in calculating the total cost of a purchase.

In this WML document segment the user enters the state abbreviation and the total for a specific purchase.

In Figure 7, the WMLScript function finds the tax rate for a given state, calculates the sales tax amount, based on that rate, totals the sales tax amount and the sales amount, and returns those values to the variables in the WML document. The function returns control to a card in the WML document that displays the results.

Figure 3. WML document used for input of state code and display of sales tax rate

```
<?xml version="1.0" encoding="utf-8"?>
<!DOCTYPE wml PUBLIC "-//WAPFORUM//DTD WML 1.3//EN"
   "http://www.wapforum.org/DTD/wml13.dtd">
<wml>
  <card id="tax_rate">
   <onevent type="onenterforward">
    <refresh>
     <setvar name="tax_rate" value=""/>
    </refresh>
   </onevent>
  <p>
   State Code
   <input name="state_code"/>
  </p>
  <do type="accept" label="TR">
   <go href="tax_rate.wmls#main('$(state_code)')"/>
  </do>
  </card>

 <card id="rate" title="Tax Rate">
  <p>
  Tax Rate = $(tax_rate)
  </p>
 </card>

 </wml>
```

Figure 4. WML document state code input

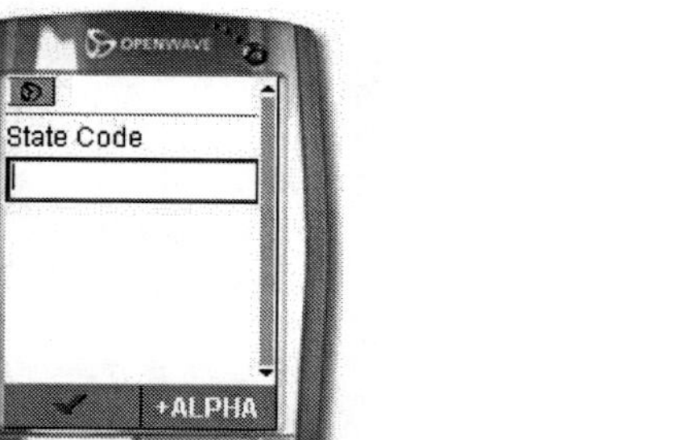

Figure 5. Device screen after input of AL (Alabama state code)

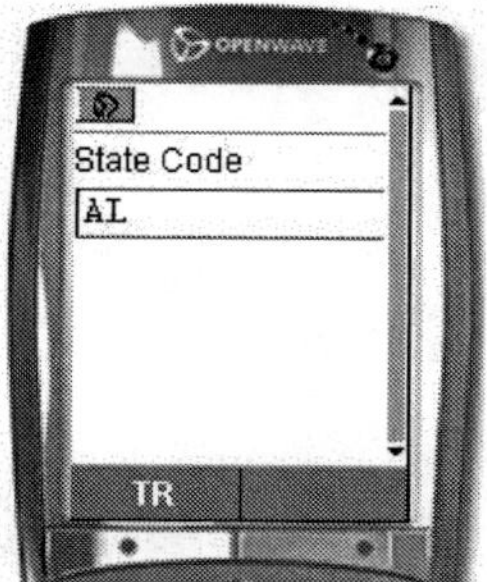

Figure 6. Sales tax rate for Alabama

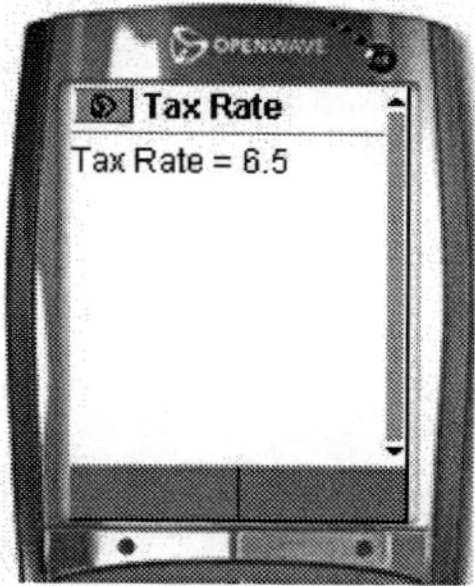

Figure 7. WMLScript function used to calculate sales tax amount and total for sale

```
extern function get_tax_rate(state_code, amount) {
    var sales_tax_rate;
    var state_id;
    var sales_amount;
    var tax_amount;
    var total_amount;


    state_id = state_code;

    if state_id = “AL” {
       sales_tax_rate = 6.5
    }

   if state_id = “MS” {
      sales_tax_rate = 7.0
   }
  sales_amount = Lang.parseInt(amount);
  tax_amount = sales_amount * sales_tax_rate;
  total_amount = sales_amount + tax_amount;
  WMLBrowser.setVar(“tax_amt”, tax_amount);
  WMLBrowser.setVar(“total”, total_amount);
  WMLBrowser.go(“example3.33.wml#result”);
}
```

Figure 8. Tax calculation/WML document

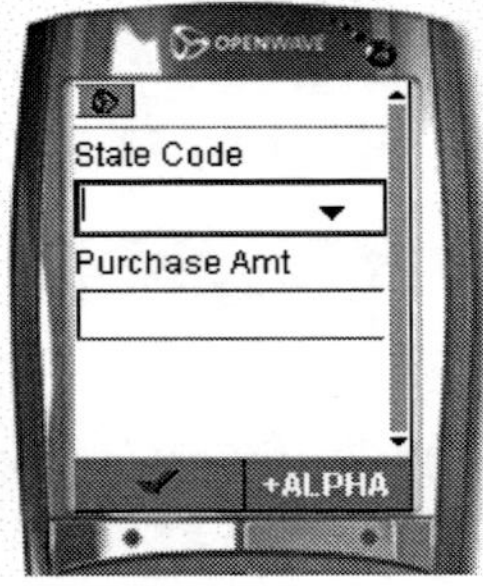

Figure 9. State code and purchase amt entered

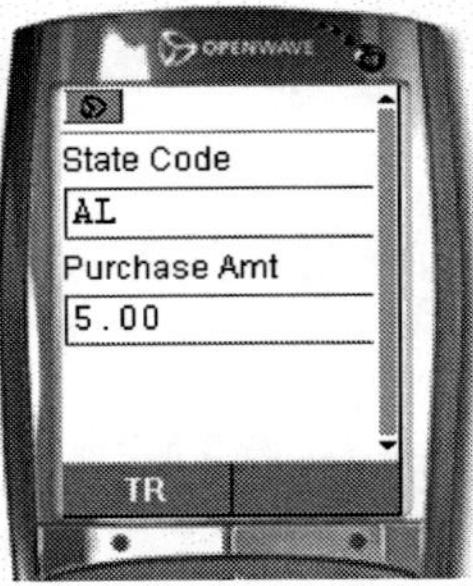

Figure 10. Result of tax calculation

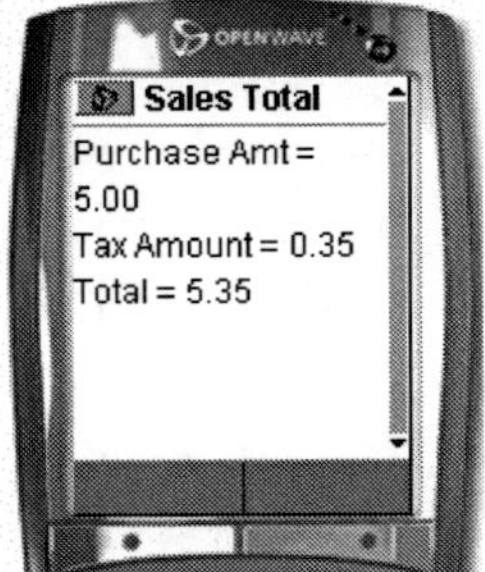

Figures 8, 9 and 10 show the results of these changes to the WML document/ WMLScript function. As you can see, WMLScript provides capabilities that WML documents lack.

Return Statement

The return statement in WMLScript programs is used to return a single value from a function. To return more than one value from a function you must use the WMLBrowser.setVar() function. You have already be introduced to this function in the previous section. One place that the return statement is helpful in the returning of values from one function to another within a WMLScript program. Figure 11 illustrates the use of the return statement to return the sales tax rate for a particular state. In this example each state's tax rate is contained in a separate function. A series of *if* statements are used to select the correct function.

Even though the example in Figure 11 is very simplistic, you can see that multiple functions can be used in WMLScript program. Only one external function is contained in this example, thus the interface between the WML document and this WMLScript program is handled by the select_state function. Since this function determines which state's tax rate is being inquired about, the sales tax rate could have been assigned to the variable at that time.

Figure 11. Returning value from function within a WMLScript program

```
extern function select_state(state_code) {

        var sale_tax_rate;

        if (state_code = "AL" ) {
            sales_tax_rate = get_AL_tax_rate()
        }

        if (state_code = "MS") {
            sales_tax_rate = get_MS_tax_rate();
        }
    WMLBrowser.setVar("tax_rate",sales_tax_rate);
    WMLBrowser.refresh();
    WMLBrowser.go("wmlcard.wmls#card_id");

function sales_AL_tax_rate() {
        return( 6.0);
    }

function sales_MS_tax_rate() {
        return (7.0);
    }
```

Pragmas

A pragma is a statement that provides a browser, gateway, or server with information about WMLScript files or units. A pragma stands alone, not being part of a function. In addition, they have their own unique syntax. WMLScript supports three different types of pragmas: 1) external file specification, 2) access control, and 3) meta-information.

External File Specification

To aid in organizing you r WMLScript files you can assign a library name to a file containing various WMLScript functions. With the "use url" pragma you can create an association between the file name and an ID. The syntax for making this association is:

```
use url ID "URL";
```

The URL pragma assigns an ID or name to the file containing the WMLScript functions. Once assigned, the individual functions within the file can be access by preceding the function name with the ID followed by a #.

Access Control

All of the examples in this chapter have been unconcerned about controlling access to the individual WMLScripts. If controlling access becomes a concern for you then you can control which WML files can access your scripts. To control access you specify in the access pragma which domains and paths are allowed to use a particular WMLScript. The syntax for the access pragma is:

```
use access domain "domain" path "path";
```

If you try to access a given WMLScript and the WML document is not in the proper location then a fatal error will be occur.

Meta-Information

Meta-information pragmas provide information relating to the code in a WMLScript file. The metadata, included in the form of a header, may be used by servers, gateways, or user agents, or can be passed as information to the function.

The *name* meta-information pragma is used by WWW servers. Information, like author's name, data a script was written, or other text information can be included in a name pragma. The general format of a meta-information name pragma is:

```
use meta "type" "property" "content" "scheme"

use meta name "Author" "Pam Programmer"
use meta name "Written" "10 October 2004"
```

Browsers ignore meta name information.

The *http equiv* meta-information pragma is used as a header in HTTP. When a header is received by a WAP gateway the information is interpreted. This information is also received by the microbrowser on a wireless device. Here the information can be used. The following gives the general form of the *http equiv* information pragma.

```
use meta http equiv "string1" "string2"
use meta http equiv "Programmer" "Carl Coder"
```

The *meta name* and the *http equiv* formats are very similar, however, only the *meta http equiv* information is forwarded to the browser.

The last type of meta-information pragmas is the *user agent*. This pragma is used to pass information to the microbrowser on a wireless device. The interpretation of this pragma is dependent upon the individual browser. The general form is:

```
use meta user agent "string1" "string2"
```

The following is an example of a *user agent* pragma.

```
use meta user agent "Start" "Run"
```

In this example two value are passed to the browser, "Start" and "Run" which the microbrowser can then use as determined.

Summary

Due the limitation of WML documents it is important that exist a means by which one can carryout calculations, decision-making, and execution control. WMLScript provides that ability. In this chapter we have examined the basic elements of WMLScript and how programs can be developed from a series of interrelated functions. The if statement supports much needed decision-making. The while and for statement allow for executing the same statements one or more times. External functions provide for communication with WML documents and internal functions support program subdivision.

Exercises

1. Discount Carpet Sales, Ltd. needs a program to assist their sales staff in creating estimates for their customers. Create a program that allows the user to enter the dimensions of a rectangular room (length and width), the cost per square yard of the carpeting, and the special charges, if any. Calculate an estimate and display the result on the screen.
2. Enhance the program you created in No. 1 to allow for an additional cost, the price of the pad. The pad is a fixed cost per square yard: $1.50.

Chapter V

WMLScript Standard Libraries

In this chapter, you will:

- Learn about how the WMLScript libraries interact with WML documents and WMLScript
- Examine the contents of the WMLScript Standard Libraries: Dialogs, Lang, Float, String, URL, and WMLBrowser

Introduction

In an effort to aid developers in the creation of WML and WMLScript applications a set of libraries, the WMLScript Standard Libraries, were developed. These libraries provide you with pretested, standardized functions aimed at easing the process of developing and testing WML-based applications. This chapter examines the primary functions in each of the different libraries. Elementary examples illustrate how the individual functions operate and how to call then from a WML document.

NOTE: To examine and use WMLScript functions with the Openwave 6.2.2 emulator, you will need to make certain that you download the 6.2.2 WAP version. Down this version from: developer.openwave.com.

Integrating WMLScript Libraries with WML and WMLScript Functions

In Chapter 4, we examined the use of WMLScript functions to enhance the usefulness of WML documents. In that chapter, you were required to develop all of the functionality that you desired. In this chapter, we will be expanding on your knowledge of WMLScript functions by adding a set of library routines that contain much of the functionality. To use the library functions you simply include them in your WMLScript functions, passing to the specific library function the argument(s) expected and then using any return value. Library functions cannot be called directly from a WML document.

To test the functionality of each of the library routines a simple WML document was developed as a driver for the library functions. This driver document, shown in Figure 1 provides a means for accessing a given function. To use this document to examine a library function you simply have to change the name of the WMLScript file in which you have the library routine embedded.

When this document is displayed on the Openwave SDK 6.2.2 WAP emulator, the document appears a shown in Figure 2.

Once, you press the button below the Call label then the associated WMLScript function is accessed. Within that function is another function call that passes control to the specified library function.

Figure 1. WML document used as driver function to test Standard Library functions

```
<?xml version="1.0" encoding="utf-8"?>
<!DOCTYPE wml PUBLIC "-//WAPFORUM//DTD WML 1.3//EN"
   "http://www.wapforum.org/DTD/wml13.dtd">
<wml>

  <card id="card1" title="Library Function Driver">
    <do type="accept" label="Call">
      <go href="alert.wmlsc#main()"/>
    </do>
  </card>
</wml>
```

Figure 2. WML document used as library function driver routine

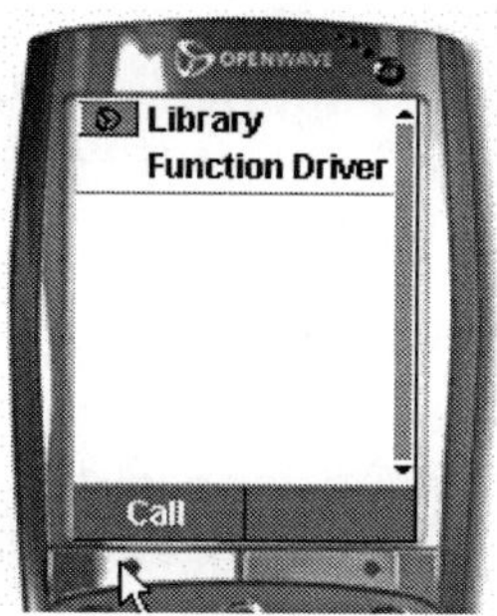

Standard Libraries

The standard libraries are divided into six different categories, each with a special set of related functions. Table 1 provides a classification of these libraries.

These libraries are composed of a variety of different functions, each with a special purpose. To understand both the content of each library and the use of each function contained in that library, we will examine each library individually in the following sections. Each section brings with it a list of all of the functions and the purpose for each function. Examples illustrate the use of the primary functions.

Table 1. WMLScript Standard Libraries

Library	Purpose
Dialogs	Functions to communicate with user from within a WMLScript function
Lang	Provides functions associated with core elements of the WMLScript language
Float	Functions associated with floating point variables and values
String	Functions for manipulating and comparing strings
URL	Functions useful in manipulating URLs for accessing Web sites
WMLBrowser	Functions for communicating directly with WML documents

Dialogs Library

The Dialogs library provides the application developer with a means of communicating with the user from within a WMLScript function. Table 2 lists the three different functions included in this library.

The Dialogs.alert( ) function gives the developer a means by which a message can be displayed on the wireless device from within a WMLScript function. This function is quite helpful when developing WMLScript functions since it can aid in the debugging of your applications. Furthermore, this function can be used to display a message to the user whenever an error occurs within a production application.

Figure 3 presents an example of using the alert( ) function with a WMLScript function.

The result of calling the Dialogs.alert( ) function appears in Figure 4. Here the message "Dialogs.Alert – WMLScript Libraries" is displayed on the wireless device. Notice that the message presented is linewrapped due to the limited size of the output window associated with the emulator. The Openwave 6.2.2 emulator opens a separate box or window when the output comes from a WMLScript function.

The Dialogs.confirm function presents the user with a Yes/No question. The user is given the opportunity to response with either a "yes" or "no" by simply pressing the corresponding key on the mobile device. The value of the reply can be applied to a variable within the WMLScript function. The resulting values are *true* for a *yes* reply and *false* for a *no* reply.

Table 2. Dialogs library functions

Function	Meaning
alert(message)	Display message to user
confirm(message,yes,no)	Request reply from user
prompt(message,default value)	Prompts user for string input; if no input then default value is used

Figure 3. Dialogs.alert( ) function used to display message

```
extern function main() {

  Dialogs.alert("Dialogs.Alert - WMLScript Libraries");

}
```

Figure 4. Output of Dialogs.alert( ) used to display message

Figure 5. WMLScript function employing Dialogs.prompt() to verify state code

```
extern function main() {

  var reply;

  reply = Dialogs.confirm("Correct State? CA ", "yes", "no");
  Dialogs.alert(reply);

}
```

Figure 6. Prompt displayed on wireless device

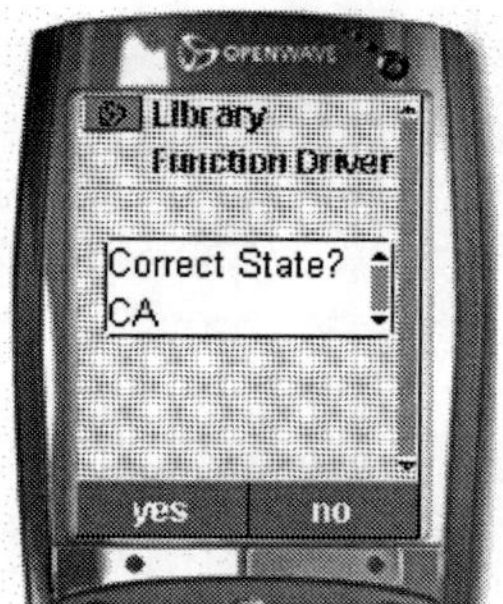

Figure 7. Result of user's response to prompt

Figure 5 illustrates the use of this function to verify that the correct state code was entered. Figure 6 shows the prompt presented on the wireless device and Figure 7 shows the response entered by the user.

The Dialogs.prompt( ) function allows the user to input a value in response to a message sent from within a WMLScript function. A message is presented to the user and the user enters a value. A default value can be assigned to the function when it is declared. The resulting value can be used within the WMLScript function. Figure 8 shows the code for enter a two-digit state code in response to the prompt sent by the Dialogs.prompt() function. Figures 9 and 10 show the results of providing a reply.

You will notice in the Dialogs.prompt() argument list that the state code for Alabama is provided as a default value. This default value appears when the

Figure 8. WMLScript function using Dialogs.prompt( ) to obtain state code

```
extern function main() {

  var reply;

  reply = Dialogs.prompt("Enter State Code","AL");
  Dialogs.alert(reply);

}
```

Figure 9. Prompt displayed by Dialogs.prompt( ) and user reply

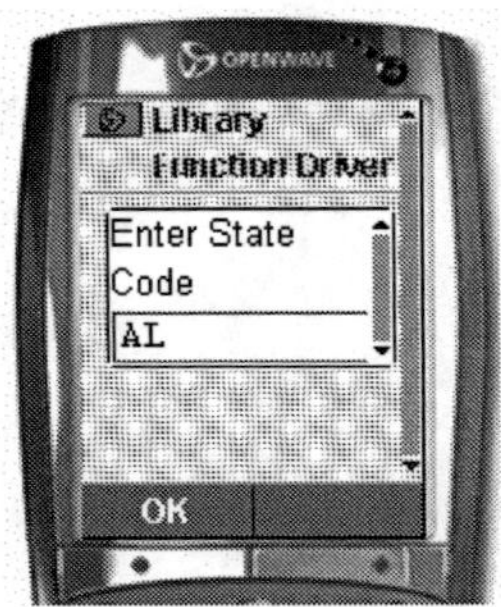

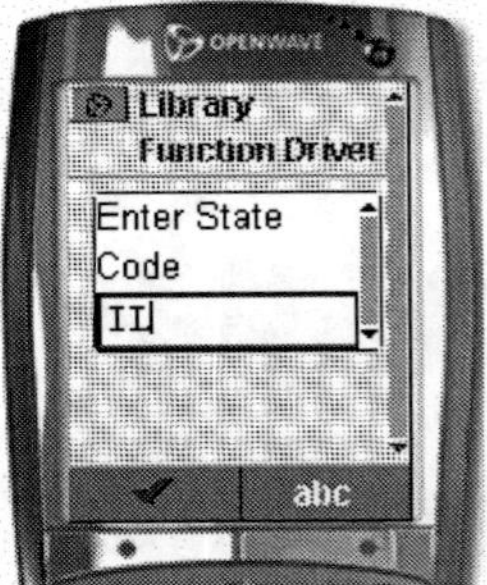

Figure 10. Dialogs.alert( ) used to display user response

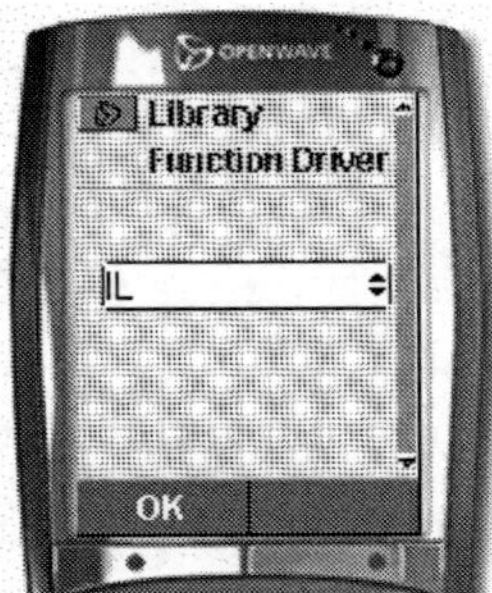

function is first executed. If you chose not to enter another state code, then this value, "AL", is returned and assigned to the variable *reply*.

In this instance, the user entered the abbreviation for the state of Illinois. After the state code is entered then the Dialogs.alert( ) function is used to display the results on the wireless device.

Lang Library

The Lang library contains a wide variety of functions that aid in the developing of helpful WMLScript functions. These library functions range from numerical functions, to program control functions, for example, Lang.abort( ).

In developing an application, it is important to understand the environment for which the application is being constructed. The Lang library functions float( ) and characterSet( ) provide the user with information about the underlying system. The float( ) function reports whether the system supports floating point operations or not. The characterSet( ) function gives you information about the particular character set supported on the given device. This function returns the

Table 3. Lang library functions

Function	Meaning
abort(message)	Terminates program
abs(number)	Returns absolute value of an integer
characterSet()	Returns MIBnum indicating type of character designated by Intern Assigned Number Authority (IANA)
exit(value)	Normal program termination
float( )	Reports if interpreter supports floating point numbers
isFloat(string)	Reports if string represents a valid floating point value
isInt(string)	Reports if string represents a valid string value
max(number1, number2)	Returns the larger of two numeric arguments
maxInt( )	Reports the maximum integer supported by the computer system
min(number1,number2)	Returns the smaller of two numeric arguments
minInt( )	Reports the minimum integer supported by the computer system
parseInt(string)	Examines a string for a valid integer value
parseFloat(string)	Examines a string for a valid floating-point value
random(range)	Returns a random number between 0 and the range, inclusively
seed(integer)	Sets the starting value (seed) for the random function

MIBenum that indicates the type of characters as designated by the Internet Assigned Number Authority (IANA).

Note: If you want to acquire more information about the different character sets, please refer to the official Web site for the registry: www.iana.org/assignments/character-sets.

The Lang.isFloat( ) and Lang.isInt( ) functions allow the program to determine for the user whether a particular string represents a valid numeric value or not. These functions are helpful when used in conjunction with user input. Figure 11 shows how these two functions are used within a WMLScript function.

This function takes two strings and stores the numeric representations of an integer and a floating point number. If a value were not a valid numeric representation then the result shown would be *false*. Figure 12 presents the driver function's display, with the left softkey labeled *Call*. Pressing the key beneath this label transfers control to the WMLScript function. The function, main( ), in turn, calls the library functions. Figure 13 shows the output of these functions.

Figure 11. Use of Lang.isInt( ), Lang.isFloat functions

```
extern function main() {
  var int_string = "1234";
  var float_string = "12.34";

  Dialogs.alert("Valid Integer = " + Lang.isInt(int_string) + " Valid Float = " +
Lang.isFloat(float_string));
}
```

Figure 12. Driver display for WMLScript Lang.isInt(), Lang.isFloat( )

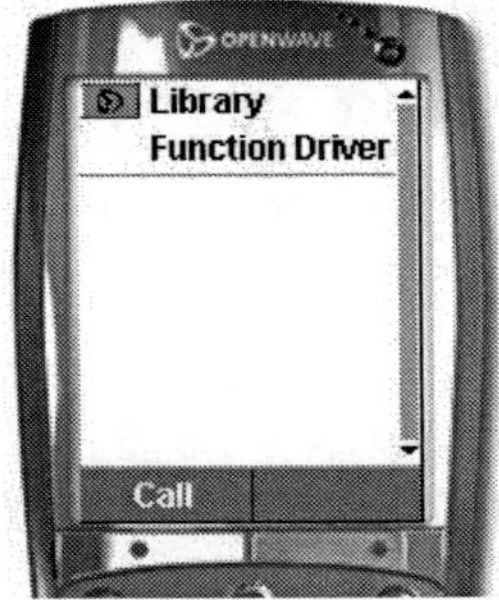

Figure 13. Result of Lang.isInt( ), Lang.isFloat( )

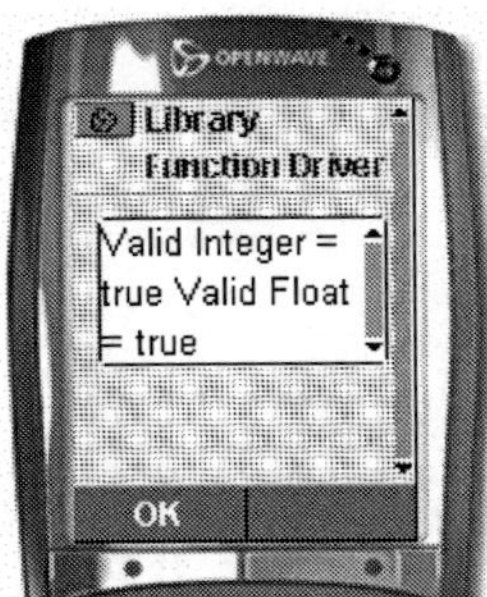

Figure 14. Lang.minInt( )

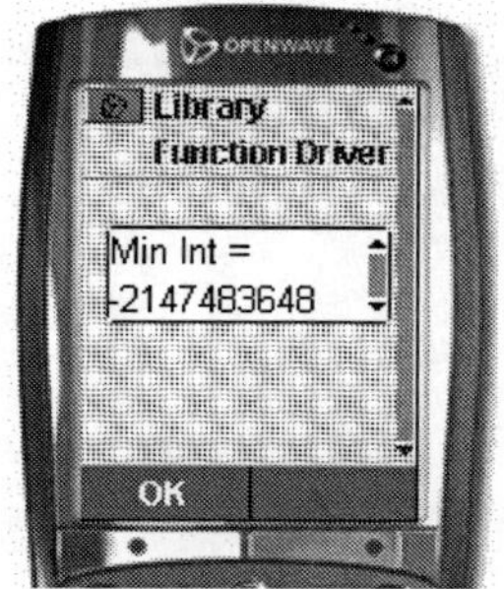

Figure 15. Lang.maxInt( )

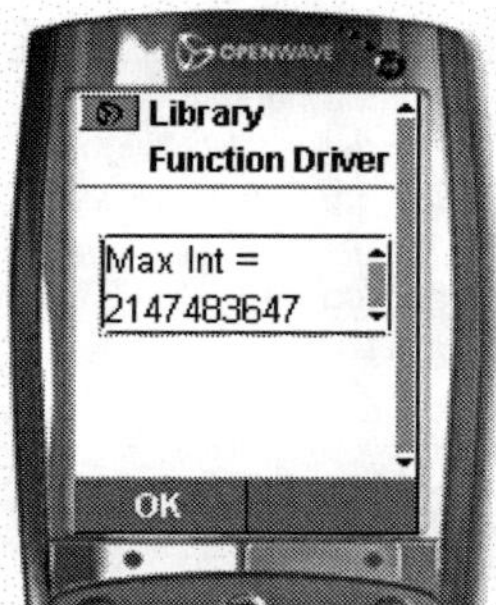

The Lang.minInt( ) and Lang.maxInt( ) functions provide information about a given system and the size of the integer values supported on that system. Figures 14 and 15 give the output of these functions on a Pentium 4 computer.

parseInt( ) and parseFloat( ) functions examine a string to determine if it contains a valid integer or floating point number respectively. If the string contains a valid value then the string is parsed returning the numeric value. Figures 16 through 18 show the results of using these functions in a WMLScript function. Figure 16 initializes the strings and Figures 17 and 18 present the results of calling the parsing functions.

NOTE: The parsing functions terminate the moment they encounter an invalid character. For this reason, the numeric representation must occur at the beginning of a string.

The Lang.abs( ) function returns the absolute value of a number, that is the number without a sign. Figure 19 illustrates the use of the Lang.abs( ) function, with Figure 20 showing the output of this function.

The Lang.exit( ) and Lang.abort( ) are two related functions that control program execution. The Lang.exit( ) function, see Figure 21, terminates the WMLScript function and returns control to the calling WMLScript function or WML document.

When the Lang.exit( ) function is encountered in this WMLScript function, control is returned to the point where this function was called.

The Lang.abort( ) function terminates the program immediately. If a message is passed to the function as an argument, then that message is displayed before the program terminates. In Figure 22, the abort function is called when a program encounters an error and a message is displayed on the wireless device.

Figure 16. Lang.parseInt( ) and Lang.parseFloat( ) used to extract integer and float point values from a string

```
extern function main() {
  var int_string = "1234value";
  var float_string = "12.34value";

  Dialogs.alert("Int = " + Lang.parseInt(int_string));
  Dialogs.alert("Float = " + Lang.parseFloat(float_string));
  }
```

Figure 17. Lang.parseInt( ) result

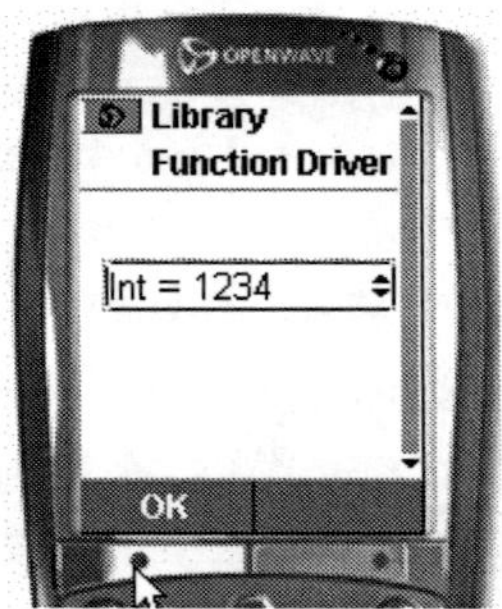

Figure 18. Lang.parseFloat( ) result

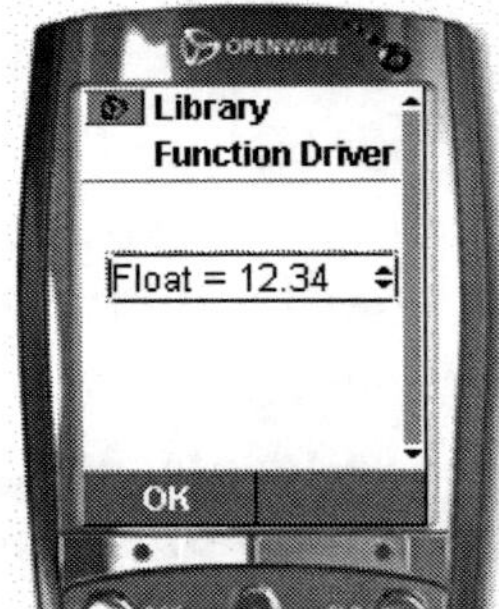

Figure 19. Lang.abs( ) function usage

```
extern function main() {
  var negative = -12.34;

  Dialogs.alert("Absolute Value " + Lang.abs(negative));
  }
```

Figure 20. Result of Lang.abs( ) function with negative argument

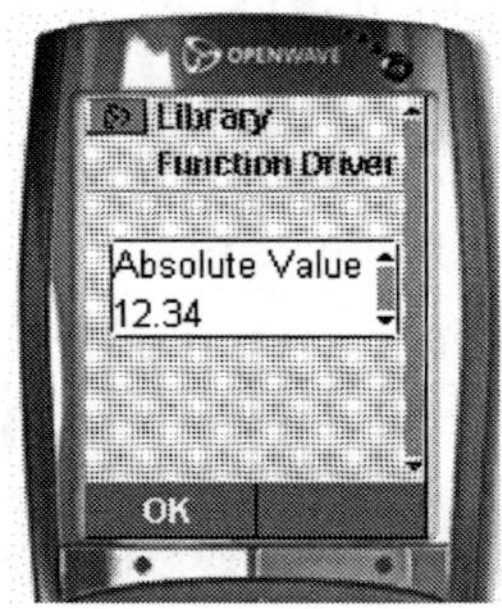

Figure 21. Use of Lang.exit( ) function

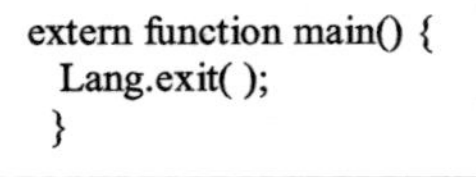

```
extern function main() {
  Lang.exit( );
  }
```

In an actual application, the error messages should be precise enough to aid the user and the developer in understanding the cause of the program's termination.

The Lang.isInt( ) and Lang.isFloat( ) functions can be used to determine whether a give value is a correct integer or floating point value. These functions return the value *true* if the values are acceptable, and *false* if they are invalid values. Figure 24 shows the result of using the Lang.isInt( ) to determine if the value 12 is a valid integer, and in Figure 25 the Lang.isFloat( ) function determines if 12.45 is a valid floating point value.

Figure 22. Use of Lang.abort( ) function to terminate program

```
extern function main() {
  Lang.abort("Error Encountered" );
  }
```

Figure 23. Use of Lang.isInt( ) and Lang.isFloat( ) to determine validity of data type

```
extern function main() {
  var int_value = 12;
  var float_value = 12.34;

   Dialogs.alert(Lang.isInt(int_value));
   Dialogs.alert(Lang.isFloat(float_value));
  }
```

Figure 24. Result of testing 12 as an integer value

Figure 25. Result of testing 12.34 as a floating point value

Figure 26. Use of Lang.min( ) and Lang.max( ) to determine smaller, larger of two values

```
extern function main() {

 var float_var = 12.45;
 var int_var = 1234;

 Dialogs.alert("Smaller No. " + Lang.min(float_var, int_var));
 Dialogs.alert("Larger No. " + Lang.max(int_var, float_var));

 }
```

Figure 27. Smaller value returned by Lang.min( )

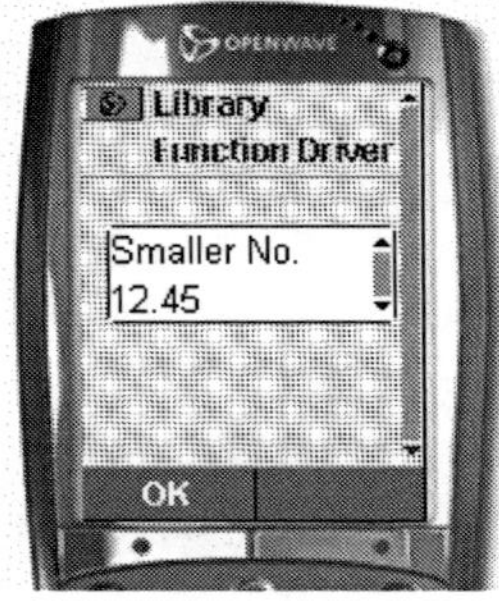

Figure 28. Larger value returned by Lang.max( )

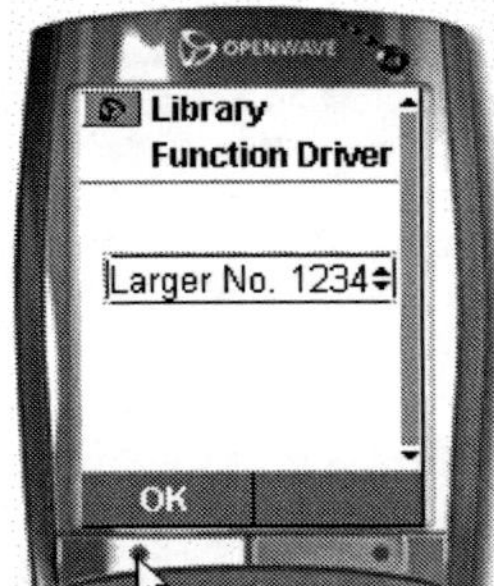

Figure 29. Lang.random( ) function set to 25 to generate random values between 0 and 25

```
extern function main() {

 Dialogs.alert("Random Number " + Lang.random(25));

 }
```

The Lang.min( ) and Lang.max( ) functions return the smaller or larger of two arguments. Figure 26 presents the WMLScript function used to call the Lang.min( ) and Lang.max( ) functions.

In Figure 27 the result of the Lang.min( ) function is shown. Here the value 12.45 is displayed. Figure 28 presents the larger of the two number where 1234 is returned by the Lang.max( ) function.

The last two functions in the Lang library are the Lang.random( ) and the Lang.random.seed( ) functions. These two functions are closely related. The Lang.random( ) function returns a random number between zero and some specified value, see Figure 29.

Figure 30. 1st run of Lang.rand( )

Figure 31. 2nd run of Lang.rand( )

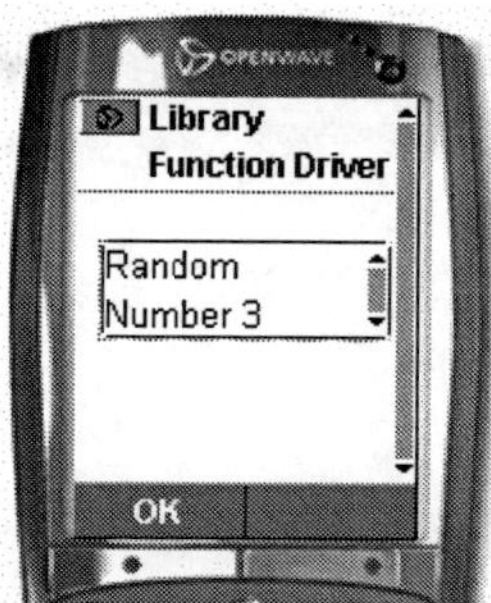

Figure 32. Use of Lang.seed( ) to control random number stream

```
extern function main() {
Lang.seed(77);
Dialogs.alert("Random Number " + Lang.random(25));
}
```

Figures 30 and 31 give the result of using the Lang.random( ) function to generate random values. The Lang.random( ) function was called in order to produce different random numbers.

In many instances, you may want or need to generate the same string of random numbers. In order to repeat the random numbers in the same order as in a prior run, you must use the same starting seed each time you start to produce the stream of numbers. The Lang.seed( ) function, illustrated in Figure 32, is used to initialize the random number to a specific starting seed. That seed is used to generate the first random number and affects the value and order of all following numbers.

In the example shown in Figures 33 and 34, the Lang.random( ) function generates the same random number each time the function is accessed.

In a real application, the random number seed would be set once and then the random number generator, Lang.random( ), would be called the desired number of times to produce the set of random numbers.

Figure 33. Use of Lang.seed( ) to control random number stream produced by Lang.random( )

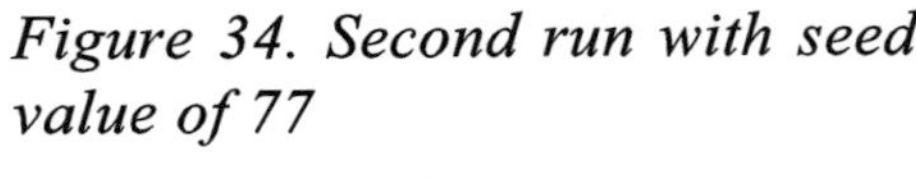
Figure 34. Second run with seed value of 77

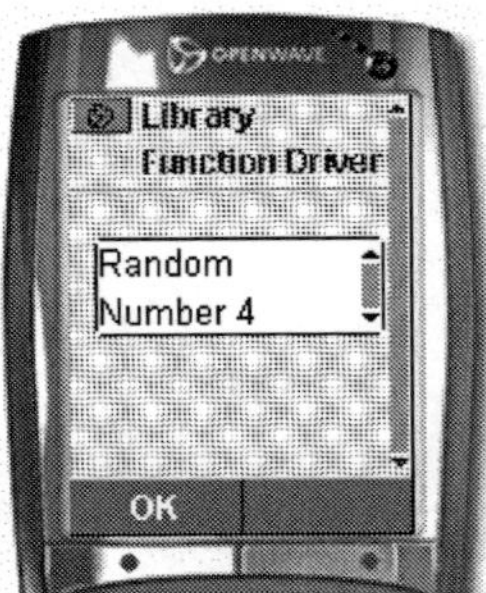

Float Library

The float library contains a number of functions which apply to floating-point values, as well as, the implementation of support for floating-point numbers on a given computer system. Table 4 lists the functions contained in this library.

The Float.ceil( ) and the Float.floor( ) functions are closely related. The ceil( ) function returns the smallest integer that is not less than or equal to the floating point value passed to the function. The floor( ) function, on the other hand, returns the largest floating point value that is not greater than or equal to the arguments passed to the function. Using the same value as an argument to these two functions, 12.34, the Float.ceil( ) and Float.floor( ) functions are used in the

Table 4. Float library functions

Function	Meaning
ceil(floating point value)	Returns smallest integer that is not less than or equal to floating point value
floor(floating point value)	Returns largest integer that is not greater than or equal to the floating point value
int(floating point value)	Returns integer equivalent to floating point value, ignoring any decimal portion
maxFloat()	Returns largest supported floating point value
minFloat()	Returns smallest floating point value
pow(base, power)	Returns result of raising floating point value to a given power
round(floating point value)	Returns integer result of rounding floating point value to nearest integer
sqrt(floating point value)	Returns square root of floating point number

Figure 35. Use of Float.ceil( ) and Float.floor( ) functions

```
extern function main() {

 var int_value = 12.34;
 Dialogs.alert("Ceiling = " + Float.ceil(int_value) + " Floor = " + Float.floor(int_value));

 }
```

Figure 36. Result of Float.ceil() and Float.floor() functions with argument of 12.34

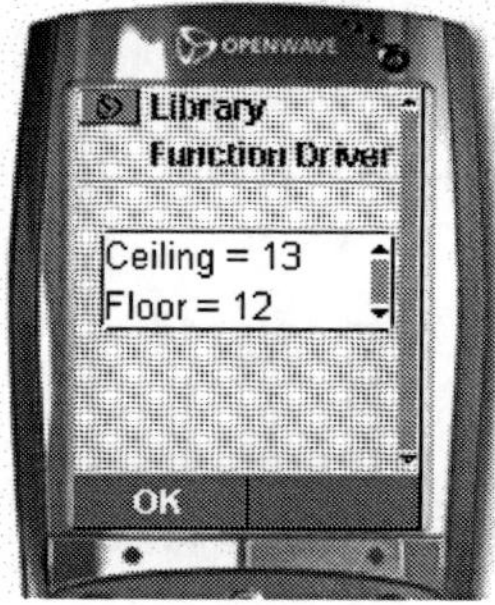

Figure 37. Float.int( ) and Float.round( ) used to return integer from floating point value

```
extern function main() {

 var float_value = 12.34;
 var float_value2 = 12.57;
 Dialogs.alert("int( ) = " + Float.int(float_value) + " round( ) = " +
Float.round(float_value2));
```

following code, Figure 35, to demonstrate their functionality. Figure 36 presents the result.

The Float.int( ) and the Float.round( ) functions are used to manipulate floating point numbers. The first function, Float.int( ), takes a floating point value and truncates it (cuts off the decimal portion) returning the integer or whole part of the number. The Float.round( ) function modifies the floating point value by rounding it to the nearest integer value. Any decimal portion greater than or equal to .5 is rounded up, else only the whole number portion of the floating

Figure 38. Result of using Float.int() for truncation and Float.round() for rounding

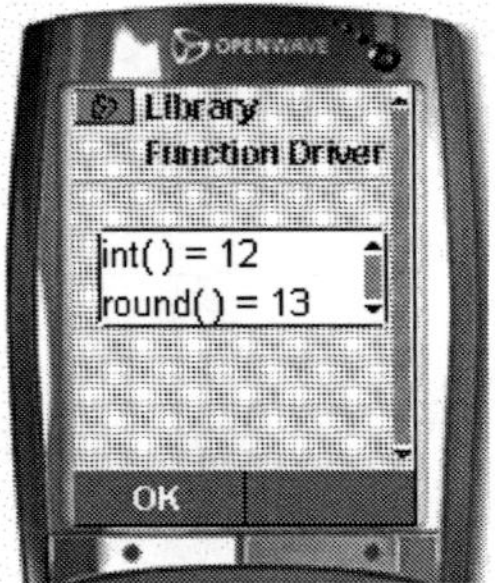

Figure 39. Use of Float.pow( ) and Float.sqrt( ) to square a value and to find the square root of the same value

```
extern function main() {

 var float_value = 16;
 var power = 2;
 Dialogs.alert("pow( ) = " + Float.pow(float_value, power) + " sqrt( ) = " +
Float.sqrt(float_value));

 }
```

point number is returned without modification by the function. If the decimal portion of a floating point number has a value of less than .5 then the Float.int() and the Float.round() functions will return the same value. Figure 37 shows the WMLScript using these two functions. Values of 7.6 and 7.4 are passed to the functions.

The Float library provides two functions relating to the raising of a value to a power and the deriving of a square root of a number. There functions are Float.pow( ),which raises a number to power, and Float.sqrt( ), which returns the square root of a number.

The last two functions in the Float library to be discussed are the Float.min( ), which returns the smallest floating point value supported by the computer on which the application is located, and Float.max( ), which returns the largest floating point value supported. To illustrate the use of these functions, this following function, see Figure 42, was executed on a Pentium 4 computer.

Figure 40. Result of squaring 16 and of finding the square root of 16

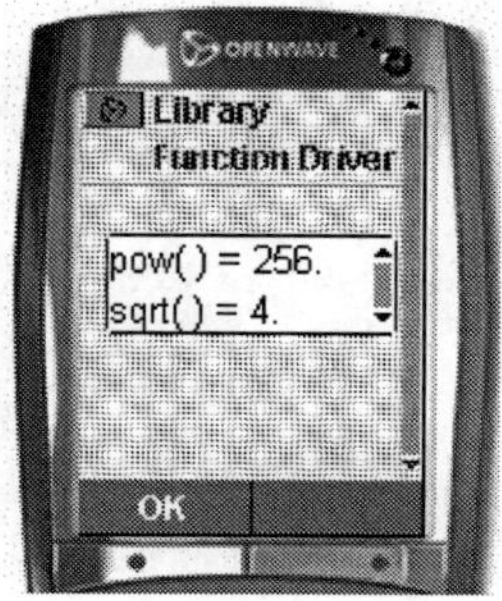

Figure 41. Float.min( ) and Float.max( ) used to find minimum and maximum floating point number supported on system

```
extern function main() {

 Dialogs.alert("minFloat( ) = " + Float.minFloat() + " maxFloat( ) = " +
Float.maxFloat());

 }
```

Figure 42. Minimum and maximum floating point values supported on Pentium 4

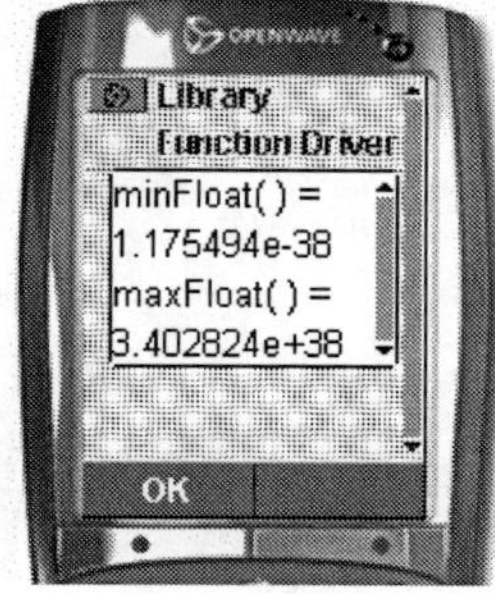

String Library

The String library, much like the Lang and Float libraries, provides the user with a set of specialized functions that correspond to a particular data type, in this case the "string". These functions, listed in Table 5, allow you to manipulate a

Table 5. String library functions

Function	Meaning
charAt(string, location)	Returns character at given location
compare(string1, string2)	Returns value indicating whether strings are equal
elementAt(string, location, separator)	Returns element at a given place in a string of elements, separator determines where elements end
elements(string, separator)	Returns count of elements in a string
find(string1, string2)	Returns the starting location of a substring within a string
format(format, value)	Performs specified formatting on a string
insertAt(string, new location, separator)	Inserts new element into a string
isEmpty(string)	Returns Boolean value indicating whether string is empty or not
length(string)	Returns integer indicating length of string
removeAt(string, index, separator)	Removes element in string at given index
replace(string, old, new)	Replaces substring with new substring
replaceAt(string, new string, location, separator)	Replaces element in string with a new element at given location
squeeze(string)	Removes the multiple instances of spaces with a single space
substring(string, start, length)	Returns substring beginning at given location for a set length
toString(value)	Converts value to a string
trim(string)	Removes the spaces from the beginning and end of a string

Figure 43. Use of String.charAt( ) to find character located at specific location in string

```
extern function main() {

 var string_value = "Hello, WAP Programmers";
 Dialogs.alert("8th Char " + String.charAt(string_value,8));

 }
```

string in a number of different ways, such as editing strings and testing the content of a string. Due to the diversity of the String library, we will again look at each of these functions, explaining their functionality.

The String.charAt( ) function is used to return a character contained in a string at a given location. Figure 43 shows how this function can be employed in WMLScript function. Figure 44 shows the result of returning the eighth character in string.

In Figure 44, the letter "A" is returned from the eighth position in the string.

Figure 44. Result of using String.charAt( ) to find eighth character in string "Hello, WAP Programmers"

Figure 45. String.compare( ) used to determine differences in two strings

```
extern function main() {

 var string_value1 = "Hello, WAP Programmers";
 var string_value2 = "Hello, WML Programmers";
 Dialogs.alert("Comparison " + String.compare(string_value1,string_value2));

 }
```

Figure 46. Result of comparing the two strings where the first string is "smaller" than the string

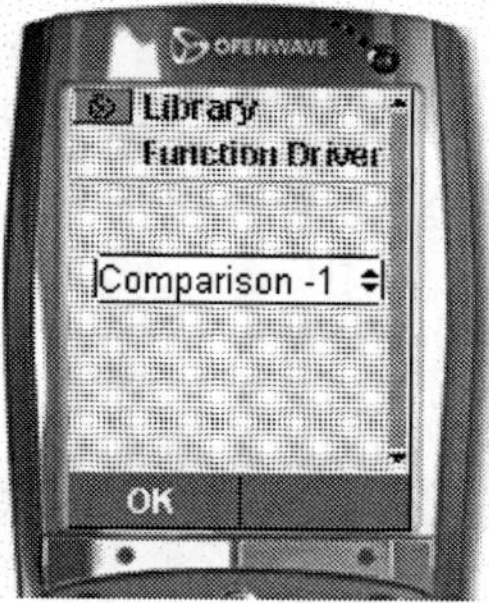

Figure 47. Use of String.elementAt( ) to find 3rd element in a comma delimited string

```
extern function main() {

 var string_value = "WAP, WML, WMLScript, XHTML";

 Dialogs.alert("3rd Element " + String.elementAt(string_value,3,","));

 }
```

The String.compare( ) function is used to compare the ASCII values of two different strings to determine if there is a difference between the two strings. If the strings are equal then the function returns a value of zero. If the first string is less than the second string then a value of -1 is returned. Finally, if the second string is less than the first string then a positive value of 1 is returned.

Note: In comparing two strings, the function examines each of the characters in both strings, one at a time. Once one of the characters does not match, then the ASCII value of the two different characters is determined and the string containing the smaller of the two values determines what result the function will return.

Figure 45 shows the use of the String.compare( ) function to examine two very similar strings, "Hello, WAP Programmers" and "Hello, WML Programmers". The two strings are of the same length, that is, they contain the same number of characters. The difference in the strings is first noted when the first "A" and "M" are compared. At that point, the "A" has a smaller ASCII value than does the "M". For this reason, the function terminates and returns a -1 indicating that string 1 is smaller than string 2. Figure 46 presents the outcome of the string comparison.

The String.elementAt( ) function is used to return a particular element contained within a string. Elements can be stored in a string in WMLScript functions. Elements are identified by the use of a separator character, often a comma. In Figure 47 a string of elements, separated by a comma, are passed to the function.

The function returns the string located at position 3.

Note: In many programming languages, a list of elements starts with the first one being numbered 0. In WMLScript, the elements contained in a string start with 0. Thus, when one is counting the number of elements in a string they will have a value this is one plus the last index value. Care has to be taken when using count to assist in modifying the elements in a string.

The String.elements( ) can aid one in determining the number of elements contained in a string. You simply pass the string, along with the separator, and the function returns the number of characters found in the string. Figure 49 shows the code for the String.elements( ) function.

The function returned a value of 4 for the number of elements in the string. Figure 50 shows this result.

The String.find( ) function returns the location of an element within a string. If the element does not exist then a -1 is returned, else the index to the element

Figure 48. Result of find third element in string shown in Figure 47

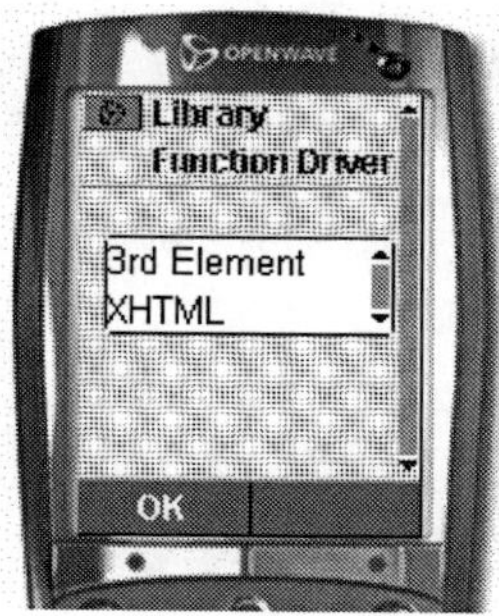

Figure 49. Use of String.elements( ) to count number of elements in string

```
extern function main() {

 var string_value = "WAP, WML, WMLScript, XHTML";

 Dialogs.alert("No. of Elements " + String.elements(string_value,","));

 }
```

Figure 50. Result of counting elements in comma delimited string

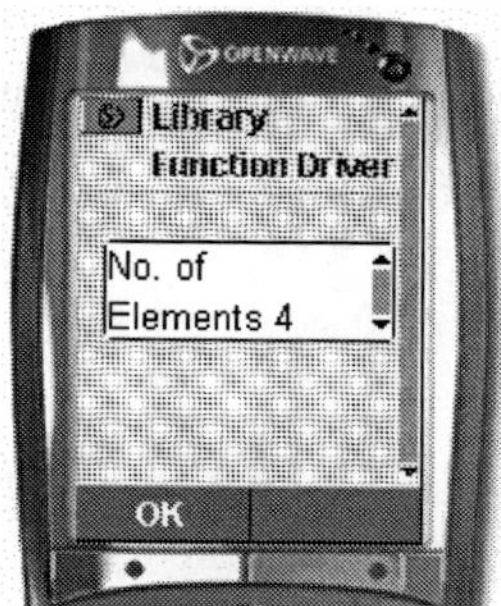

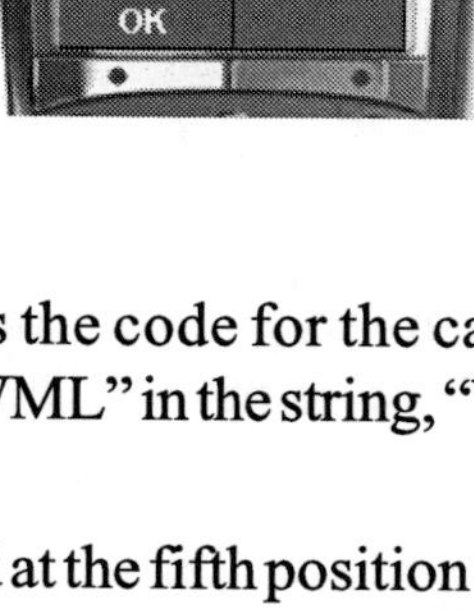

is returned. Figure 51 provides the code for the calling of the String.find( ) function to locate the element "WML" in the string, "WAP, WML, WMLScript, XHTML".

In this example, WML is located at the fifth position in the string, see Figure 52.

String.insertAt( ) is used to insert an element into a list contained within a string. You simply pass the new element, along with its location and the separator, and

Figure 51. Use of String.find( ) to locate position of element in a string

```
extern function main() {

var string_value = "WAP, WML, WMLScript, XHTML";

Dialogs.alert("Find WML " + String.find(string_value,"WML"));

}
```

Figure 52. Result of using String.find( ) to locate element in a string

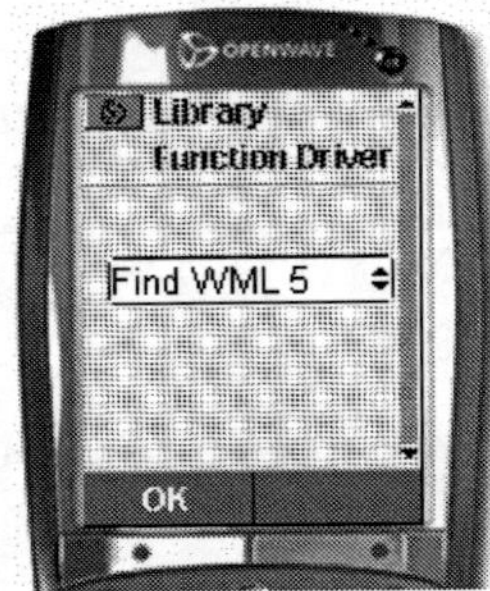

Figure 53. Use of String.insertAt to add element to string list

```
extern function main() {

var string_value = "WAP, WML, WMLScript, XHTML";
var string_value2;
string_value2 = String.insertAt(string_value,"Java",3,",");
Dialogs.alert("After Insert At " + string_value2);

}
```

the function returns the modified string. Figure 53 gives an example of using String.insertAt( ) where "Java" is inserted in the string, after "WMLScript". Remember that you are using the location starts with the first element being element 0, not element 1.

The String.format( ) function can be used to format string values, decimal values, and floating point values. The general form of the format command is as follows:

Figure 54. Result of inserting element, "Java", into existing string at position 4

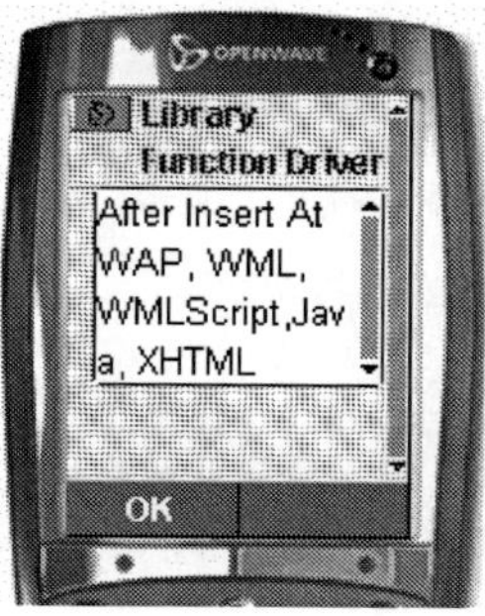

Figure 55. String.length( ) used to determine number of characters in a string

```
extern function main() {
 var string_value = "WMLScript Standard Libraries are quite helpful.";
 Dialogs.alert("Length of String " + String.length(string_value));
}
```

String.format("Name: %s",string_variable);
String.format("Decimal %.nf",decimal value);
String.format("Floating Point %n.nd",numeric value);

Once the function has completed execution, it returns the new string, which in this case is assigned to string_value2. Figure 54 shows the results of performing the insert into the string.

The String.length( ) function is quite helpful with its results often being used to perform string manipulation. The String.length( ) function accepts a string and returns the number of characters contained in that string. Figure 55 uses String.length( ) to return the number of characters in a lengthy string.

In this instance, String.length returns 47 as the number of characters in the string argument, see Figure 56.

The String.replace( ) function is used to edit the content of a string. With this function, you can replace one or more instances of a string with a new string. In

Figure 56. Number of characters in string returned by String.length( )

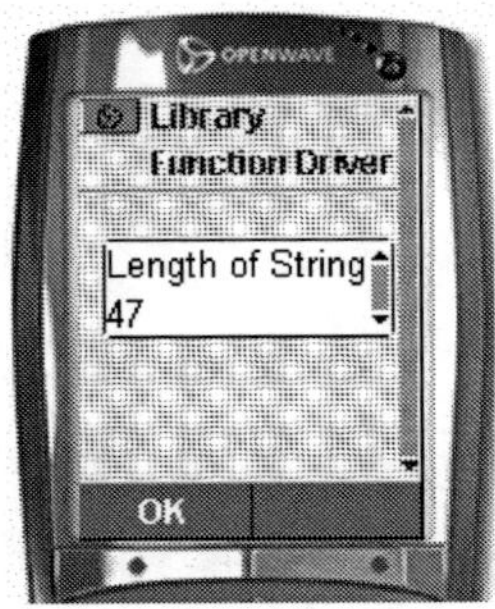

Figure 57. String.replace( ) used to replace string "quite" with string "very"

```
extern function main() {

 var string_value = "WMLScript Standard Libraries are quite helpful.";

 string_value = String.replace(string_value, "quite", "very");
 Dialogs.alert("New String " + string_value);

}
```

Figure 58. Result of modifying string, replacing "quite" with "very"

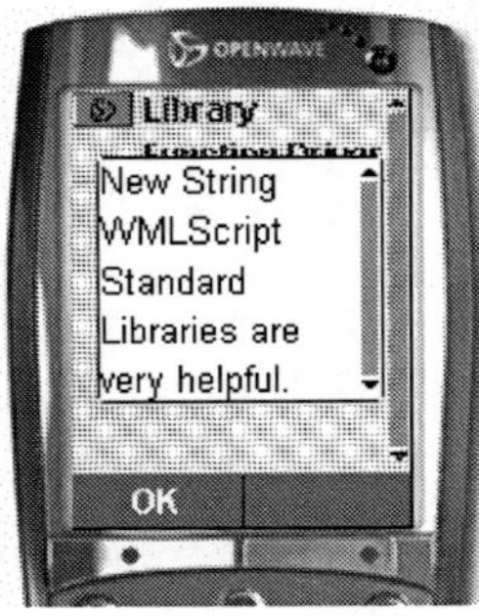

this example, Figure 57, we replace the instance of "quite" with "very" in the string value.

When the function is executed, the modified string is returned. Here the Dialogs.alert( ) function is used to display the modified string, see Figure 58.

Another means of formatting strings, particularly helpful when displaying text on a wireless device, is to use the String.squeeze( ) function. This function,

Figure 59. Use of String.squeeze( ) to remove unnecessary spaces from string

```
extern function main() {

var string_value = "WMLScript    Standard    Libraries    are    quite    helpful.";

string_value = String.squeeze(string_value);
Dialogs.alert("String squeezed: " + string_value);

}
```

Figure 60. Result of using String.squeeze( )

Figure 61. String.replaceAt( ) used to modify element in a string

```
extern function main() {

var string_value = "WML, WMLScript, Java, XHTML, WAP";

string_value = String.replaceAt(string_value, "XHTML Basic",3,",");
Dialogs.alert("Modified String: " + string_value);

}
```

demonstrated in Figure 59, removes the extra spaces contained in a string and thereby, reducing the amount of screen space required to display the string.

In this example, the string contains a number of embedded spaces. Using the String.squeeze( ) function, the resulting string, shown in Figure 60, is shorten and requires less space to display on the wireless device.

To modify the content of a string containing elements you use the String.replaceAt( ) function illustrated in Figure 61. The list of elements,

Figure 62. Result of replacing 'XHTML' with 'XHTML Basic' in string of elements

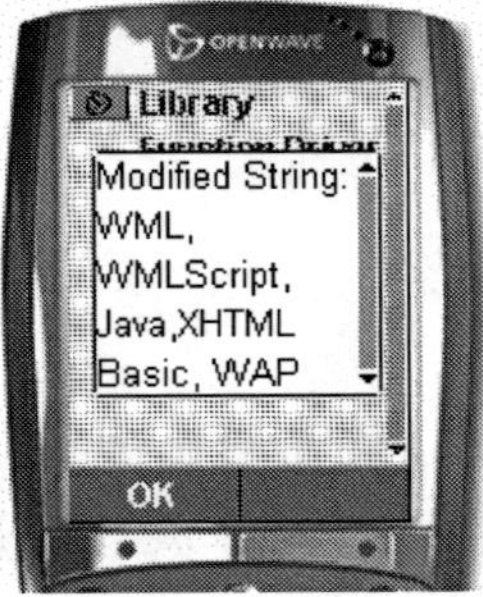

Figure 63. Use of String.subString( ) to acquire portion of string

```
extern function main() {

 var string_value = "WAP, the Wireless Application Protocol";
 var sub_string;

 sub_string = String.subString(string_value,9, 8);
 Dialogs.alert("SubString: " + sub_string);

}
```

separated by commas, is passed to the function, along with the new element and the desired location.

Once the string is modified, it is returned. The result of using this function is given in Figure 62.

NOTE: Remember you use a value of 0 for the first element in the list. Therefore, if you count to see which element you want to replace you may have to subtract one from that value.

The String.subString( ) function returns a string of characters of a specified length located at a given location. In the example in Figure 63, the "Wireless" substring is retrieved from the original string.

Once the function is executed, the value is returned. The sub_string is then displayed by the Dialogs.alert( ) function, Figure 64.

The last String library function to be examined is the String.trim( ) function shown in Figure 66. Similar in operation to the String.squeeze( ) function, this function removes spaces from the beginning and end of a string. When

Figure 64. Result of using String.subString( ) to acquire substring

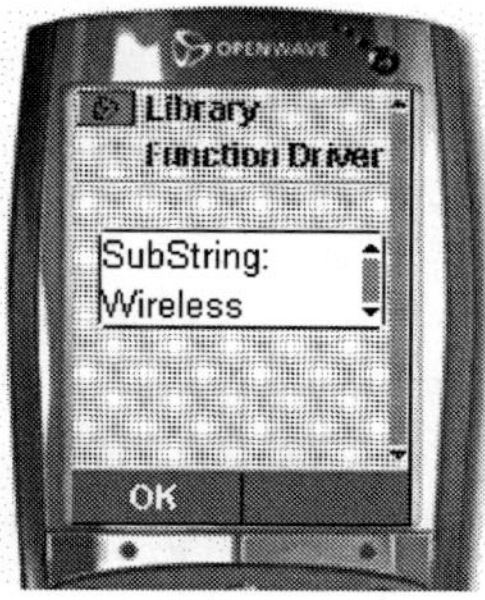

Figure 65. String.trim( ) to remove spaces from end of string

```
extern function main() {

 var string_value = "WAP, the Wireless Application Protocol              ";
 var trimmed_string;

 trimmed_string = String.trim(string_value);
 Dialogs.alert("Trimmed: " + trimmed_string);

}
```

Figure 66. Result of using String.trim( ) remove spaces from end of string

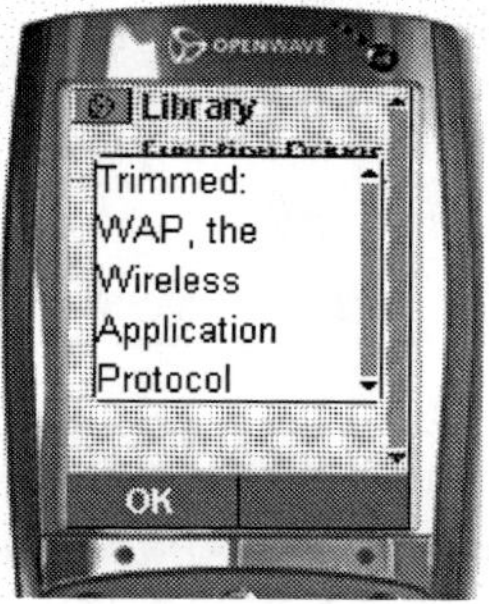

displaying text on a wireless device it is helpful to remove any unnecessary spaces. Combining both functions, String.squeeze( ) and String.trim( ), should be considered when displaying large text messages. Figure 66 uses String.trim( ).

Figure 66 shows the display of the string after the trailing spaces are removed.

Figure 67. WML document containing state code calling of WMLScript function

```
<?xml version="1.0" encoding="utf-8"?>
<!DOCTYPE wml PUBLIC "-//WAPFORUM//DTD WML 1.3//EN"
   "http://www.wapforum.org/DTD/wml13.dtd">
<wml>


 <card id="card1" title="Library Function Driver">
  <onevent type="onenterforward">
  <refresh>
   <setvar name="st_code" value = "MS" />
  </refresh>
  </onevent>
   <do type="accept" label="Call">
      <go href="getvar.wmlsc#main()"/>
   </do>
 </card>
</wml>
```

URL Library

The URL Library contains a number of functions that are helpful in manipulating URLs. These functions make it possible for one to modify a URL based on some event or value within a program. The actual use of these functions is not examined within the context of this text, however, in developing advanced WML applications, you may find these functions to be helpful. Table 6 presents the functions, along with their purpose.

WMLBrowser Library Functions

The WMLBrowser functions provide for close integration of WMLScirpt functions and WML documents. Unlike the functions associated with the WMLScript Dialogs library, of which we have employed the Dialogs.alert() function to display results, the WMLBrowser functions affect the variables in a WML document, as well as, provide navigation to a card in a WML deck. Table 7 lists the contents of the WMLBrowser library.

The WMLBrowser.getVar() function allows you to access the value stored in a variable in a WML document. Using the getVar() function is an alternative method to the passing of arguments to a WMLScript function. Figure 68 shows

Table 7. WMLBrower library functions

Function	Meaning
getCurrentCard( )	Returns URL of current card
getVar(variable name)	Return value stored in WML variable
go(url)	Branches to particular location or card
newContext( )	Clears browser context
prev( )	Returns to card on top of history stack, previous card
refresh( )	Performs a WML refresh
setVar(variable name, value)	Sets variable to a specific value

Table 6. URL library functions

Function	Meaning
escapeString(string)	Returns string in which characters in the original string have been changed to their two-digit hexadecimal ASCII values
getBase( )	Returns URL for the WMLScript unit
getFragment(url)	Returns fragment in a URL parameters, e.g. #card1
getHost(url)	Returns host from URL passed to function; 'invalid' returned if host cannot be extracted
getParameters(url)	Returns parameters associated with URL
getPath(url)	Returns path from URL
getPort(url)	Returns port number is one is include in URL
getQuery(url)	Returns query portion of URL
getReferer( )	Returns URL of unit that called WMLScript
getScheme(url)	Returns scheme portion of URL
isValid(url)	Checks syntax of URL, returns 'true' if correct, 'false' if incorrect
loadString(url,type)	Converts URL and its content type to string
resolve(base, relative)	Converts relative URL to an absolute URL
unescapeString(string)	Converts ASCII hex coding to characters

the use of the getVar( ) to acquire the two-character state code from a WML document given in Figure 67.

The WMLScript is called and the WMLBrowser.getVar( ) function is used to acquire the state code from within the WMLScript function.

The example of getting the value of a state code could be enhanced by allowing the user to input their desire value. Figure 70 shows the modification of the WML document allowing the user to enter the desired state code.

The WMLBrowser.setVar( ) function is essentially the opposite of the getVar( ) function. With this new function, you can assign a value to a variable in a WML document from within a WMLScript function. Figure 73 illustrates the use of setVar( ) function to the return the capital information for the state of New York.

Figure 68. WMLBrowser.getVar( ) function used to access state code value in WML document

```
extern function main() {

  var state_code="";

 state_code = WMLBrowser.getVar("st_code");
 Dialogs.alert("State Code: " + state_code);

}
```

Figure 69. Result of using WMLBrowser.getVar( ) to acquire state code

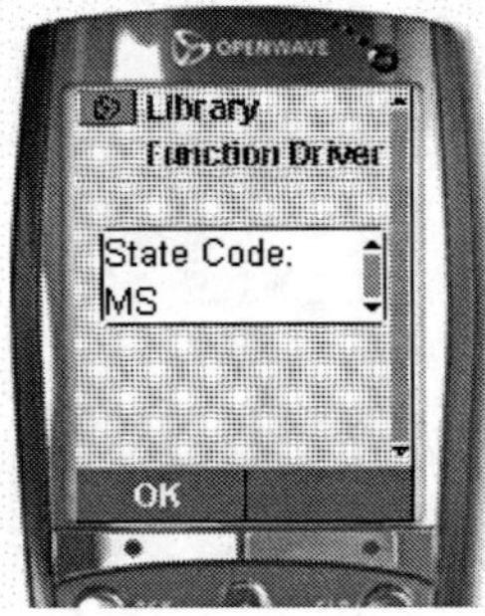

Figure 70. Modification to WML document for use of WMLBrowser.getVar()

```
<?xml version="1.0" encoding="utf-8"?>
<!DOCTYPE wml PUBLIC "-//WAPFORUM//DTD WML 1.3//EN"
   "http://www.wapforum.org/DTD/wml13.dtd">
<wml>
 <card id="card1" title="Library Function Driver">
 <onevent type="onenterforward">
  <refresh>
     <setvar name="st_code" value="" />
  </refresh>
 </onevent>

 <onevent type="onenterbackward">
  <refresh>
     <setvar name="st_code" value="" />
  </refresh>
 </onevent>
     <p>
    State Code
     <input name="st_code"/>
   </p>
 <do type="accept" label="Call">
      <go href="getvar.wmlsc#main()"/>
   </do>
 </card>
</wml>
```

Figure 71. Use of WMLBrowser.getVar( ) to access value stored in WML document variable, st_code

```
extern function main() {

 var state_code="";

state_code = WMLBrowser.getVar("st_code");
Dialogs.alert("State Code: " + state_code);

}
```

Figure 72. Value of st_code as displayed by Dialogs.alert( ) in WMLScript function

The WMLBrowser Standard Library contains another helpful function, the go( ) function which allows you to transfer program control to another location, in this case, in Figure 73, to "card2" in the WML document. The syntax for the go( ) function is quite simple, the URL for the location to which you want to transfer control, for example,

WMLBrowser.go("filename.wml#card_id").

Through the use of the WMLBrowser.setVar( ) and the WMLBrowser.go( ) function the result of selecting the state capital information contained in the WMLScript function is displayed on the wireless device as shown in Figures 74 and 75.

The WMLBrowser library contains a couple of additional functions that can be used to affect the associated WML document and can return the shortest relative URL for the current WML card. The WMLBrowser.newContext( )

Figure 73. Use of WMLScript function to test for state code and to return New York information if state code equals "ny", else return message "State Unknown"

```
extern function main() {

 var state_code="";

 state_code = WMLBrowser.getVar("st_code");
 if (state_code == "ny")
    {
    WMLBrowser.setVar("city","Albany");
    WMLBrowser.setVar("county","Albany");
    WMLBrowser.setVar("pop","95,658");
    WMLBrowser.go("driver2.wml#card2");
    }
 else
   {
    Dialogs.alert("State Unknown");
   }
}
```

Figure 74. Use of WML document to pass state code to WMLScript function

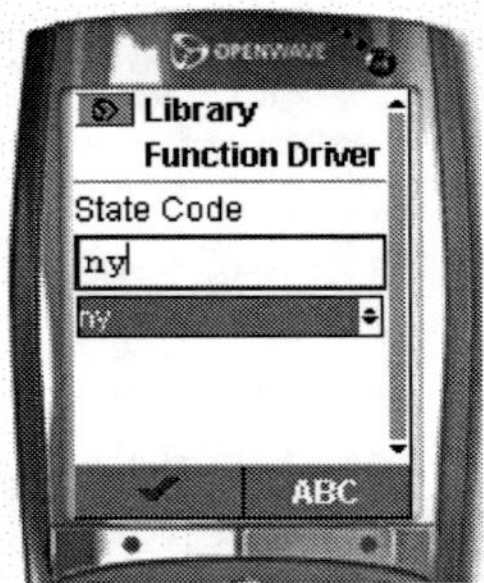

Figure 75. Result of using WMLBrowser.setVar( ) to return capital information for state of New York

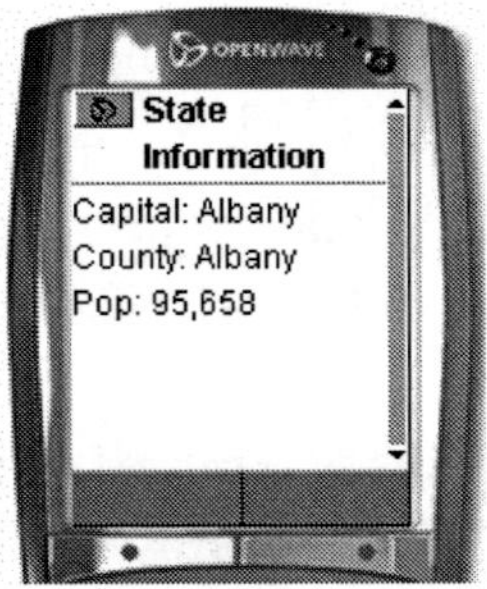

Figure 76. Result of inputting unknown state code to WMLScript function

function operates in a like manner to the WML newcontext attribute. This function causes the browser's context to be cleared. An empty string is returned by the function. The WMLBrowser.getCurentCard( ) function returns the shortest relative URL for the current WML card.

Summary

This chapter focused on the WMLScript Standard Libraries: Dialogs, Lang, Float, String, URL and WMLBrowser. Various examples were presented that illustrated the use of many of these functions. The integration of WML, WMLScript and the WMLScript libraries was used throughout the chapter:

- The Dialogs Standard Library provides for communication between the user and the WMLScript function.
- The Lang Standard Library contains a number functions used for checking variable types and type conversions, as well as, controlling program execution.
- The Float Standard Library has functions that are directly related to the use of floating point values with WMLScript programs.
- The String Standard Library presents functions related to string manipulation and the storage of elements in strings.
- The URL Standard Library provides functions used for the manipulation of URLs.

- The WMLBrowser Standard Library holds functions one can use for communication between WML documents and WMLScript functions.

Exercises

1. Your boss would like to have a program to improve his memory and response time. Create a simply program that uses the Lang.random( ) function to generate a random number between 1 and 15. The user is then allowed to enter a guess. Keep a count of the number of times the user guesses the number before she gets the right number. When the number is guessed, display on the screen the number of guesses required.
2. Having studied the WMLScript language and the WMLScript library functions, what additional functions would your recommend for inclusion in the standard library? Discuss why you believe these functions should be added. Is it possible for you to develop your own set of library functions to be used like the WMLScript Standard Libraries?
3. Design a simple calculator that could be used on a wireless device using the functions in the WMLScript Standard Libraires. Your calculator should be capable of handing the following functions: addition, subtraction, multiplication, and division.

Chapter VI

XHTML Basic

In this chapter, you will:

- Learn about XHTML Basic
- Describe the elements supported in XHTML Basic
- Learn how to integrate XHTML Basic and WML/WMLScript functions
- Examine the use of Cascading Style Sheets and their use with XHTML

Introduction to XHTML

XHTML is a derivative of XML and HTML. HTML has long been the standard for development of Web sites. With the creation of XML and its use as a foundation for portable documents, language definitions began to appear. XHMTL is one of those important document types. XHMTL documents can be used to create WML documents and is becoming a standard replacement for HTML.

The standard specifications for HTML and XHTML are the responsibility of the World Wide Web Consortium (W3C). To locate information about the standards and recommendations for HTML and XHTML you can visit their Web site at www.w3.org.

Due the voluntary nature of the W3C group, the different versions of XHTML and HTML are treated as merely recommendations, not standards that have to be strictly followed.

XHTML Basic

XHTML Basic is a limited subset of XHTML designed specifically for wireless devices. This subset was developed in order to accommodate the limited capabilities and memory of mobile devices such as cell phones. Version 1.0 was recommended by the W3C in January 2000. The advantage of using XHTML Basic over WML relates to the fact that one can create a single version of an application that can be viewed by either a PC-based browser like Netscape's or Microsoft's or the microbrowser on a handheld device. This reduces development time, while at the same time standardizing the Web site's appearance.

XHTML is case sensitive. An XHTML document is able to distinguish between a lowercase word and the same word in uppercase. This fact means that, when developing documents in XHTML, one has to be extra careful that both the syntax and the format are correct.

XHMTL, due to its reliance on XML, must be syntactically defect free in order to display. Any syntax error causes the document to not be displayed. In contrast, incorrect HTML documents will, in many instances, be displayed with the incorrect HTML text being ignored. Table 1 lists the elements supported in XHTML Basic.

The key elements supported in XHTML Basic are text, forms, tables, style sheets, and images. These elements provide a solid foundation when developing Web sites which may be accessed by both mobile devices and workstation-based browsers.

Table 1. Elements supported in XHTML Basic

Module	Elements (tags) supported
Structure	<body>, <head>, <html>, <title>
Text	<abbr>,<acronym>,<address>,<blockquote>, ,<cite>,<code>, <dfn>,<div>,<em>,<h1>,<h2>,<h3>,<h4>,<h5>,<h6>,<kbd>, <pn>,<pre>,<q>,<samp>,<span>,<string>,<var>
Hypertext	<a>
List	<dl>,<dt>,<dd>,<ul>,<li>
Basic Forms	<form>,<input>,<label>,<select>,<option>,<textarea>
Basic Tables	<caption>,<table>,<td>,<tr>,<th>
Image	<img>
Object	<object>,<param>
Meta Information	<meta>
Link	<link>
Base	<base>

Regular text is supported in XHTML Basic which includes the formatting of that text. Formatting includes paragraphs, headers, breaks, and lists. You can apply emphasis to your text, however, italics are not supported.

XHTML Basic supports the fundamental elements of forms which includes form, input, select, option, and textarea. Other elements of forms supported under the full version of XHTML are not included in XHTML Basic.

Tables under XHTML Basic allow for the fundamental elements of tables which are caption, table, td (table data), tr (table row), and th (table headers).

External style sheets, which allow for formatting of XHTML Basic documents, can be accessed with the link attribute. The elements supported in the style sheets are: div, span, and class. What is important to consider, when using style sheets, is that not all handheld devices support them. You will have to take that fact into consideration when applying style sheets in your application.

Fundamental Structure of a XHTML Basic Document

As mentioned above, XHTML Basic documents must comform to, validate, and contain specific syntax in order for the browser to display them. The guidelines to which the document must conform are:

a. must be a valid XHTML Basic document

b. must contain a valid DOCTYPE definition (DTD)

c. the root element must be html

d. the root element must contain XHTML's default namespace

Figure 1 presents an elementary XHTML Basic document.

Figure 1. Simple XHTML Basic document

```
<?xml version="1.0" ?>
<!DOCTYPE html PUBLIC "-//WC3//DTD XHTML Basic 1.0// xml:lang="en" >

<html xmlns=http://www.w3.org/1999/xhtml xml:lang="en" >
<head>
  <title> Example </title>
</head>
 <body>
     <p> XHTML Basic </p>
</body>
</html>
```

Figure 2. XHTML Basic document

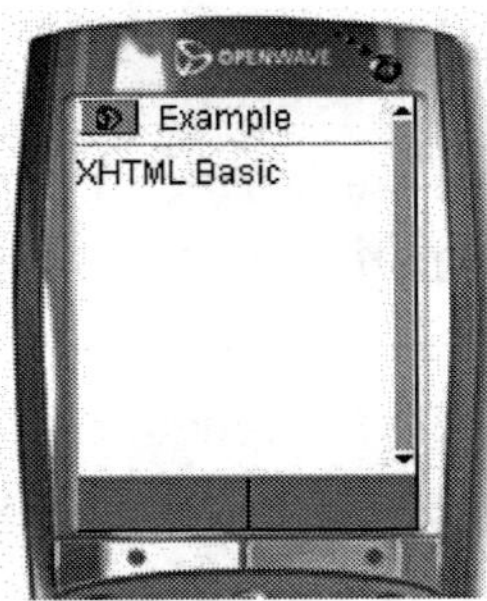

Figure 3. Viewing XHTML Basic document with Internet Explorer

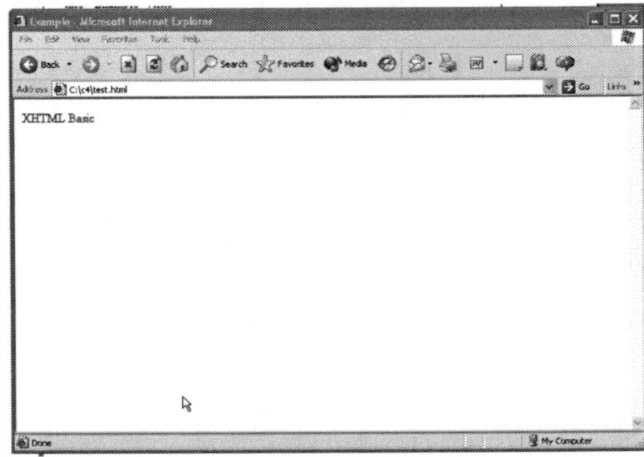

Viewing this document using the Openwave emulator produces this output in Figure 2.

Using Microsoft's Internet Explorer to view the same document produces the same output (see Figure 3).

This example shows the flexibility of using XHMTL Basic for creating Web pages that will be accessed by more than the mobile users. One can save considerable amount of time in creating and maintaining Web sites by employing XHTML Basic.

XHTML Basic can be used to format output and provide for simple user interaction. First, XHMTL Basic uses the same type of headers as does HTML. Bolded text in different sizes is supported through the use of the header tags - <h*n*> .. </h*n*> where represent the size of the header. The values range from 1 to 6, where 1 is the largest of the headers and 6 is the smallest. Figure 4 illustrates the code needed to use each of the headers. Figure 5 shows the output from displaying this XHMTL Basic document.

The use of headers can be helpful in establishing the size of text. Advanced formatting for XHMTL is provided through the use of style sheets which are discussed later in this chapter. By using style sheets, you can affect the size and style of text throughout a XHTML document.

Another means by which text can be formatted in a XHTML document is through the use of lists. XHTML provides for the use of unnumbered, ordered

Figure 4. XHTML Basic code for use of headers

```
<?xml version="1.0" encoding="utf-8"?>
<!DOCTYPE html PUBLIC "-//WAPFORUM//DTD XHTML Mobile 1.0//EN"
    "http://www.wapforum.org/DTD/xhtml-mobile10.dtd" >

<html xmlns="http://www.w3.org/1999/xhtml">
  <head>
    <title>Headers</title>
  </head>
  <body>
    <h1> Header 1 </h1>
    <h2> Header 2 </h2>
    <h3> Header 3 </h3>
    <h4> Header 4 </h4>
    <h5> Header 5 </h5>
    <h6> Header 6 </h6>
  </body>
</html>
```

Figure 5. Output from XHMTL Basic use of headers

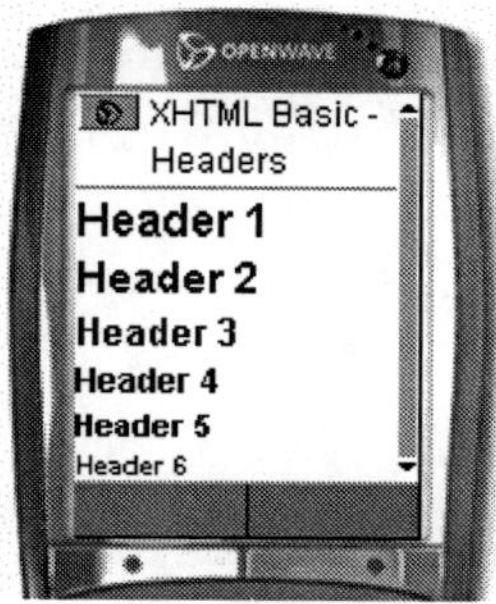

Figure 6. Use of unnumbered list in XHMTL Basic

```
<?xml version="1.0" encoding="utf-8"?>
<!DOCTYPE html PUBLIC "-//WAPFORUM//DTD XHTML Mobile 1.0//EN"
    "http://www.wapforum.org/DTD/xhtml-mobile10.dtd" >

<html xmlns="http://www.w3.org/1999/xhtml">
  <head>
    <title>XHTML Basic - Headers</title>
  </head>
  <body>

    <li> Northeast </li>
    <li> Southeast </li>
    <li> Midwest </li>
    <li> Southwest </li>
    <li> West </li>
  </body>
</html>
```

Figure 7. Output of list in XHTML

and numbered lists, as well as definition lists and terms. Figure 6 provides a simple example of an unnumbered list for the regions of the United States.

A list can be used for a number of different purposes in a document. It is quite helpful to use a list to organize data, as well as links.

XHTML Basic provides only basic forms for use in allowing input by the user. The basic forms module is used for input by the user. Data is input and stored in the variable associated with each input field. In addition to the assignment of values to a variable, you can identify the type and size of the data allowed to be entered in a given field. Figure 8 shows the basic structure of a form that allows the user to enter a two-digit state code.

Figure 9 shows the resulting screen from viewing the XHMTL Basic document.

Figure 8. Basic form module used for input of state code

```
<?xml version="1.0" encoding="utf-8"?>
<!DOCTYPE html PUBLIC "-//WAPFORUM//DTD XHTML Mobile 1.0//EN"
     "http://www.wapforum.org/DTD/xhtml-mobile10.dtd" >

<html xmlns="http://www.w3.org/1999/xhtml">
  <head>
     <title>State Code</title>
  </head>
  <body>
    <form method="post" >
     State Code: <input type="text" name="statecode" size="2" maxlength="2"/>
    </form>
  </body>
</html>
```

Figure 9. Input of state code using form in XHTML Basic

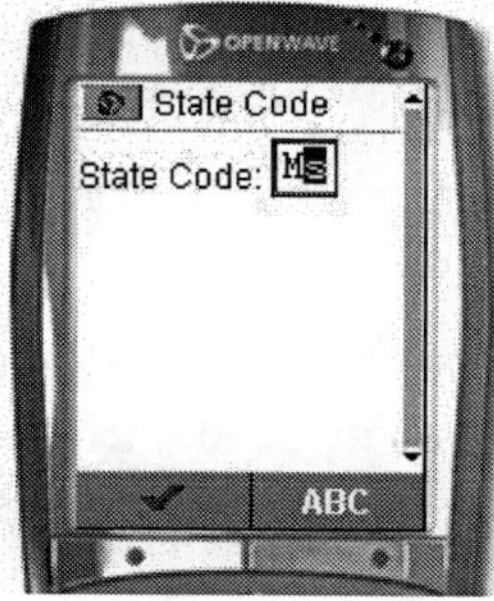

Here the user is provided with a simple form that is used to enter the two-character state code, in this instance "MS" for Mississippi. You will note that by using the keypad on the phone, "MS" was entered as "Ms".

Integrating XHMTL Basic and WML/WMLScript

XHTML Basic does not support the use of scripts within a document, nor can you call one externally such as WMLScript functions. In order to overcome this limitation, you can navigate from a XHTML documents to a WML document and then call the WMLScript to complete your application. To illustrate this technique, we will develop an application that uses a XHTML Basic document

Figure 10. XHML document linking to WML document

```
<!xml version="1.0"?>
<!DOCTYPE html PUBLIC "-//OPENWAVE//DTD XHTML MOBILE 1.0//EN"
http://www.openwave.com/DTD/xhtml-mobile10.dtd>

<html xmlns=http://www.w3.org/1999/xhtml xml:lang="en">
   <head><title>XHMTL Basic</title></head>
   <body>
         <a href="WMLdocument.wml">Call WML</a>
   </body>
   </head>
</html>
```

as the main document accessed by the user. Once that document is viewed then the user can select the navigation link that takes them to a WML document. Finally, the WMLScript is executed and the result of being there is displayed by use of the Dialogs.alert( ) function.

The first document created is shown in Figure 10. Here, a simple XHTML Basic document is used to link to a WML document.

Accessing the XHMTL document and then branching to the WML document appears as shown in Figures 11 and 12.

As can be seen in this example, the link to the WML document is placed in the XHMTL document. Pressing the key below the checkmark sends the control from the XHTML document to the WML document. Adding a link to the WMLScript file completes the process of linking from an XHTML Basic document to a WMLScript function.

Figure 11. XHTML document with link to WML document

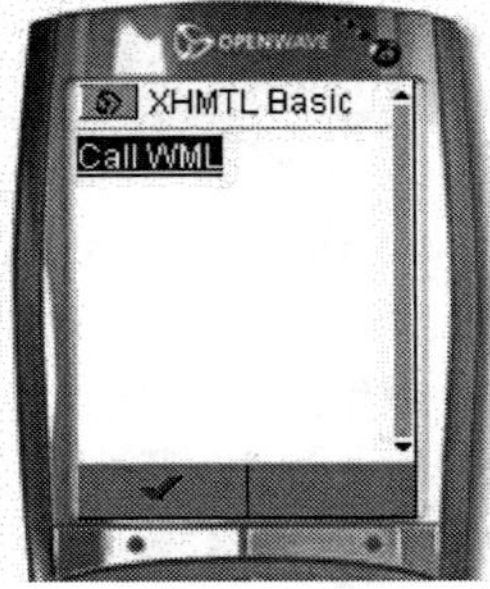

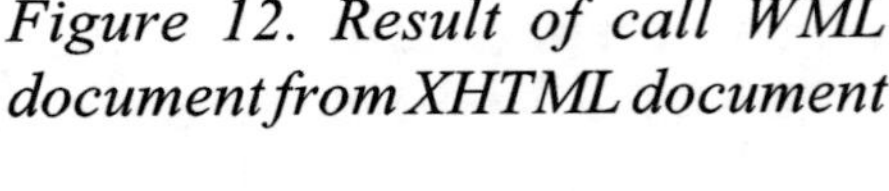

Figure 12. Result of call WML document from XHTML document

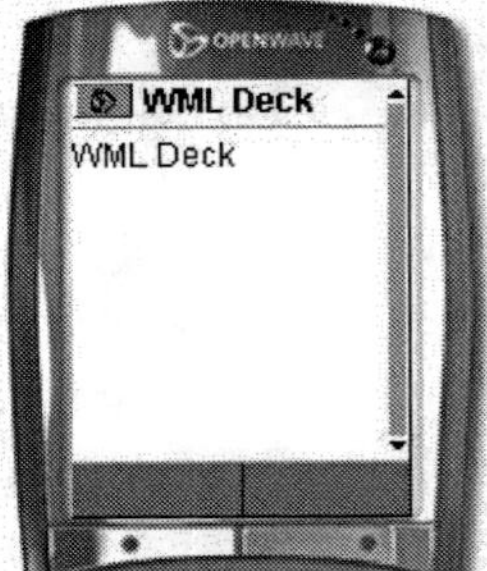

Note, at this point you will encounter a problem with the Openwave 6.2.2 emulator. For this reason, a different toolkit is employed to illustrate the linking of XHTML Documents with WML and WMLScript. The Nokia Mobile Internet Toolkit (NMIT) supports the use of XHTML Basic, WML documents, and WMLScript functions. In order to acquire this toolkit, you must register at the Nokia Forum, www.forum.nokia.com. After registering, you can download the 4.0 toolkit.

There are a couple of important things to remember, in order to have the process work correctly. First, XHMTL Basic documents cannot access WMLScript functions directly. Second, to call a WMLScript function in the toolkit, the WMLScript function may have to be compiled and the reference to the WMLScript function indicate that the WMLScript file is compiled, for example, .wmlsc. The following example illustrates the use of a XHTML Basic document to call a WMLScript function, by first calling a WML document that automatically calls the WMLScript function. The WML document is not visible to the user since we are applying an event, <onenterforward>.

To illustrate the calling of a WMLScript from a XHTML document, the following example is provided. The WML document, shown in Figure 13 automatically calls the WMLScript function without displaying the WML document first. The WMLScript function, shown in Figure 14, displays a message and then returns to the original XHTML Basic document.

Figure 13. WML document automatically calling WMLScript function

```
<?xml version="1.0"?>
<!DOCTYPE wml PUBLIC "-//WAPFORUM//DTD WML 1.1//EN"
"http://www.wapforum.org/DTD/wml_1.1.xml">
<wml>
 <card id="card1" title="Test wmls">
  <onevent type='onenterforward'>
    <go href="call.wmlsc#displayalert()"/>
  </onevent>
 </card>
</wml>
```

Figure 14. WMLScript function called from WML document

```
extern function display_message()
{
Dialogs.alert("WMLScript Called");
}
```

Figure 15. Output from WMLScript function called from WML document

Figure 16. XHTML code used to call WML document which in turn calls WMLScript function

```
<?xml version="1.0"?>
<!DOCTYPE html PUBLIC "-//WAPFORUM//DTD XHTML Mobile 1.0//EN"
"http://www.wapforum.org/DTD/xhtml-mobile10.dtd" >
<html xmlns="http://www.w3.org/1999/xhtml">

  <head>
    <title>XHTML Basic</title>
  </head>
  <body>
    <p>
        <a href="Document.wml">Call WMLScript</a>
    </p>
  </body>
</html>
```

Note that many of the microbrowsers require that the WMLScript functions be compiled. This case is true for the NMIT. NMIT provides one with a means of compiling WMLScript functions. Once the function is compiled then it can be accessed from the WML document. Please note that the reference to the WMLScript function used the compiled version: <go href="call.wmlsc#displayalert()"/>, indicated by the "c" following the wmls file extension.

The result of calling this function is shown in Figure 15.

To complete the entire process, an XHTML Basic document is used to access the WML document. The code for the XHTML document is presented in Figure 16.

Figure 17. WML document using <onevent> to call WMLScript function

```
<?xml version="1.0" encoding="utf-8"?>
<!DOCTYPE wml PUBLIC "-//WAPFORUM//DTD WML 1.3//EN"
   "http://www.wapforum.org/DTD/wml13.dtd">
<wml>
 <card id="card1" title="TEST" >

<onevent type='onenterforward'>
   <go href="call.wmlsc#displayalert()"/>
</onevent>

  </card>
</wml>
```

Figure 18. XHTML Basic document displayed after returning from WMLScript function

Note: As noted above, not all emulators support the integration of XHMTL documents, WML documents, and WMLScript functions. You may encounter situations where the XMHTL document will transfer control to the WML document, however, the WML document will not be able to call the WMLScript function. At the same time and with the same emulator, you will be able to call the WMLScript function directly from the WML document, just not from the XHTML document through the intervening WML document. This situation makes testing of software difficult at best.

The WML document, shown in Figure 17, is designed to immediately call the WMLScript function without the WML document being displayed.

Notice, in this WML document, that the <onevent> onenterforward is used to cause the WML document to immediately call the WMLScript function, "displayalert( )" before the document can be displayed. This technique allows one to develop a XHTML document that uses WMLScript functions.

Once the WMLScript function is accessed, the following screen is displayed (see Figure 18).

Cascading Style Sheets (CSS) and XHTML Basic

To format the output of a XHTML Basic document, it is recommended that you use a Style Sheet. To fully understand Style Sheets, what they are and how to use them, this section examines Cascading Style Sheets (CSS) and their usage with XHMTL Basic documents.

Cascading Style Sheets are a means by which one can have a consistent design and establish common formatting across all pages of a document. One is able to affect the typeface, background, text size, link colors, margin controls, and the placement of objects on a page.

CSS are applied to all of the pages in a document. To properly assist you in making changes to a document's appearance you simply have to change the associated CSS and the change will affect all of the pages.

The elements that makeup a CSS are selectors, properties, and values. A selector represents the element of the XHTML Basic document that is to receive the properties, for example, <p> for paragraph or <h1> for header. Selectors are listed in Table 1. Properties relate to a particular selector. You assign a desired value to the property which in turn, when applied to an XHTML document, affects the format of its output.

Figure 19 shows an example of a CSS. Here the format of the paragraph is impacted, along with the title for the page.

Figure 19. Cascading style sheet

```
title {
  font-style: italic;
}

p {
  font-size: small;
  font-weight: bold;
}
```

To fully understand the use of CSS to format an XHMTL document, this particular style sheet is applied to the XHTML Basic document which contains a state's information. To make the example more realistic, the XHTML document also contains the necessary elements to place the information in a table. The XHTML document, with the CSS, is shown in Figure 20.

Applying this CSS to the state capital information page results in the output shown in Figure 21. In this example, you can see that the title, Mississippi, was

Figure 20. Linking CSS to XHTML Basic document

```
<?xml version="1.0"?>
<!DOCTYPE html PUBLIC "-//OPENWAVE//DTD XHTML Mobile 1.0//EN"
"http://www.openwave.com/DTD/xhtml-mobile10.dtd">

<!-- XHTML-MP 1.0 file created by the Openwave SDK -->

<html xmlns="http://www.w3.org/1999/xhtml" xml:lang="en">
        <head><title>Mississippi</title>
    <link rel=stylesheet href="style_sheet1.css" type="text/css" />
    </head>
      <body>
    <table>
    <tr>
    <td> <p>City:</p> </td>
    <td> <p>Jackson</p> </td>
    </tr>
    <tr>
    <td> <p>County:</p></td>
    <td> <p>Hinds</p></td>
    </tr>
    <tr>
    <td><p> Pop:</p></td>
    <td><p> 250,000</p> </td>
    </tr>
    </table>

   </body>
</html>
```

Figure 21. Result of applying CSS to state capital info XHTML Basic document

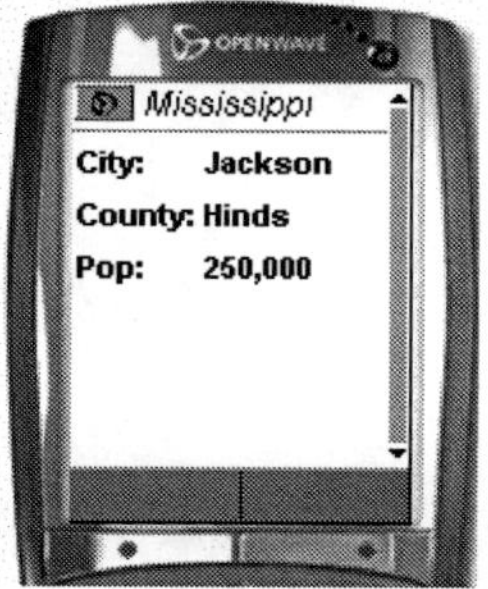

italicized and the text for the table was bolded and placed in a small sized font. Changes to the display of the text can be modified quickly by simply modifying the CSS. Furthermore, as will shown later in this chapter, the CSS is applied to all documents in the file so one can standardize the appearance of a XHTML Basic Web site.

XHTML State Capitals Example

To understand fully the use of XHMTL for wireless Internet applications, the state capitals example that we examined in Chapters 3 and 4 is implemented using XHTML Basic.

To begin the first screen is developed and tested. This document provides the user with a list of regions of the United States from which they can select the one for which the want to display the state capital's information.

The first XHMTL document, shown in Figure 22 provides the list of regions as hyperlinks to the individual region document. The individual region documents do not exist at this point so the hyperlinks are inactive.

Figure 22. XHTML Basic document for regions menu

```
<?xml version="1.0"?>
<!DOCTYPE html PUBLIC "-//OPENWAVE//DTD XHTML Mobile 1.0//EN"
"http://www.openwave.com/DTD/xhtml-mobile10.dtd">

<!-- XHTML-MP 1.0 file created by the Openwave SDK -->

<html xmlns="http://www.w3.org/1999/xhtml" xml:lang="en">
        <head><title>State Capitals</title></head>
        <body>
          <p>
            <a href="southeast.html">Southeast</a>
          </p>
          <p>
            <a href="northeast.html">Northeast</a>
          </p>
          <p>
            <a href="midwest.html">Midwest</a>
           </p>
          <p>
            <a href="southwest.html">Southwest</a>
         </p>
          <p>
            <a href="west.html">West</a>
          </p>
        </body>
</html>
```

Once this code is implemented, you can display the results using the Openwave emulator. The emulator presents the following result as shown in Figure 23.

As you can see from the above example, the use of XHTML Basic produces the same type of result you received when using WML. Adding the individual states for the Southeast region allows for the linking to the individual state's information. Figure 24 illustrates the completion of the state capital program where you can link to the individual state's data.

The individual state data is included in a separate XHTML Basic document. For this example, the state of Mississippi was chosen and a document was developed to contain the city, county, and population data. Figure 25 contains the code for Mississippi.

Figure 23. State capitals region menu developed in XHTML Basic

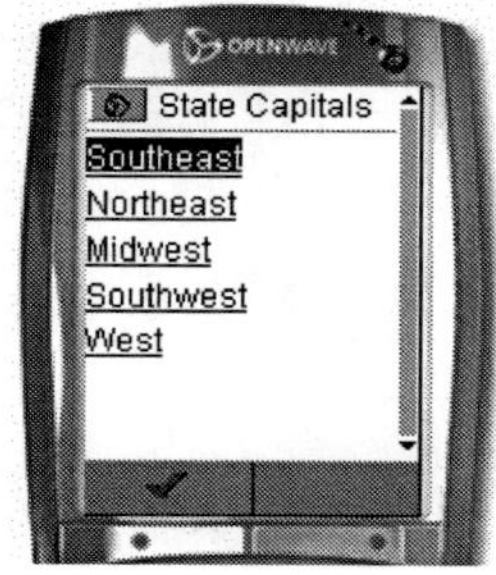

Figure 24. Southeast region states presented in XHTML Basic

Figure 25. XHMTL document used to display capital information

```
<?xml version="1.0"?>
<!DOCTYPE html PUBLIC "-//OPENWAVE//DTD XHTML Mobile 1.0//EN"
"http://www.openwave.com/DTD/xhtml-mobile10.dtd">

<!-- XHTML-MP 1.0 file created by the Openwave SDK -->

<html xmlns="http://www.w3.org/1999/xhtml" xml:lang="en">
<head><title>Mississippi</title></head>
   <body>
    <p>
      City: Jackson
    </p>
    <p>
      County: Hinds
    </p>
    <p>
      Pop: 250,000
    </p>
    </body>
</html>
```

Figure 26. Result of access XHTML Basic document shown in Figure 24

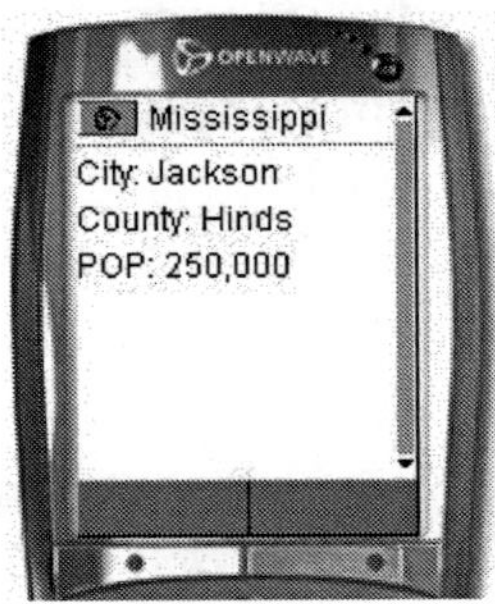

This document is accessed by selecting Mississippi from the state listing. Using the Openwave 6.2.2 emulator, information is displayed as shown in Figure 26.

This display could be enhanced through the use of a table for the data fields. The output containing the table would be similar to that show Figure 21.

Summary

In this chapter, we have examined XHTML Basic and how it can be used to create Web sites supported by both microbrowsers on a mobile device and on desktop PCs using an Internet browser. This feature assists in the development of a common interface for both mobile devices and for LAN based applications.

XHTML Basic supports the use of cascading style sheets (CSS) which are used to apply a common formatting to all of the pages in an XHMTL document. Only external styles sheets are supported in XHMLT Basic.

XHTML Basic can support the calling of WMLScript functions as long as you employ an intermediate WML document. Control can be returned from the WMLScript function to the XHTML document. To make the process transparent to the user, you can use an <oneventforward> event which will avoid having the WML document appear on the mobile device.

Exercises

1. XHTML and XML are becoming important languages in the development of Web-based applications. What are the advantages of using these languages over WML and WMLScript? Are their any disadvantages? Additional information on this topic can be found on the Web and in particular at www.w3.org.
2. Use XHTML Basic to replicate the phone directory you developed in Exercise 4 in Chapter 3.
3. Create a style sheet to format the following text. Bold the header, set the paragraph in italics, and place the entire text in a small font size.

   Wireless App. Dev.

   WML, WMLScript, and XHTML Basic are important languages when developing applications to run on a mobile wireless device. It is important to understand the syntax and use of these languages.

Chapter VII

Dynamic Wireless Application Development I: Developing Wireless Applications Using ColdFusion

In this chapter, you will:

- Learn the techniques of designing and developing wireless applications for Pocket PC and mobile handsets
- Learn to use the tags of CFML
- Learn to interact with a database using ColdFusion
- Learn about cookie and session variables
- Learn to interact with email services using ColdFusion
- Learn to develop a shopping cart application

Introduction

A wireless application is designed to function when the device is connected to networks (e.g., the Internet) or other devices wirelessly. An example of such an application is a directory service, such as Indigo, found on handsets and PDAs with wireless Web services. These applications allow users to access and even manipulate data on the move. More and more organizations are beginning to develop wireless applications for their employees so they can access critical corporate data whenever and wherever the service is available. The primary advantage of a wireless application over a mobile application is that the user can have access to the most up-to-date information; therefore, if the information in an organization frequently changes, a wireless application is more appropriate in this situation.

A limitation of a wireless application is its reliability. The reliability of the application depends on a variety of factors including the reliability of the network and the servers. Information becomes inaccessible when the wireless network service is not available at the location. The speed of a wireless application can also vary depending on the network traffic and throughput.

Wireless applications are typically delivered to users via Web browsers on PDAs (e.g., Internet Explorer for Pocket PC) or microbrowsers on wireless handsets. Therefore, the design and development of these applications are very similar to those of Internet applications. However, due to the limited display area, processing power, and inputting capabilities of mobile devices, designers must take into account a number of usability and technical considerations when developing wireless applications. In this chapter, we will design and develop a sales force automation system for Wireless Solutions. By doing so, we will illustrate the techniques for designing and developing wireless applications.

Sales Force Automation System (SAS)

The salespeople at Wireless Solutions spend a lot of their time on the road visiting clients and acquiring new clients. They believe that they will be able to do their jobs more efficiently and effectively if they can access the most up-to-date information when they are away from their desks. Timely access to information will allow them to better serve their clients and take advantage of cross-selling and up-selling opportunities more effectively. Every salesperson at Wireless Solutions is equipped with a mobile phone and a Pocket PC. Wireless Solutions decides to develop a SAS that can function on these devices.

The salespeople would like to have a number of key functions in the SAS: 1) access information on customers, products, and other salespeople; 2) find the customer's contact information as well as purchase history so that they can recommend products to their clients; 3) access product specification and availability, and order products for clients using SAS; 4) search for salespeople's contact information and send emails using SAS; and 5) report travel expenses so that salespeople can make use of the time in transit to report travel expenses rather than upon their return home.

The type of wireless device also determines the functions of the application. In general, wireless devices are more suitable for transaction-oriented tasks (e.g., search for the nearest gas station or placing an order for a product). This is because the small display screens of wireless devices make information-oriented tasks difficult (e.g., reading a report). Mobile phones are most limited as they have the smallest displays and limited input capability. Therefore, only a subset of all the features in the SAS will work decently on a mobile phone as compared to a PDA with larger displays.

Another important consideration for wireless applications is security. Adequate security measures must be in place to prevent unauthorized users from accessing sensitive corporate data. Therefore, Wireless Solutions requires every salesperson to login before using any function in the SAS.

Building the Database

We will start the project by designing the database. The database will have the following tables and fields, and Figure 1 is a schematic representation of the database tables and their relationships.

Figure 1. Database tables and relationships

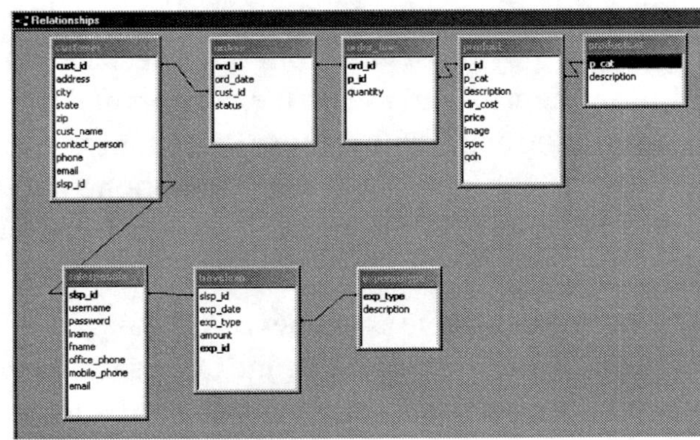

CUSTOMER (Cust_id, address, city, state, zip, cust_name, contact_person, phone, email, slsp_id)

ORDERS (ord_id, ord_date, cust_id, status)

ORDER_LINE (ord_id, p_id, quantity)

PRODUCT (p_id, p_cat, description, dlr_cost, price, image, spec, qoh)

PRODUCTCAT (p_cat, description)

SALESPEOPLE (slsp_id, username, password, lname, fname, office_phone, mobile_phone, email)

TRAVELEXP (exp_id, slsp_id, exp_date, exp_type, amount)

EXPENSETYPE (exp_type, description)

Selecting the Development Tools

When developing applications for wireless devices, the first consideration in technology selection is to find a technology platform that will work with a wide range of client devices. Wireless Application Protocol (WAP) offers an ideal solution because 1) it is supported by a wide variety of client devices, and 2) it leverages the existing Internet infrastructure and content, thus making the development process simpler. While WML, the primary language of WAP, can be interpreted by both a microbrowser and Internet Explorer for Windows CE, it is not as versatile and flexible as HTML in developing multimedia content for larger screens (e.g., Pocket PC). Therefore, we will use WML for wireless handsets and HTML for Pocket PC devices.

A server-side technology is ideal for wireless applications for the following two reasons. First, wireless devices often have little processing power. Second, server-side technology functions regardless of client devices, making it possible to write once and use it anywhere. A wide variety of server-side technologies exist to deliver applications over the Internet. All of them will work equally well in most cases. In this example, we choose to use Macromedia ColdFusion as the server-side technology because 1) it is becoming one of the predominant development tools for corporate Web development, and 2) it is easy to learn and use, especially for applications that interface with databases.

To develop ColdFusion applications, you will need the following items:

- ColdFusion server installed on your Web server
- A text editor (e.g., Notepad) or HTML/WML generator for coding
- An FTP program for uploading files to the Web server

As most readers will have Notepad on their computer, we will use Notepad for all demonstrations in the following sections.

Creating an ODBC Connection

The first thing we need to do is to create an ODBC connection for our database. If you do not have access to the ColdFusion server administration tools, ask the administrator to create the ODBC connection for you. If you have access to the administration tools, follow the steps below to create an ODBC connection.

1. Upload the database file to the Web server.
2. Enter the administration tool (http://yourservername/cfide/administrator/index.cfm) by entering the right password.
3. Click "**ODBC**" on the left panel.

Figure 2. Creating ODBC data source

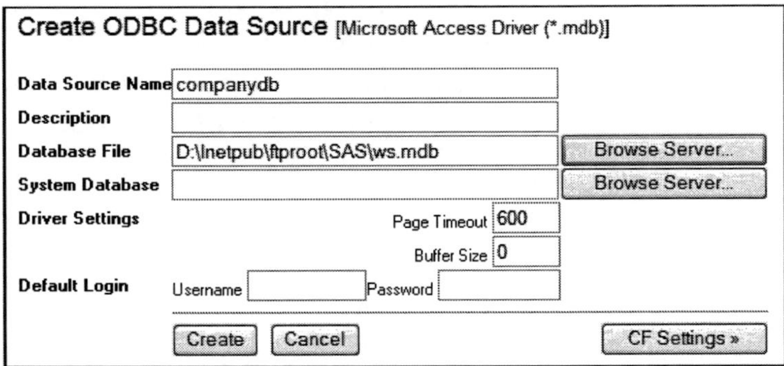

4. Type "**companydb**" as the datasource name. Select "**Microsoft Access Driver**" as the ODBC driver. Click the **Add** button.
5. Locate the database file by browsing the file system of the server. Click the **Create** button (see Figure 2).
6. You will see that the new datasource has been added to the list. If the status is "**verified**", your ODBC connection has been created successfully.

From now on, you will refer to your database by using its datasource name, "companydb".

Creating the SAS Heading

To provide easy navigation to users, the same heading with links to different functions of the SAS will be displayed on every page throughout the application. If the heading is individually programmed into each and every page of the application, a minor change in the heading will result in major work. To avoid this maintenance, we will take advantage of the application framework of ColdFusion. ColdFusion's application framework allows you to use a special file called "application.cfm". When a ColdFusion file in a folder is requested, the ColdFusion server executes the application.cfm file in the folder before the requested file is executed. If application.cfm file is not found in the folder, the ColdFusion server will instead execute the application.cfm file in the root directory, provided there is one.

The application.cfm file has many useful features that we will discuss in the later part of this chapter. Here, we will use it to create a heading for the application that will appear on every page.

1. Open a new document in Notepad. Save the document as "application.cfm". Enter the statementsshown in the following page into the document.

```
<!DOCTYPE HTML PUBLIC "-//W3C//DTD HTML 4.0 Transitional//EN">

<TABLE width = 230>
   <TR>
      <TD><IMG src="logo.gif"></TD>
   </TR>
   <TR>
      <TD>
      <FONT size="-1">
      <A href ="index.cfm">home</A> | 
      <A href ="productsearch.cfm">products</A> | 
      <A href ="customersearch.cfm">customers</A> | 
      <A href
      ="salespeoplesearch.cfm">salespeople</A> | 
      <A href ="travelexp.cfm">report expenses</A> | 
      <A href ="viewcart.cfm">view cart</A> | 
      <A href ="logout.cfm">logout</A>
      </FONT>
      </TD>
   </TR>
</TABLE>
```

2. Save the file and upload it to the Web server.

Creating the Customer Search Feature

Performing a search in a Web application is a two-step process. First, the user will be presented with a form to enter search criteria. Second, the ColdFusion application will search the database and display records that meet the criteria. For wireless applications, you want to use prepopulated ComboBoxes whenever it is possible so that the user does not have to type the search criteria. To search a database, you need to understand three important CFML tags.

```
<CFQUERY datasource = "[datasource name]" name = "[query name]">
    [SQL statement]
</CFQUERY>
```

<CFQUERY> is one of the most important CFML tags, as it executes SQL statements. The datasource attribute tells the ColdFusion server which database will be queried. The query is uniquely identified by the query name in the document.

Another important CFML tag is <CFOUTPUT>. It is used to display ColdFusion variable or a query result. The syntax for <CFOUTPUT> is as follows:

```
<CFOUTPUT {query="[query name]"}>
    #[query name].[field name]#
</CFOUTPUT>
```

Another way to display query results is using <CFLOOP>. <CFLOOP> will display only a subset of the query result if you choose to do so.

```
<CFLOOP {query="[query name]" startrow="[row number]" endrow="[row
number]"} >
    <CFOUTPUT>
    #[query name].[field name]#
</CFOUTPUT>
</CFLOOP>
```

Now, let's create the customersearch.cfm file.

1. Open a new file in Notepad. Save the file as "customersearch.cfm". Enter the following statements in the document.

```
<!--Retrieve customer names from the customer table-->

<CFQUERY datasource="companydb" name="getname">
SELECT cust_name FROM customer
</CFQUERY>

<TABLE width="230">
   <TR>
      <TD>
      Select the customer's company name:
      <P>

<!--Supply search criteria to customersearchresult.cfm-->

      <FORM action="customersearchresult.cfm" method=post>

<!--A drop-down list of customer names-->

      <SELECT name="custname" size=1>
         <CFOUTPUT query="getname">
         <OPTION value="#getname.cust_name#">#getname.cust_name#
         </CFOUTPUT>
      </SELECT>
      <BR>
      <INPUT type="submit" value="Search">
      </FORM>
      </TD>
   </TR>
</TABLE>
```

Figure 3. Searching for a customer

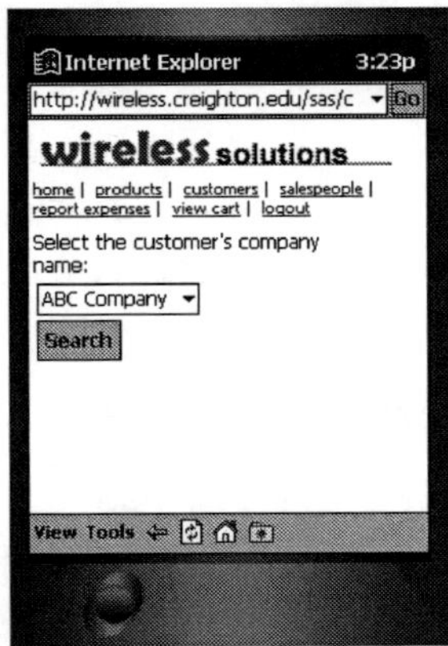

2. Save the file. Upload the file to the Web server and test it. Your form should look like the form in Figure 3.

The Internet is a stateless system, that is, one Web page is not aware of the processes occurring in another Web page. There are two ways to pass data from one page to another. The first method uses the form variable. The passing page must contain a form, and the "action" attribute of the form tag is assigned to the filename of the target page. The form variable is passed from one page to the target when the user presses the submit button. To access the form variable in the target page, you use "#FORM.variable name#".

The second method uses the URL variable. As the name suggests, the value of the variable is passed to the target page as part of the URL. For example, the URL http://www.ws.com/product.cfm?pid=002&qty=20 passes two variables to product.cfm. The two variables are "pid" and "qty". The variable-value sets and the URL of the target page are separated by a question mark, and the URL variable-value sets are separated by an ampersand. To access the URL variable in the target page, you use "#URL.[variable name]#".

In the following example, we will use the form variable to create the Customersearchresult.cfm file.

1. Open a new document in Notepad. Save the file as "customersearchresult.cfm". Enter the following statements. The SQL statement retrieves the information to be displayed to the user.

```
<CFQUERY datasource="companydb" name="getcust">

SELECT customer.cust_id, customer.cust_name, customer.address,
customer.city, customer.state, customer.zip,
customer.contact_person, customer.phone, customer.email,
salespeople.slsp_id, salespeople.lname, salespeople.fname
FROM customer, salespeople
WHERE cust_name = '#FORM.custname#'
AND customer.slsp_id = salespeople.slsp_id
ORDER BY cust_name

</CFQUERY>
```

2. Enter the following statements to display the results in a table.

```
<TABLE width="230">
   <TR>
      <TD>
      Search results:
      <P>
      <CFOUTPUT>
      <B>#getcust.cust_name#</B>
      </CFOUTPUT>
      </TD>
   </TR>
   <TR>
      <TD>
      <CFOUTPUT>
      #getcust.address#<BR>
      #getcust.city#, #getcust.state# #getcust.zip#<BR>
      </CFOUTPUT>
      </TD>
   </TR>
   <TR>
      <TD>
      <CFOUTPUT>
      Contact person: #getcust.contact_person#<BR>
      Phone: #getcust.phone#<br>
      email: #getcust.email#<br>
      Sales rep:<A href="Omit for now">
      #getcust.lname#, #getcust.fname#</A><BR>
      <A href="Omit for now">
      What has the customer purchased before?
      </A><BR>
      </CFOUTPUT>
      </TD>
   </TR>
</TABLE>
```

3. Save the changes and upload the file to the Web server. Test the page. Your page should produce results similar to Figure 4.

Figure 4. Customer search result

Creating the Salespeople Search Feature

Searching for salespeople is a three-step process. The user will first choose from a list of last names of salespeople. The user is then provided with a list of names of salespeople with the same last name. The user clicks on the name of the salesperson he or she is looking for to get detailed information about the salesperson. This process minimizes the amount of user input the user has to provide.

1. Open a new document in Notepad. Save the document as "salespeoplesearch.cfm". Enter the following statements.

```
<CFQUERY datasource="companydb" name="getlast">
SELECT lname FROM salespeople
</CFQUERY>

<TABLE width="200">
   <TR>
      <TD>
      Select the sales representative's last name:
      <P>
      <FORM action="salespeoplesearchresult.cfm" method=post>
      <SELECT name="slsplast" size=1>
         <OPTION value="ALL" selected>All
         <CFOUTPUT query="getlast">
         <OPTION value="#getlast.lname#">#getlast.lname#
         </CFOUTPUT>
      </SELECT>
      <BR>
      <INPUT type="submit" Value="Search">
      </FORM>
      </TD>
   </TR>
</TABLE>
```

2. Save the file.
3. Open a new document in Notepad. Save the document as **"salespeoplesearchresult.cfm"**. Enter the following statements in the file.

```
<CFQUERY datasource="companydb" name="getslsp">
SELECT * FROM salespeople
<CFIF #FORM.slsplast# NEQ "ALL">
      WHERE lname = '#FORM.slsplast#'
</CFIF>
ORDER BY lname
</CFQUERY>
```

<CFIF> is an important CFML tag. It allows the program to conditionally execute a block of statements. Condition statements contain logical expressions. Table 1 contains a list of logical operators accepted in ColdFusion.

The syntax for <CFIF> is as follows:

```
<CFIF [condition]>
    [statements]
{<CFELSE>
    [statements]}
</CFIF>
```

4. Enter the following statements.

```
<TABLE width="230">
   <TR>
      <TD>
      Search results:
      <P>
      <CFIF #getslsp.recordcount# IS 0>
            No records were found matching your criteria
      <CFELSE>
            <CFOUTPUT>
            Your search returned #getslsp.recordcount# record(s).
            </CFOUTPUT>
      </CFIF>
      <P>
      <OL>
         <CFOUTPUT query="getslsp">
         <LI>
         <A
         href="salespeopledetail.cfm?slspid=#getslsp.slsp_id#">
         #getslsp.lname#, #getslsp.fname#
         </A>
         </CFOUTPUT>
      </OL>
      </TD>
   </TR>
</TABLE>
```

Table 1. Logical operators

Operator		Operator	
EQ	Equal to	NEQ	Not equal to
LT	Less than	GT	Greater than
LE	Less than or equal to	GE	Greater than or equal to
NOT	Not	AND	And
OR	or		

The statement “<A href=“salespeopledetail.cfm?slspid=#getslsp.slsp_id#”>” passes a URL variable “slspid” to the taget page, salespeopledetail.cfm. When the name of a salesperson is selected, the corresponding salespeople ID will be passed to the detail page.

5. Save the changes. Upload both salespeoplesearch.cfm and salespeoplesearchresult.cfm to the Web server. Test the pages. Your pages should be similar to Figure 5.

In the following section, we will create the salespeopledetail.cfm file to retrieve and display detailed information about a salesperson.

Figure 5. Salespeople search pages

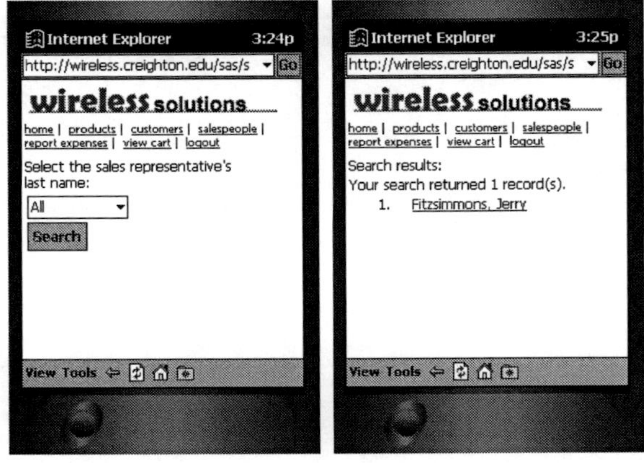

6. Open a new document in Notepad. Save the document as "salespeopelsearchdetail.cfm". Enter the following statements. The SQL statement below uses the URL variable, "slspid", which was passed as part of the URL from salespeoplesearchresult.cfm.

```
<CFQUERY datasource="companydb" name="getslsp">
SELECT * FROM salespeople
WHERE slsp_id = '#URL.slspid#'
</CFQUERY>
```

7. Enter the following statements.

```
<TABLE width="230">
   <TR>
      <TD>
      <CFOUTPUT>
      <B>#getslsp.lname#, #getslsp.fname#</B>
      </CFOUTPUT>
      </TD>
   </TR>
   <TR>
      <TD>
      <CFOUTPUT>
      Phone (office): #getslsp.office_phone#<BR>
      Phone (mobile): #getslsp.mobile_phone#<BR>
      Email: <A
      href="email.cfm?email=#getslsp.email#">#getslsp.email#</A>
      </CFOUTPUT>
      </TD>
   </TR>
</TABLE>
```

Figure 6. Salespeople detail

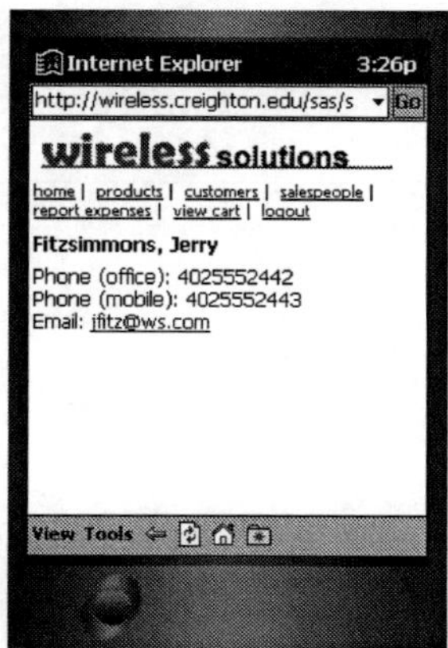

A URL variable, "email", is being passed to email.cfm, which provides the user with a form to compose an email to the salesperson. We will develop the email.cfm file at a later time.

8. Save and upload the file. Test the page. Your page should look like Figure 6.

Completing the Customer Search Feature

1. Open customersearchresult.cfm in Notepad. Modify the highlighted area in the code. Then save and upload the file to the Web server.

```
<CFOUTPUT>
Contact person: #getcust.contact_person#<BR>
Phone: #getcust.phone#<BR>
email: #getcust.email#<BR>
Sales rep:<A
href="salespeopledetail.cfm?slspid=#getcust.slsp_id#">
      #getcust.lname#, #getcust.fname#</A><BR>
<A href="purchasehistory.cfm?custid=#getcust.cust_id#">
What has the customer purchased before?
</A><BR>
</CFOUTPUT>
```

This first highlighted statement passes the URL variable, "slspid", to salespeopledetail.cfm, which displays the information about the corresponding salesperson. The second highlighted statement passes the URL variable, "custid", to purchasehistory.cfm. Purchasehistory.cfm displays the customer's purchase history. This information enables a salesperson to make product recommendations to the customers more effectively. Let's develop purchasehistory.cfm now.

2. Open a new document in Notepad. Save the document as "purchasehistory.cfm". Enter the following statements.

```
<CFQUERY datasource="companydb" name="gethistory">
SELECT orders.ord_date, order_line.quantity, product.description
FROM orders, order_line, product
WHERE orders.cust_id = '#URL.custid#'
AND orders.ord_id = order_line.ord_id
AND order_line.p_id = product.p_id
ORDER BY orders.ord_date
</CFQUERY>
```

3. Enter the following statements at the end of the file.

```
<TABLE>
   <TR>
      <TD>
      This customer has purchased the following products before:
      <P>
      <CFIF #gethistory.recordcount# IS 0>
            No records were found.
      <CFELSE>
            <CFTABLE query="gethistory" colheaders>
            <CFCOL header="<b>Date</b>" width ="10"
            text="#ord_date#">
            <CFCOL header="<b>Product</b>" width="30"
            text="#description#">
            <CFCOL header="<b>Qty</b>" width="5"
            text="#quantity#">
            </CFTABLE>
      </TD>
   </TR>
</TABLE>
</CFIF>
```

When we develop applications for wireless devices, we want to make every effort to ensure that the content can fit inside the display area in such a way that scrolling is not necessary. However, this is not always practical or possible. For example, a purchase history will be best displayed in a tabular form for easy viewing. <CFTABLE> and <CFCOL> are useful CFML to display data in a tabular form.

4. Save the changes and upload the file. Test the page. Your page should be similar to Figure 7.

Figure 7. Purchase history

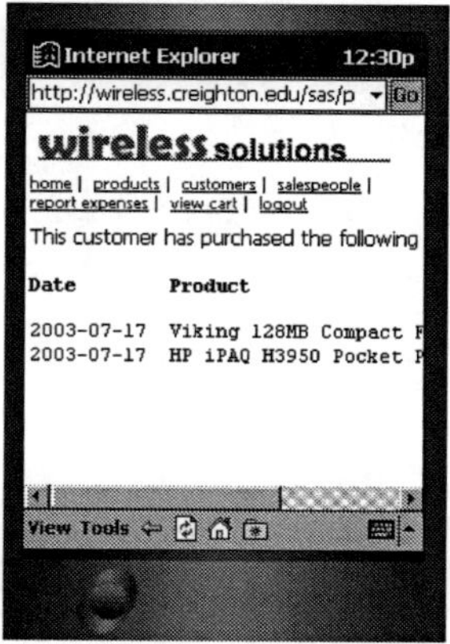

Creating the Product Search Feature

An important feature of the SAS is that a user can access the most up-to-date product and product availability information. Since this feature is likely to be frequently used, we want to improve its usability by providing the user with multiple methods to search for a product: 1) search by product ID; 2) search by product name; and 3) search by product category. We will first create a form for the user to enter search criteria.

1. Open a new document in Notepad. Save the document as "productsearch.cfm". Enter the following statements.

```
<CFQUERY datasource="companydb" name="getcat">
SELECT p_cat, description FROM ProductCat
</CFQUERY>

<TABLE width="200">
   <TR>
      <TD>
      You can search by product ID, product name, or product
      category:
      <p>

      <FORM action="productsearchresult.cfm" method=post>
      Product ID: <INPUT type="text" name="productid"
      size=10><BR>
      Product Name: <INPUT type="text" name="productname"
      size=10><BR>
      Product Category:
      <SELECT name="productcat" size=1>
         <OPTION value="ANY" selected>ANY
         <CFOUTPUT query="getcat">
         <OPTION value="#getcat.p_cat#">#getcat.description#
         </CFOUTPUT>
      </SELECT>
      <BR>
      <INPUT type="submit" value="Search">
      </FORM>
      </TD>
   </TR>
</TABLE>
```

2. Save and upload the file to the Web server. Your product search page should resemble Figure 8.
3. Open a new document in Notepad. Save the document as "productsearchresult.cfm". Enter the following statement in the document.

```
<CFQUERY datasource="companydb" name="getproduct">
SELECT p_id, description FROM Product
WHERE 0=0
<CFIF #form.productid# IS NOT "">
      AND p_id = '#FORM.PRODUCTID#'
</CFIF>
<CFIF #FORM.PRODUCTNAME# IS NOT "">
      AND description LIKE '%#FORM.PRODUCTNAME#%'
</CFIF>
<CFIF #FORM.PRODUCTCAT# IS NOT "ANY">
      AND p_cat = '#FORM.PRODUCTCAT#'
</CFIF>
ORDER BY p_id
</CFQUERY>
```

<CFIF> tag can be embedded within other CFML to render statements based on conditions. The clause "WHERE 0=0" is a dummy "Where" clause, but without it we will not be able to embed <CFIF> tags in the SQL statement.

The statement "AND description LIKE '%#FORM.productname#%'" allows the user to search without knowing the exact name for the product. The logical operator "LIKE" does not require an exact match of text. The "%" sign is a wildcard character, which represents any number of characters or numbers.

The search result page gives the user a list of products that meet the search criteria. Each product is also a link to productdetail.cfm, which displays detail information about a product. In order to let productdetail.cfm know which product information to display, we will pass the product ID of the selected product as a URL variable to productdetail.cfm.

Figure 8. Product search

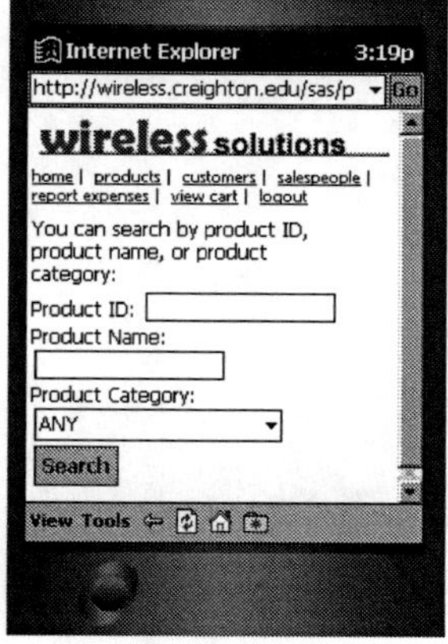

4. Enter the following statements at the end of the document.

```
<TABLE width="230">
   <TR>
      <TD>
      Search results:
      <P>
      <CFIF #getproduct.recordcount# IS 0>
         No records were found matching your criteria
      <CFELSE>
         <CFOUTPUT>
         Your search returned #getproduct.recordcount# record(s).
         </CFOUTPUT>
      </CFIF>
      <P>
      <OL>
         <CFOUTPUT query="getproduct">
         <LI>
         <A
         href="productdetail.cfm?productid=#getproduct.p_id#">
         #getproduct.p_id#</A>
         <BR>#getproduct.description#
         </CFOUTPUT>
      </OL>
      </TD>
   </TR>
</TABLE>
```

5. Save and upload the file. Open productsearch.cfm in the browser and select "handhelds" for product category. Click the Search button. Your product search result page should look like Figure 9.

Figure 9. Product search result

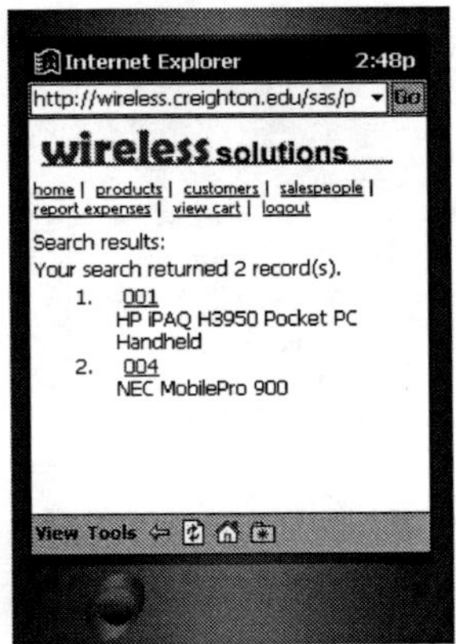

6. Open a new document in Notepad. Save the new document as "productdetail.cfm". Enter the following statements in the document.

```
<CFQUERY datasource="companydb" name="getproduct">
SELECT * FROM Product
WHERE p_id = '#URL.PRODUCTID#'
</CFQUERY>

<CFFORM action="submitorder.cfm" method=post>
<TABLE width="230">
   <TR>
      <TD>
      <CFOUTPUT>
      <B>#getproduct.description#</B>
      </CFOUTPUT>
      </TD>
   </TR>
   <TR>
      <TD>
      <CFOUTPUT>
      Quantity on hand: #getproduct.qoh#
      </CFOUTPUT>
      </TD>
   </TR>
   <TR>
      <TD>
      <CFOUTPUT>
      Our price: #DollarFormat(getproduct.price)#
      </CFOUTPUT>
      </TD>
   </TR>
   <TR>
      <TD>
      <CFOUTPUT>
      #getproduct.spec#
      </CFOUTPUT>
      </TD>
   </TR>
   <TR>
      <TD>
      <CFOUTPUT>
      <IMG src="/sas/images/#getproduct.image#">
      </CFOUTPUT>
      </TD>
   </TR>
</TABLE>
```

7. Save and upload the document. Click on the link to product 001 in productsearchresult.cfm. Your productdetail.cfm should resemble Figure 10.

Creating Application Level Security

One requirement for the SAS is that only authorized users be permitted to view the information. The most common way to provide this type of security is via usernames and passwords. Hence we need to develop a login function for the application.

Processing login is a two-step process. In the first step, the user is asked to enter his or her username and password in a form. In the second step, the entered username and password are checked against the database to see if they are valid. If the username or password is not valid, the user will be asked to try

Figure 10. Product detail

again. If they are valid, the user will be allowed to use any features of the SAS. We would like the salespeople to login before they start using the SAS; therefore, it is natural to place the login form in the first page of the application, index.cfm.

1. Open a new document in Notepad. Save the document as "index.cfm". Enter the following statements in the document.

```
<HTML>
<HEAD>
<TITLE>Company SAS</TITLE>
</HEAD>
<BODY>
<TABLE width = 200>
   <TR>
      <TD>
      <BR>
      <FONT size="-1"><B>Welcome to Company SAS -- Salesforce
      Automation System!  Please login.</B></FONT>
      <P>
      </TD>
   </TR>
   <TR>
      <TD>
      <CFFORM action="loginprocess.cfm">
      <FONT size="-1">
      Username: <CFINPUT type="text" name="username" size="20"
      required="yes" message="You must enter the username!">
      <BR>
      Password: <CFINPUT type="password" name="password"
      size="20" required="yes" message="You must enter the
      password!">
      <BR>
      <INPUT type="submit" value="Login">
      </CFFORM>
      </FONT>
      </TD>
   </TR>
</TABLE>
</BODY>
</HTML>
```

When developing a form in ColdFusion, you can use either HTML form tags or ColdFusion Form tags. The only syntax difference between these two types of tags is that ColdFusion Form tags begin with "CF" (e.g., <CFFORM> and <CFINPUT>). Using ColdFusion Form tags has a very important benefit. You can use built-in data validation tools to check user input before submitting the data.

The most common data validation check is a completion check. To perform a completion check, you assign the value "yes" to the attribute "required" in the <CFINPUT> or <CFSELECT> tag. If you would like to provide a custom error message, you can do so by using the "message" attribute. The syntax for a ColdFusion input tag is:

> <CFINPUT type = "element type" {name = "[element name]" required = "[yes]/[no]" message = "[error message]">

The username and password entered by the user are sent as form variables to loginprocess.cfm. Loginprocess.cfm evaluates the username and password supplied by the user. If the username and password match those in the database, the user is allowed to view subsequent Web pages. If the username and password do not match those in the database, the user should be given another chance to login.

2. Open a new document in Notepad. Save the document as "loginprocess.cfm". Enter the following statements in the document.

```
<CFQUERY datasource="companydb" name="checkData">
SELECT * FROM Salespeople
WHERE UCase(username) = '#UCase(FORM.Username)#'
AND
UCase(password) = '#UCase(FORM.Password)#'
</CFQUERY>

<TABLE width="200">
   <TR>
      <TD>
      <CFIF checkData.recordCount GT 0>
```

continued on the following page

```
            <FONT size="-1">
            Logon successful!
            <P>Choose one of the following options:
            <P>
            <OL>
               <LI><A href="productsearch.cfm">Search
               product</A><BR>
               <LI><A href="customersearch.cfm">Search
               customer</A><BR>
               <LI><A href="salespeoplesearch.cfm">Search
               Salespeople</A><BR>
               <LI><A href="travelexp.cfm">Report Travel
               Expenses</A><BR>
            </OL>

         <CFELSE>

            Incorrect username or password.  Click the back button
            on the toolbar and try again.

         </CFIF>

         </TD>
      </TR>
   </TABLE>
```

This file checks if a record in the database matches the username and password combination entered by the user. If a match is found, the user is allowed into a page with links to different features of the system. If no match is found, the user is asked to go back and re-enter the username and password.

3. Save and upload the document. Test the login function. Enter "jfitz" as the username. Enter "8888" as the password. The page in Figure 11 should appear.

Figure 11. Login page

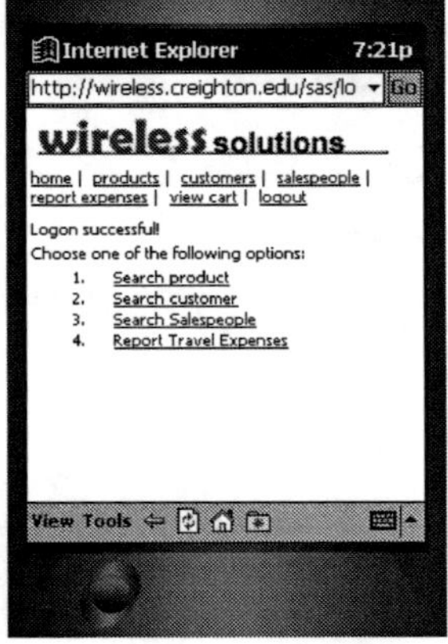

Managing State Using Cookies

There is one problem with the current login system. If an unauthorized user knows the exact URL of any of the Web pages, he or she will be able to bypass the login page. How can we prevent unauthorized users from accessing restricted areas of the Web site while allowing authorized users to navigate the Web site effortlessly? The solution: a cookie.

A cookie is a small file that is saved on the client device by the Web server. Only the Web server that sets the cookie can read the cookie. A cookie builds state for a Web site as it records important information such as the user's navigation history in a file that can be accessed in the future. A cookie exists on the client device for a specified period of time. While cookies are controversial due to consumers' privacy concerns, they are very useful tools for developing secure and personalized Web sites.

To set a cookie in ColdFusion, use the following syntax:

```
<CFCOOKIE name = "[cookie name]" value = "[cookie value]" {expires =
"[period]"}>
```

The "expires" attribute specifies when the cookie will be deleted from the client device. This attribute is optional, and its value can be a date, a period, "NOW", or "NEVER". When the attribute is set to "NOW", the cookie is immediately deleted.

To access a cookie programmatically in ColdFusion, use the following syntax:

```
#COOKIE.[cookie name]#
```

The login process can use a cookie to record if the user is logged in or not. If the user is logged in, the user will be allowed to access any page without having to enter the username and password again. If the user is not logged in, the user will be asked to login first no matter which page he or she requests. To do this, we need to revisit application.cfm. Application.cfm is executed before any requested page is executed.

1. Open application.cfm in Notepad. Add the highlighted statements in your file.

```
<CFPARAM name="cookie.loggedin" default="no">
<CFPARAM name="cookie.username" default="">

<CFIF cookie.loggedin IS "no">
   <CFIF GetFileFromPath(CGI.SCRIPT_NAME) IS "index.cfm" OR
   GetFileFromPath(CGI.SCRIPT_NAME) IS
   "loginprocess.cfm">

   <CFELSE>
      <CFLOCATION url="index.cfm">
   </CFIF>
</CFIF>

<TABLE width = 230>
   <TR>
      <TD>
      <IMG src="logo.gif">
      </TD>
   </TR>

...
```

<CFPARAM> is similar to <CFSET> because it also assigns values to variables, but it is used in different situations. <CFPARAM> checks to see if a particular variable already exists. If it does not exist, the variable will be declared, and a value can be assigned. If the variable already exists, nothing happens. <CFPARAM> is used when a variable's existence is uncertain and its non-existence will result in errors.

The function GetFileFromPath( ) returns the file name of the file without the path. CGI.SCRIPT_NAME is a special variable that stores the full path of the file requested by the user. The program checks if the user is requesting "index.cfm" or "loginprocess.cfm". This prevents the program from getting into an infinite loop.

2. Save and upload the file.

To finish building the login pages, we also need to change "loginprocess.cfm".

3. Open loginprocess.cfm in Notepad. Add the highlighted statements to the document.

```
...
<TABLE width="200">
   <TR>
      <TD>
      <CFIF checkData.recordCount GT 0>
      <CFCOOKIE name="loggedin" value="yes">
      <CFCOOKIE name="username" value="#FORM.Username#">
      <FONT size="-1">
      Logon successful!
...
```

These statements set cookies for the user if the login is successful.

4. Save and upload the file. Try to access any file by typing the URL. The program should always return you to the login page. Login using the right username and password. The program should allow you to access all pages now.

The login feature should always be accompanied by the logout option. To logout a user, the program simply has to delete the cookie from the client device.

5. Open a new document in Notepad. Save the document as “logout.cfm”. Enter the following statements in the document.

```
<!DOCTYPE HTML PUBLIC "-//W3C//DTD HTML 4.0 Transitional//EN">

<CFCOOKIE name="loggedin" expires="NOW">
<CFCOOKIE name="username" expires="NOW">

<TABLE width=200>
   <TR>
      <TD>
      Logout successful! Goodbye.
      </TD>
   </TR>
</TABLE>
```

6. Save and upload the file.

Interacting with E-Mail Service

ColdFusion allows your program to interact with other services such as email, file system and Web services. In this project, we will take advantage of this capability to allow salespeople to send emails to each other.

To interact with e-mail service, you need to use <CFMAIL>. The syntax of <CFMAIL> is as follows:

<CFMAIL to = "[recipient's email address]" from = "[sender's email address]" server = "[server name]" {subject = "[email subject]" timeout = "[second]" mimeattach = "[file path]"}>

[Body of the e-mail message]

</CFMAIL>

The following steps create the e-mail feature in the SAS.

1. Open a new document in Notepad. Save the document as "email.cfm". Enter the following statements in the document.

```
<CFQUERY datasource="companydb" name="getemail">
SELECT email FROM salespeople
WHERE username = '#cookie.username#'
</CFQUERY>

<CFFORM action="sendemail.cfm" method=post>

<TABLE width=230>
   <TR>
      <TD>
      <CFOUTPUT>
      FROM: <CFINPUT type="text" name="fromemail" size=10
      value="#getemail.email#">
      </CFOUTPUT>
      <BR>
      TO: <CFINPUT type="text" name="toemail" size=10
      value="#URL.email#">
      <br>
      SUBJECT: <CFINPUT type="text" name="subject" size=10>
      <BR>
      MESSAGE:
      <TEXTAREA name="messagebody" col=20 row=10></TEXTAREA>
      <BR>
      <INPUT type="submit" value="Send"><input type="reset"
      value="Clear">
      </TD>
   </TR>
</TABLE>

</CFFORM>
```

2. Save and upload the file.

Email.cfm is a form in which users can input or edit information for the email. To send this email, an action page is needed. Email.cfm sends the information to the action page as form variables. We will now create the action page, sendemail.cfm.

3. Open a new document in Notepad. Save the document as "sendemail.cfm". Enter the following statements in the document.

```
<CFMAIL from="#FORM.fromemail#" to="#FORM.toemail#"
server="yourmailservername" subject="#FORM.subject#">

#FORM.messagebody#

</CFMAIL>

You email has been sent successfully!
```

4. Save and upload the file. Test the page by searching salespeople. Click the email address in salespeopledetail.cfm. Your page should resemble Figure 12.

Figure 12. E-mail feature

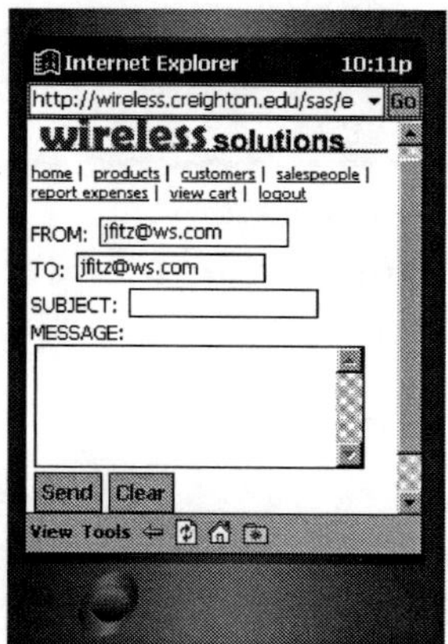

Creating a Feature to Report Travel Expenses

Reporting travel expenses requires inserting, updating and deleting data. You can use SQL statements to manipulate the data in a database. The SQL statement to insert data in a database table is:

INSERT INTO [table name] ([field1 name], [field2 name], ...)
VALUES ([value1], [value2], ...)

The SQL statement to update data in a database table is:

UPDATE [table name]
SET [field1 name] = [value1], [field2 name] = [value2], ...
{WHERE [condition]}

The SQL statement to delete data from a database table is:

DELETE FROM [table name]
{WHERE [condition]}

These SQL statements can be used in conjunction with <CFQUERY> tag to manipulate data in a database.

Inserting Travel Expenses

1. Open a new document in Notepad. Save the document as "travelexp.cfm". Enter the following statements in the document.

```
<CFQUERY datasource="companydb" name="gettype">
SELECT exp_type, description FROM Expensetype
</CFQUERY>

<CFQUERY datasource="companydb" name="getid">
SELECT slsp_id FROM Salespeople
WHERE Username = '#Cookie.Username#'
</CFQUERY>
```

To simplify data entry for the salespeople, the first query will retrieve a list of valid expense types from the database. This list will be used later in the program to create a combo box. The second query retrieves the salesperson ID based on the username the salesperson used to login.

We will now create a form for the user to enter travel expense information.

2. Append the following statements to the end of the document.

```
<TABLE width="230">
   <TR>
      <TD>
      <CFFORM action="submitexp.cfm" method=post>
      <CFOUTPUT>
      Slsp ID: #getid.slsp_id#
      <INPUT type="hidden" name="slspid" value="#getid.slsp_id#">
      <BR>
      Date:
      <CFINPUT type="text" name="expdate" size=10 required="yes"
      message="You must enter the date!"
      value="#DateFormat(Now(), "mm/dd/yyyy")#">
      <BR>
      Amount:
      <CFINPUT type="text" name="amount" size=10 required="yes"
      message="You must enter the amount!">
      </CFOUTPUT>
      <BR>
      Exp type:
      <SELECT name="exptype" size=1>
         <CFOUTPUT query="gettype">
         <OPTION value="#gettype.exp_type#">#gettype.description#
         </OUTPUT>
      </SELECT>
      <BR>
      <INPUT type="submit" Value="Submit Expense">
      </CFFORM>
      </TD>
   </TR>
</TABLE>
```

As you may have noticed, a hidden form element is used here. By using a hidden element, it is invisible to the user but can be passed to the action page as a form variable. We do not make it a textbox simply to prevent users from making accidental or deliberate changes to the data.

To simplify data entry, today's date is entered in the date field by default. The DateFormat function formats date variables according to the mask. Another useful function is TimeFormat. It is used to format variables that describe time.

3. Save and upload the file.

We will now make the action page, submitexp.cfm, to insert a travel expense in the "travelexp" table.

4. Open a new document in Notepad. Save the document as "submitexp.cfm". Enter the following statements in the document.

```
<CFQUERY datasource="companydb" name="getexpid">
SELECT Max(exp_id) +1 AS newexpid FROM travelexp
</CFQUERY>
```

Every new travel expense will have a unique expense ID. This query will find the largest expense ID in the table and add 1 to the expense ID. The result is used as the new expense ID.

5. Enter the following statements at the end of the document.

```
<CFQUERY datasource="companydb">
INSERT INTO travelexp
(slsp_id, exp_date, exp_type, amount, exp_id)
VALUES
('#FORM.slspid#', ###FORM.expdate###, '#FORM.exptype#',
#FORM.amount#, #getexpid.newexpid#)
</CFQUERY>
```

This set of statements inserts the data entered by the user into the database. Notice that FORM.expdate has three "#"s in front of it and three "#"s behind it. Microsoft Access requires that data values be enclosed in "#"s. As "#" has special meaning in ColdFusion, you need to type two "#"s to symbolize one "#".

6. Add the following statements to the end of the document.

```
<CFQUERY name="GetDesc" datasource="companydb">
SELECT description FROM expensetype
WHERE exp_type = '#FORM.exptype#'
</CFQUERY>

The following travel expense has been entered successfully.
<P>
<CFOUTPUT>
Exp ID: #getexpid.newexpid#<BR>
Slsp ID: #FORM.slspid# <BR>
Date: #FORM.expdate#<BR>
Exp type: #GetDesc.description#<BR>
Amount: #DollarFormat(FORM.amount)#
<P>
Click <A
href="edittravelexp.cfm?expid=#getexpid.newexpid#">here</A> if
you want to edit this expense.
<BR>Click <A
href="deleteexp.cfm?expid=#getexpid.newexpid#">here</A> if you
want to delete this expense.
<BR>Click <A href="travelexp.cfm">here</A> to enter another
expense.
</CFOUTPUT>
```

Figure 13. Inserting travel expenses

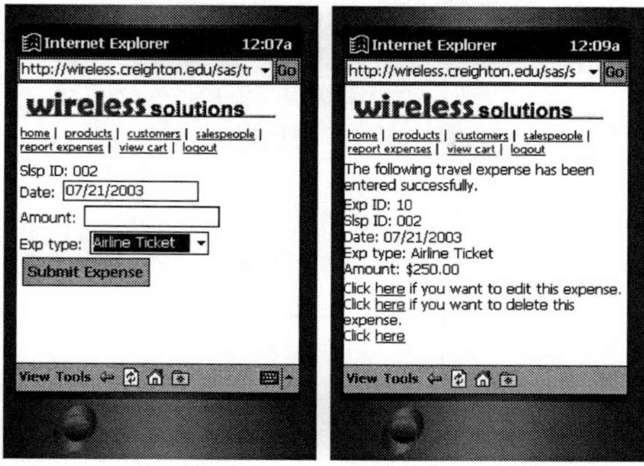

7. Save and upload the file. Test the function. Your pages should look like Figure 13.

Once the data has been inserted into the database, a confirmation is given to the user along with a chance to review the data. The user can modify or delete the data if necessary. In the following sections, we will create edittravelexp.cfm and deleteexp.cfm.

Updating Travel Expenses

Edittravelexp.cfm gives the user a chance to make changes to the submission. It is a two-step process. In the first step, the user can view the submission and make changes. The second step updates the database.

1. Open a new document in Notepad. Save it as "edittravelexp.cfm". Enter the following statements in the document.

```
<CFQUERY datasource="companydb" name="gettype">
SELECT exp_type, description FROM Expensetype
</CFQUERY>

<CFQUERY datasource="companydb" name="getdata">
SELECT * FROM travelexp
WHERE exp_id = #URL.expid#
</CFQUERY>

<CFIF getdata.recordcount EQ 0>
No such expense was found.
<CFABOUT>
</CFIF>
```

For easy data entry, the first query retrieves a list of expense types to be used to populate a combo box. The second query retrieves data about the expense that the user wants to edit. The <CFIF> statement tests to see if the record exists. If the record doesn't exist, an error message is displayed and all subsequent operations are aborted. <CFABORT> terminates the program.

2. Add the following statements to the end of the document.

```
<TABLE width="230">
   <TR>
      <TD>
      <CFFORM action="updateexp.cfm" method=post>
      <CFOUTPUT>
      Exp ID: #INT(getdata.exp_id)#
      <INPUT type="hidden" name="expid"
      value="#INT(getdata.exp_id)#">
      <BR>
      Slsp ID: #getdata.slsp_id#
      <INPUT type="hidden" name="slspid"
      value="#getdata.slsp_id#">
      <BR>
      Date: <cfinput type="text" name="expdate" size=10
      value="#DateFormat(getdata.exp_date, "mm/dd/yyyy")#">
      <BR>
      Amount: $ <cfinput type="text" name="amount" size=10
      value="#DecimalFormat(getdata.amount)#">
      </CFOUTPUT>
      <BR>
      Exp type:
      <SELECT name="exptype" size=1>
         <CFOUTPUT query="gettype">
         <OPTION value="#gettype.exp_type#">#gettype.description#
         </CFOUTPUT>
      </SELECT>
      <BR>
      <INPUT type="submit" Value="Update Expense">
      </CFFORM>
      </TD>
   </TR>
</TABLE>
```

3. Save and upload the file.

Now let's create the action page, updateexp.cfm.

4. Open a new document in Notepad. Save the file as "updateexp.cfm". Enter the following statement. This statement updates the information in the database.

```
<CFQUERY datasource="companydb">
UPDATE travelexp
SET slsp_id='#FORM.slspid#',
exp_date=###FORM.expdate###,
exp_type='#FORM.exptype#',
amount=#FORM.amount#
WHERE
exp_id=#FORM.expid#
</CFQUERY>
```

5. Add the following statements to the end of the document. These statements allow the user to view the changes.

```
<CFQUERY name="GetDesc" datasource="companydb">
SELECT description FROM expensetype
WHERE exp_type = '#FORM.exptype#'
</CFQUERY>

The following travel expense has been updated successfully.
<P>
<CFOUTPUT>
Exp ID: #FORM.expid#<br>
Slsp ID: #FORM.slspid# <br>
Date: #FORM.expdate#<br>
Exp type: #GetDesc.description#<br>
Amount: #FORM.amount#
<P>
Click <A href="edittravelexp.cfm?expid=#FORM.expid#">here</A> if
you want to edit this expense.
<BR>Click <A href="deleteexp.cfm?expid=#FORM.expid#">here</A> if
you want to delete this expense.
<BR>Click <A href="travelexp.cfm">here</A> to enter another
expense.
</CFOUTPUT>
```

6. Save and upload the file. Test the function. Your pages should look like Figure 14.

Deleting Travel Expenses

1. Open a new document in Notepad. Save the file as "deleteexp.cfm". Enter the following statements (see following page).

```
<CFQUERY datasource="companydb">
DELETE FROM travelexp WHERE exp_id=#URL.expid#
</CFQUERY>
Data deleted successfully.
Click <A href="travelexp.cfm">here</A> to enter another expense.
```

2. Save and upload the file. Try to enter a new travel expense and then delete it. Your page should resemble Figure 15.

Figure 14. Updating travel expenses

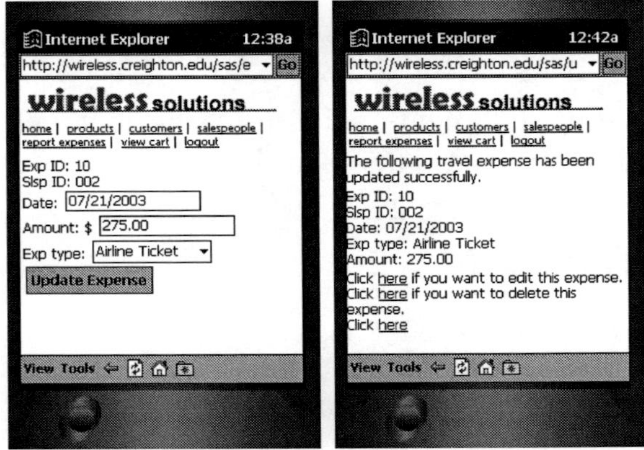

Figure 15. Deleting travel expense

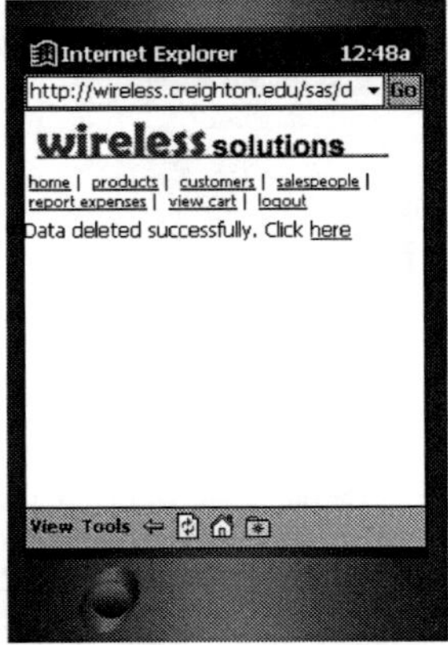

Building a Shopping Cart

Another feature that the salespeople want is a way to order products at the client's site. To do this, we need to develop a basic shopping cart application. The shopping cart application should allow the salespeople to view products, submit orders, and view the shopping cart at any time.

We have already built a product viewing function and we can build on this to create the shopping cart function.

1. Open productdetail.cfm in Notepad. Add the highlighted statements to the file. These statements create an order form. The hidden element, "pid", sends the ID of the product as a form variable to submitorder.cfm.

```
<CFFORM action="submitorder.cfm" method=post>
<TABLE width="230">
   <TR>
      <TD>
      <CFOUTPUT>
      <B>#getproduct.description#</B>
      </CFOUTPUT>
      </TD>
   </TR>
   <TR>
      <TD>
      <CFOUTPUT>
      Quantity on hand: #getproduct.qoh#
      </CFOUTPUT>
      </TD>
   </TR>
   <TR>
      <TD>
      <CFOUTPUT>
      Our price: #DollarFormat(getproduct.price)#
      </CFOUTPUT>
      </TD>
   </TR>
   <TR>
      <TD>
      <CFOUTPUT>
      #getproduct.spec#
      </CFOUTPUT>
      </TD>
   </TR>
   <TR>
      <TD>
      <CFOUTPUT>
      <IMG src="/sas/images/#getproduct.image#">
      </CFOUTPUT>
      </TD>
   </TR>
</TABLE>
Quantity to order: <CFINPUT name="qty" type="text" size="5"
required="yes" message="You must enter the quantity!">
<CFOUTPUT>
<INPUT type="hidden" name="pid" value="#URL.Productid#">
</CFOUTPUT>
<BR>
<INPUT type="submit" Value="Submit Order">
</CFFORM>
```

Figure 16. The new product detail page

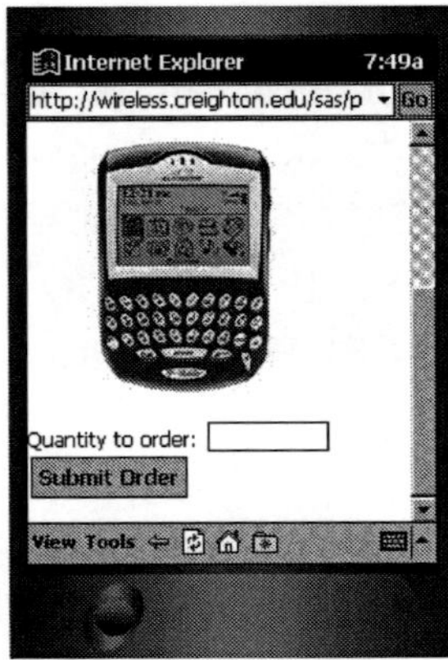

2. Save and upload the page. Now your productdetail.cfm should look like the page in Figure 16.

Session Variables

When an order is placed, the salesperson must specify the customer for this order. Another important business rule is that one order may contain multiple products. Rather than repeatedly enter the customer for each product in an order, we can eliminate this cumbersome and inefficient task by having the application "remember" the customer. The salesperson will specify the customer once when the first product is added to the shopping cart.

The most common solution used in this situation is a session variable. A session refers to a set of interactions between a client browser and a Web server. Each session has a timeout limit. If the timeout limit elapses without any interaction between the browser and the Web server, the session is ended. Session variables create state. They store values during a session. When the session expires, session variables are deleted. In our shopping cart application, session variables can be used to store customer and order information.

To use session variables, you must first enable session management using the <CFAPPLICATION> tag. To enable session management, you must assign "yes" to sessionmanagement. Sessiontimeout specifies the length of time that needs to elapse since the user's last interaction with the server for the session variable to be deleted. The syntax for enabling session management is:

```
<CFAPPLICATION name = "[name]" sessionmanagement = "[yes/no]"
sessiontimeout = #CreateTimeSpan([days, hours, minutes, seconds]#>
```

<CFAPPLICATION> tag can be used to set a number of default settings for the whole application; therefore, it is always included in application.cfm.

Now, let's modify the application.cfm file.

1. Open application.cfm in Notepad. Add the following statements at the beginning of the document.

```
<cfapplication name="OrderRequest" sessionmanagement="Yes"
sessiontimeout=#CreateTimeSpan(0,0,20,0)#>
```

2. Save and upload the file.

The syntax for creating a session variable is as follows:

```
<CFSET session.[variable name] = [value]>
```

The syntax for assigning a default value to a session variable is as follows:

```
<CFPARAM name = "session.[variable name]" default = [default value]>
```

A session variable can be accessed using:

```
#session.[variable name]#
```

A session variable is a shared resource. To prevent a session variable from being processed by multiple requests simultaneously or in the wrong order, a lock must be used to ensure that only one request can be processed at a time. To do this, you use the <CFLOCK> tag. The syntax for the <CFLOCK> tag is as follows:

```
<CFLOCK timeout = "[timeout in seconds]" scope = "[application/server/
session]" name = "[lock name]">
[statements]
</CFLOCK>
```

For a session variable, the scope attribute must be set as "session".

Submitting Orders

In this section, we will create the submitorder.cfm file for a user to submit orders.

1. Open a new document in Notepad. Save the file as "submitorder.cfm". Enter the following statements in the document.

```
<CFLOCK scope="SESSION" timeout="20">

<CFPARAM name="session.custid" default="">

<CFQUERY datasource="companydb" name="getname">
SELECT * FROM customer
</CFQUERY>

<CFIF session.custid EQ "">
      <CFOUTPUT>
      <FORM action="confirmord.cfm?pid=#FORM.pid#&qty=#FORM.qty#"
      method=post>
      </CFOUTPUT>
      This order is for the following customer: <br>
      <SELECT name="custid" size=1>
      <CFOUTPUT query="getname">
         <OPTION value="#getname.cust_id#">#getname.cust_name#
      </CFOUTPUT>
      </SELECT>
      <INPUT type="hidden" name=pid value="#FORM.pid#">
      <INPUT type="hidden" name=qty value="#FORM.qty#">
      <BR>
      <INPUT type="submit" Value="Submit">
<CFELSE>
      <CFLOCATION
      url="confirmord.cfm?pid=#FORM.pid#&qty=#FORM.qty#">
</CFIF>

</CFLOCK>
```

These statements check to see if a customer has been selected. If a customer has been selected, the user is redirected to confirmorder.cfm along with two

URL variables that store the product ID and the quantity ordered. To redirect the user to another URL, you can use the <CFLOCATION> tag as shown in the example. If a customer has not been selected, the user is given the opportunity to do so here.

2. Save and upload the file.
3. Open a new document in Notepad. Save the document as "confirmord.cfm". Enter the following statements in the document.

```
<CFLOCK scope="SESSION" timeout="20">

<CFIF session.custid EQ "">
      <CFSET session.custid = FORM.custid>
</CFIF>
```

Confirmord.cfm checks to see if a session variable for customer ID exists. If it doesn't, then the customer ID passed from submitord.cfm is assigned to session.custid.

4. Append the following statements to the documents.

```
<CFQUERY datasource="companydb" name="getproduct">
SELECT description
FROM product
WHERE p_id = '#URL.pid#'
</CFQUERY>

<FORM action="confirm.cfm" method=post>

<TABLE border=1 width=230>
   <TR>
      <TD>
      <B>Product</B>
      </TD>
      <TD>
      <B>Quantity</B>
      </TD>
   </TR>
   <TR>
      <TD>
      <CFOUTPUT>
      #getproduct.description#
      <INPUT type="hidden" name="pid" value = "#URL.pid#">
      </OUTPUT>
      </TD>
      <TD>
      <CFOUTPUT>
      <INPUT type="text" size="6" name="qty" value="#URL.qty#">
      </CFOUTPUT>
      </TD>
   </TR>
</TABLE>

<BR>
<INPUT type="submit" Value="Place Order">

</FORM>

</CFLOCK>
```

The product description and order quantity are displayed. Notice the order quantity is displayed in a textbox; that way the user can make changes to the quantity if necessary. Product ID (pid) and quantity (qty) are submitted to confirm.cfm as form variables.

5. Save and upload the file. Test submitord.cfm and confirmord.cfm. They should resemble Figure 17.

Confirming Orders

The final step in the ordering process includes a series of tasks. When the user presses the "Place Order" button, the following tasks should occur:

- An order ID is assigned if it does not already exist.
- One record is appended to the "orders" table in the database.
- One record is appended to the "order_line" table in the database.
- Quantity on hand is reduced by quantity ordered.

Figure 17. Submitting an order

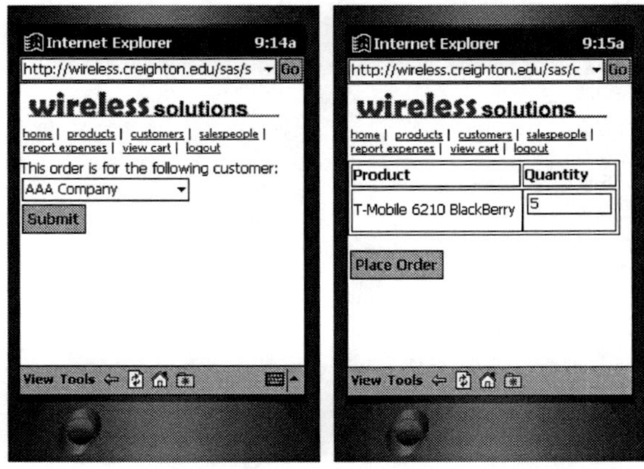

When these tasks are being performed, all tasks must be performed successfully or none of them should be performed.

The reliability of Web-based applications depends on many factors including client device performance, server performance, and network performance. A fatal error can occur and terminate processes when any of the factors fail to perform. <CFTRANSACTION> is a CFML tag that ensures that either all related tasks are performed successfully or none of the tasks are performed in case of an error. The syntax for <CFTRANSACTION> is as follows:

```
<CFTRANSACTION>
[database operations]
</CFTRANSACTION>
```

Let's create the confirm.cfm file.

1. Open a new document in Notepad. Save the document as "confirm.cfm". Enter the following statements in the document.

```
<CFPARAM name="session.ordid" default=0>

<CFTRANSACTION>

<CFIF session.ordid EQ 0>
      <CFQUERY datasource="companydb" name="getnewid">
      SELECT MAX(ord_id) +1 AS ordid
      FROM orders
      </CFQUERY>
      <CFSET session.ordid= getnewid.ordid>
</CFIF>
```

These statements check to see if the session variable for order ID exists. If it does exist, it means that an order ID has already been assigned to this order, and nothing happens. If it does not exist, a new order ID (maximum order ID in the database table plus 1) is assigned to the session variable.

2. Append the following statements to the document.

```
<CFQUERY datasource="companydb" name="getordid">
SELECT * FROM orders
WHERE ord_id = #session.ordid#
</CFQUERY>

<CFOUTPUT>
<CFIF getordid.recordcount EQ 0>
      <CFQUERY datasource="companydb">
      INSERT INTO orders
      (ord_id, ord_date, cust_id)
      VALUES
      (#session.ordid#, ###DateFormat(Now(), "mm/dd/yyyy")###,
      '#session.custid#')
      </CFQUERY>
</CFIF>

<CFQUERY datasource="companydb">
INSERT INTO order_line
(ord_id, p_id, quantity)
VALUES
(#session.ordid#, '#FORM.pid#', #FORM.qty#)
</CFQUERY>

<CFQUERY datasource="companydb">
UPDATE product
SET qoh= qoh - #FORM.qty#
WHERE
p_id='#FORM.pid#'
</CFQUERY>

</CFOUTPUT>

</CFTRANSACTION>
```

If the order ID does not already exist in the database table, a new record is inserted in the "orders" table. A new record is then inserted in the "order_line" table. Order quantity (qty) is then subtracted from quantity on hand (qoh) in the product table.

3. Append the following statements to the document.

```
The order has been successfully entered. <BR>
Click <A href="productsearch.cfm">here</A> to continue shopping.
<BR>
Click <A href="viewcart.cfm">here</A> to view the entire order.
<BR>
```

These statements confirm that the order has been entered. The user is given the choice to either continue shopping or view the shopping cart.

Figure 18. Confirming an order

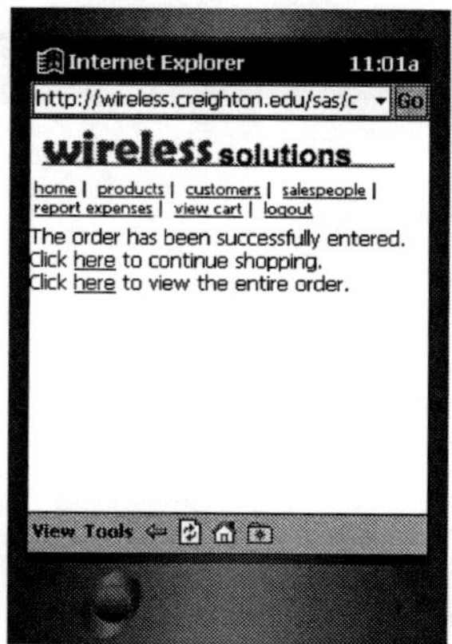

4. Save and upload the file. Place an order for a product. Your confirm.cfm should resemble Figure 18.

Viewing the Shopping Cart

We will now create the viewcart.cfm file for the user to view the shopping cart.

1. Open a new document in Notepad. Save the document as "viewcart.cfm". Enter the following statements in the document.

```
<CFPARAM name="session.ordid" default=0>
<CFSET subtotal = 0>

<CFQUERY datasource="companydb" name="getorder">
SELECT customer.cust_name, product.price, product.description,
order_line.quantity
FROM customer, orders, order_line, product
WHERE order_line.ord_id = #session.ordid#
AND customer.cust_id = orders.cust_id
AND orders.ord_id = order_line.ord_id
AND order_line.p_id = product.p_id
</CFQUERY>
```

To avoid getting an error message in case session variable "ordid" does not exist, we first assign a default value to "session.ordid". We then create another variable, "subtotal", with the value of zero. The variable "subtotal" will be used to calculate a total for the entire order. Finally, the data related to the order is retrieved from the database.

2. Append the following statements to the document.

```
<CFIF #getorder.recordcount# EQ 0>
      The shopping cart is empty.
<CFELSE>
<CFOUTPUT>
<B>Customer Name:</B> #getorder.cust_name#
</CFOUTPUT>
<P>
<TABLE width=230 border=1>
   <TR>
      <TD>
      <B>Product</B>
      </TD>
      <TD>
      <B>Quantity</B>
      </TD>
   </TR>
   <CFOUTPUT query="getorder">
   <TR>
      <TD>
      #getorder.description#</td><td>#getorder.quantity#
      </TD>
   </TR>
   <CFSET subtotal=subtotal +
   #getorder.price#*#getorder.quantity#>
   </CFOUTPUT>
   <TR>
      <TD align=right>
      Subtotal:
      </TD>
      <TD>
      <CFOUTPUT>
      #DollarFormat(subtotal)#
      </CFOUTPUT>
      </TD>
   </TR>
</TABLE>
</CFIF>
```

If the query returns no record, the message "The shopping cart is empty" is displayed. If the query returns record(s), the products and quantity ordered are displayed in a table. The last row of the table provides a subtotal of the entire order.

3. Save and upload the file. Order a few products and then view the shopping cart. Your shopping cart should be similar to that in Figure 19.

Figure 19. Viewing the shopping cart

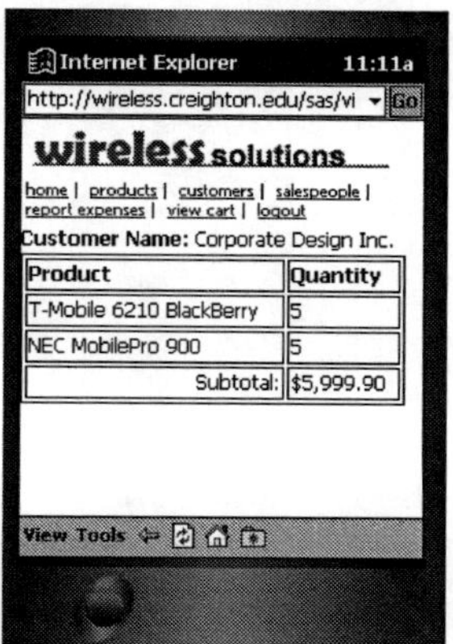

The portion of the SAS that functions on Pocket PC devices is now complete. Due to the differences in devices, this application, however, cannot readily be used for other devices such as mobile phones. Nevertheless, converting part of the SAS to be used by mobile phones is not difficult. Instead of rendering HTML documents that can be displayed in Web browsers, SAS needs to generate WML documents in order to be read on mobile phones. In the following sections, we will convert the customer search, salespeople search and product search to be WAP-compatible.

Developing SAS for Mobile Handsets

Due to the input and display limitations of mobile handsets, not all functions in SAS will be included. Therefore, the WAP-compatible version of SAS will only have three functions often used by salespeople on the move. These three functions are product search, customer search and company directory. The same database (ws.mdb) and its datasource ("companydb") will be used to shorten the development cycle.

The first step is to design the structure of the SAS WAP site. Figure 20 illustrates the structure of the site.

As you may have noticed, the WAP version uses limited and different search options compared to the PocketPC version. These search options were

Figure 20. The site structure for the SAS WAP site

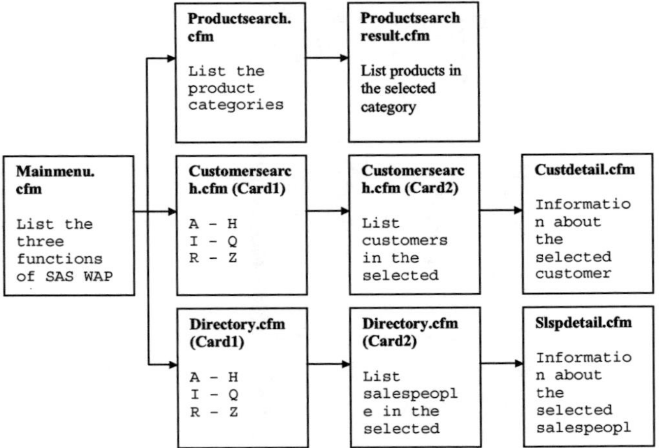

selected because they would require the least amount of user input. Usability is an important consideration when designing a WAP site.

Creating the Main Menu

The main menu page provides users with a list of the functions of SAS.

1. Open a new document in Notepad. Save the document as "mainmenu.cfm". Enter the following statements in the file.

```
<CFCONTENT TYPE="text/vnd.wap.wml">
<?xml version="1.0"?>
<!DOCTYPE wml PUBLIC "-//WAPFORUM//DTD WML 1.1//EN"
"http://www.wapforum.org/DTD/wml_1.1.xml">

<WML>
<CARD id="home">
<P>
<B>Main Menu</B>
<BR/>
<CFOUTPUT>
#DateFormat(Now(), "mmmm dd, yyyy")#
</CFOUTPUT>
<BR/>
<A accesskey = "1" href="productsearch.cfm">1. Product
        Search</A><BR/>
<A accesskey = "2" href="customersearch.cfm">2. Customer
        Search</A><BR/>
<A accesskey = "3" href="directory.cfm">3. Company
        Directory</A><BR/>
</P>
</CARD>
</WML>
```

Figure 21. Main menu

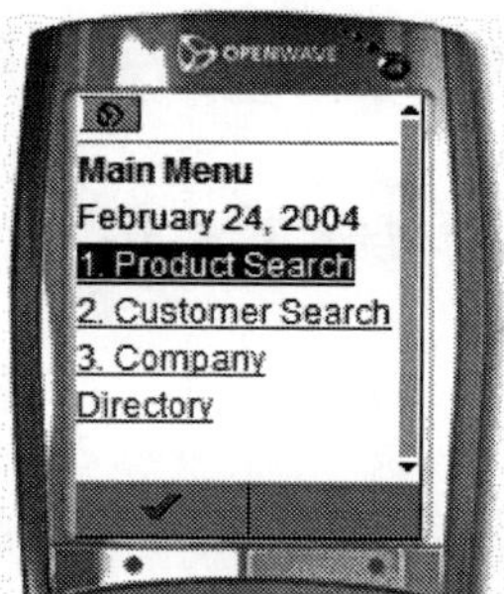

CFML can be embedded in WML files in the same way that it is embedded in HTML files. The main menu will display the current date and three options for the user to choose from.

2. Save the file and upload it to the Web server.
3. Launch Openwave SDK 6.2.2. Type the URL of the WAP site in the location bar and press "Enter" to open the page in the microbrowser. The page should look like Figure 21.

Building the Product Search Feature

To search for a product, a user will select one of the product categories to view a list of products. This requires the least amount of user input, hence it is an effective search option of mobile devices.

1. Open a new document in Notepad. Save the file as "productsearch.cfm". Enter the following statements.

```
<CFCONTENT TYPE="text/vnd.wap.wml">
<?xml version="1.0"?>
<!DOCTYPE wml PUBLIC "-//WAPFORUM//DTD WML 1.1//EN"
"http://www.wapforum.org/DTD/wml_1.1.xml">
<WML>

<TEMPLATE>
	<DO type = "options" label = "MENU">
		<GO href = "mainmenu.cfm" />
	</DO>
</TEMPLATE>
```

Consistency is the key to high usability. The <TEMPLATE> tag will affect every card in the deck. In this case, the right soft key on the handset will always take users back to the main menu.

2. Enter the following statements at the end of the file to program the left soft key.

```
<CARD id="productsearch">

<DO type="accept" label="Select">
      <GO href="productsearchresult.cfm?prodcat=$productcat" />
</DO>
```

These statements program the left soft key so that a user can select a product category and go to "productsearchresult.cfm" by pressing the key. A URL variable "prodcat", which contains the product category code, will be passed to "productsearchresult.cfm".

3. Append the following statements at the end of the file. These statements retrieve and display a list of product categories.

```
<CFQUERY datasource="companydb" name="getcat">
SELECT p_cat, description FROM ProductCat
</CFQUERY>

<P>
Select a product category:<BR/>

<SELECT name="productcat">
   <CFOUTPUT query="getcat">
   <OPTION value=#getcat.p_cat#>#getcat.description#</OPTION>
   </CFOUTPUT>
</SELECT>
</P>

</CARD>
</WML>
```

4. Save the file. Upload the file to the Web server.
5. Open another new document in Notepad. Save it as "productsearchresult.cfm". This document will provide the user with a list of products in the selected category. Enter the following statements in the file.

```
<CFCONTENT TYPE="text/vnd.wap.wml">
<?xml version="1.0"?>
<!DOCTYPE wml PUBLIC "-//WAPFORUM//DTD WML 1.1//EN"
"http://www.wapforum.org/DTD/wml_1.1.xml">
<WML>
<TEMPLATE>
      <DO type = "accept" label = "BACK">
            <PREV />
      </DO>

      <DO type = "options" label = "MENU">
                        <GO href = "mainmenu.cfm" />
      </DO>
</TEMPLATE>
```

These statements program the left and right soft keys of a handset. The left soft key will take a user to the previous page while the right soft key takes the user to the main menu.

6. Enter the following statements at the end of the file. These statements perform a query using the URL variable "prodcat" and display the results on the screen.

```
<CARD id="detail">

<CFQUERY datasource="companydb" name="getprod">
SELECT * FROM Product
WHERE p_cat='#URL.prodcat#'
</CFQUERY>

<CFOUTPUT query="getprod">
* #getprod.p_id# #getprod.description#<br />
</CFOUTPUT>

</CARD>

</WML>
```

7. Save the file. Upload it to the Web server. Test both "productsearch.cfm" and "productsearchresult.cfm". Your screens should look like Figure 22.

Building the Customer Search Feature

The customer search feature allows a user to find information about a customer.

1. Open a new document in Notepad. Save the file as "customersearch.cfm". Enter the following statements. These statements will allow the user to go

Figure 22. Searching for a product

back to the main menu by pressing the right soft key. The template will apply to all cards in the deck.

```
<CFCONTENT TYPE="text/vnd.wap.wml">
<?xml version="1.0"?>
<!DOCTYPE wml PUBLIC "-//WAPFORUM//DTD WML 1.1//EN"
"http://www.wapforum.org/DTD/wml_1.1.xml">
<WML>

<TEMPLATE>
      <DO type = "options" label = "MENU">
            <GO href = "mainmenu.cfm" />
      </DO>
</TEMPLATE>
```

2. Customersearch.cfm contains four cards. The first card lets the user narrow down the search. Enter the following statements to create the first card.

```
<CARD id="home">
<P>
The customer's name starts with:<BR/>

      <A accesskey = "1" href="#cust_atoh">1. A - H</A><BR/>
      <A accesskey = "2" href="#cust_itoq">2. I - Q</A><BR/>
      <A accesskey = "3" href="#cust_rtoz">3. R - Z</A><BR/>
</P>
</CARD>
```

3. The three options will take the user to three different lists of customer names. Enter the following statements to create the “cust_atoh” card.

```
<CARD id="cust_atoh">
<CFQUERY datasource="companydb" name="atoh">
SELECT cust_name, cust_id
FROM customer
WHERE cust_name BETWEEN 'A' and 'H'
</CFQUERY>

<CFIF atoh.recordcount EQ 0>
      <P>No record were found.</P>
<CFELSE>
      <CFOUTPUT query="atoh">
      <A
href="custdetail.cfm?custid=#atoh.cust_id#">#atoh.cust_name#</A>
      </CFOUTPUT>
</CFIF>
</CARD>
```

4. Enter the following code to create the "cust_itoq" and "cust_rtoz" cards.

```
<CARD id="cust_itoq">
<CFQUERY datasource="companydb" name="itoq">
SELECT cust_name, cust_id
FROM customer
WHERE cust_name BETWEEN 'I' AND 'Q'
</CFQUERY>

<CFIF itoq.recordcount EQ 0>
      <P>No record were found.</P>
<CFELSE>
      <CFOUTPUT query="itoq">
      <A
href="custdetail.cfm?custid=#itoq.cust_id#">#itoq.cust_name#</A>
      </CFOUTPUT>
</CFIF>

</CARD>

<CARD id="cust_rtoz">
<CFQUERY datasource="companydb" name="rtoz">
SELECT cust_name, cust_id
FROM customer
WHERE cust_name BETWEEN 'R' AND 'Z'
</CFQUERY>

<CFIF rtoz.recordcount EQ 0>
      <P>No record were found.</P>
<CFELSE>
      <CFOUTPUT query="rtoz">
      <A
href="custdetail.cfm?custid=#rtoz.cust_id#">#rtoz.cust_name#</A>
      </CFOUTPUT>
</CFIF>

</CARD>

</WML>
```

5. Save the document and upload it to the Web server. Open the page in the microbrowser. Your screens should look like Figure 23.

The function allows the user to drill down and get more information about the selected customer. Let's create the "custdetail.cfm" find for displaying detailed customer information.

Figure 23. Searching for a customer

6. Open another new file in Notepad. Save it as "custdetail.cfm". Enter the following statements.

```
<CFCONTENT TYPE="text/vnd.wap.wml">
<?xml version="1.0"?>
<!DOCTYPE wml PUBLIC "-//WAPFORUM//DTD WML 1.1//EN"
"http://www.wapforum.org/DTD/wml_1.1.xml">
<WML>

<TEMPLATE>
      <DO type = "accept" label = "BACK">
            <PREV />
      </DO>

      <DO type = "options" label = "MENU">
            <GO href = "mainmenu.cfm" />
      </DO>
</TEMPLATE>

<CARD id="detail">

<CFQUERY datasource="companydb" name="detail">
SELECT cust_name, address, city, state, zip, contact_person,
phone, email
FROM customer
WHERE cust_id = '#URL.custid#'
</CFQUERY>

<CFIF detail.recordcount EQ 0>
      <P>No record were found.</P>
<CFELSE>
      <CFOUTPUT query="detail">
      #detail.cust_name# <BR />
      #detail.address# <BR />
      #detail.city#, #detail.state# #detail.zip# <BR />
      #detail.contact_person# <BR />
      <A href="wtai://wp/mc;#detail.phone#"
      title="Call">#detail.phone# </A>
      <BR/>
      #detail.email#
      </CFOUTPUT>
</CFIF>

</CARD>
</WML>
```

Figure 24. Displaying detailed customer information

The highlighted statement uses Wireless Telephony Applications Interface (WTAI) to allow the user to dial the phone number from the handset. WTAI enables applications to perform typical functions of a mobile telephone such as making a phone call.

7. Save the document and upload it to the server. Test the page in the microbrowser. The screen should look like Figure 24.

Building the Company Directory Feature

The development techniques employed in the company directory function are very similar to those used to create the customer search function.

1. Open a new document in Notepad. Save the file as "directory.cfm". Enter the following statements in the document.

```
<CFCONTENT TYPE="text/vnd.wap.wml">
<?xml version="1.0"?>
<!DOCTYPE wml PUBLIC "-//WAPFORUM//DTD WML 1.1//EN"
"http://www.wapforum.org/DTD/wml_1.1.xml">
<WML>

<TEMPLATE>
      <DO type = "options" label = "MENU">
            <GO href = "mainmenu.cfm" />
      </DO>
</TEMPLATE>

<CARD id="home">
<P>
```

continued on the following page

```
The salespeople's last name starts with:<BR/>

      <A accesskey = "1" href="#slsp_atoh">1. A - H</A><BR/>
      <A accesskey = "2" href="#slsp_itoq">2. I - Q</A><BR/>
      <A accesskey = "3" href="#slsp_rtoz">3. R - Z</A><BR/>
</P>
</CARD>

<CARD id="slsp_atoh">
<CFQUERY datasource="companydb" name="atoh">
SELECT lname
FROM salespeople
WHERE lname BETWEEN 'A' AND 'H'
</CFQUERY>

<CFIF atoh.recordcount EQ 0>
      <P>No record were found.</P>
<CFELSE>
      <CFOUTPUT query="atoh">
      <P>Search result:</P>
      <A
href="slspdetail.cfm?lastname="#atoh.lname#">#atoh.lname#</A>
      </CFOUTPUT>
</CFIF>
</CARD>

<CARD id="slsp_itoq">
<CFQUERY datasource="companydb" name="itoq">
SELECT lname
FROM salespeople
WHERE lname BETWEEN 'I' AND 'Q'
</CFQUERY>

<CFIF itoq.recordcount EQ 0>
      <P>No record were found.</P>
<CFELSE>
      <CFOUTPUT query="itoq">
      <P>Search result:</P>
      <A
href="slspdetail.cfm?lastname="#itoq.lname#">#itoq.lname#</A>
      </CFOUTPUT>
</CFIF>
```

```
</CARD>

<CARD id="slsp_itoq">
<CFQUERY datasource="companydb" name="itoq">
SELECT lname
FROM salespeople
WHERE lname BETWEEN 'I' AND 'Q'
</CFQUERY>

<CFIF itoq.recordcount EQ 0>
      <P>No record were found.</P>
<CFELSE>
      <CFOUTPUT query="itoq">
      <P>Search result:</P>
      <A
href="slspdetail.cfm?lastname="#itoq.lname#">#itoq.lname#</A>
      </CFOUTPUT>
</CFIF>
```

Figure 25. Searching for salespeople

2. Save the file. Upload it to the Web server and test it. Your screens should look like Figure 25.

Summary

This chapter discusses the techniques for developing wireless applications for PocketPC devices and mobile handsets. While a wide range of server-side development tools can be used, Macromedia ColdFusion, a server-side technology, is used in this chapter to demonstrate the techniques.

Using a sample application, Sales Force Automation System (SAS), this chapter introduces you to the ColdFusion Markup Language (CFML). CFML is a tag-based language that can be embedded in an HTML document to create dynamic Web applications.

This chapter discusses a number of ways to manage state in the Web environment. Form and URL variables are used in the example to pass data from one Web page to another. Cookies and session variables are used to store data in the main memory for a relatively longer period.

The chapter further extends the SAS application to the mobile handset platform. The application was modified to render WML files, the file format that is supported by most microbrowsers. As mobile handsets have very small displays and limited input capabilities, only a subset of the features of SAS is provided via this platform for usability reasons.

Project

According to the 1997 U.S. Census, there were nearly 61,000 real estate agent and broker establishments, employing over 219,000 employees. There were nearly 1.2 million employees in other real estate functions, including property management and appraisers. Your team is commissioned to develop and deploy a wireless application that allows real estate agents to manage properties, prospects, sales opportunities, and contact information while on the move. The wireless application is expected to provide real estate agents and brokers reliable point of contact for all mobile information needs and increase productivity and service levels by providing access to key customer service tools

The wireless application should have the following features:

HomeSearch: HomeSearch is a mobile search function providing immediate access to information about listed properties. HomeSearch enables users to search for properties by MLS number, type, location, and other criteria such as price, minimum square footage, number of bedrooms and bathrooms, waterfront properties, and new construction.

Prospects: This feature allows real estate agents to manage prospect data such as contact information and client requirements.

Stats: The statistics function generates an immediate market analysis for specified geographic areas, such as neighborhoods, cities, counties, and the state, and can compare this data to a select property. It can provide information such as the average number of days on market, average square footage, number of beds and baths, living area, and lot size for a given neighborhood.

Use the techniques discussed in this chapter to develop the wireless application described above.

Chapter VIII

Dynamic Wireless Application Development II: Developing ASP .NET Mobile Web Applications Using Visual Studio .NET

In this chapter, you will:

- Learn how to develop ASP .NET mobile Web applications using Visual Studio .NET
- Learn to create WML cards in Visual Studio .NET
- Learn to retrieve data from a database using the OleDbDataAdapter and Dataset objects
- Learn to read from a database using the OleDbDataCommand and OleDbDataReader objects
- Learn to insert records into a database using the OleDbDataCommand object
- Learn how to develop database-driven wireless applications

Introduction

In the previous chapter, we created an m-business application using ColdFusion. Besides ColdFusion, many other development tools can be used to develop m-business applications. Visual Studio .NET, an integrated development environment by Microsoft, has become an increasingly popular corporate application development tool due to its ease of use and support for a wide range of programming languages. Besides traditional Windows and Web applications, Visual Studio .NET also allows developers to build mobile and wireless applications with relative ease. The focus of this chapter is to discuss the tools and techniques for developing wireless applications using Visual Studio .NET. Wireless applications are developed using the ASP .NET Mobile Web Application template. The template provides developers with WYSIWYG tools for creating user interfaces for various mobile devices. These tools work seamlessly with ASP.NET, which uses a form-based approach to build server-side applications for processing user requests and interacting with databases. In this chapter, we will develop a business-to-consumter wireless application using Visual Studio .NET.

Parking Finder Application

Parking at the central business districts of most large cities in the U.S. has long been a costly problem for consumers. The existing process of finding parking is described in Figure 1. The process in Figure 1 is inefficient and ineffective due to the following reasons:

- Precious time and effort are wasted when the consumer drives around aimlessly looking for a parking lot.
- The consumer often parks in the first parking lot he or she finds without checking out competitors. This allows parking lots with location advantage to charge a premium due to the consumer's lack of good information.
- Precious time and effort are wasted for consumers who choose to drive around and comparison shop for parking services.
- The consumer is forced to decide whether to park, on the spot, with enormous time pressure.

To solve this problem, we would like to create a prototype for a wireless application that helps consumers locate parking lots in the central business district of a cosmopolitan area. The wireless application can be accessed using WAP-enabled handsets by consumers. As previously discussed, the lack of parking lot information available to the consumer leads to the breakdown in the

Figure 1. The process of finding parking without the Parking Finder

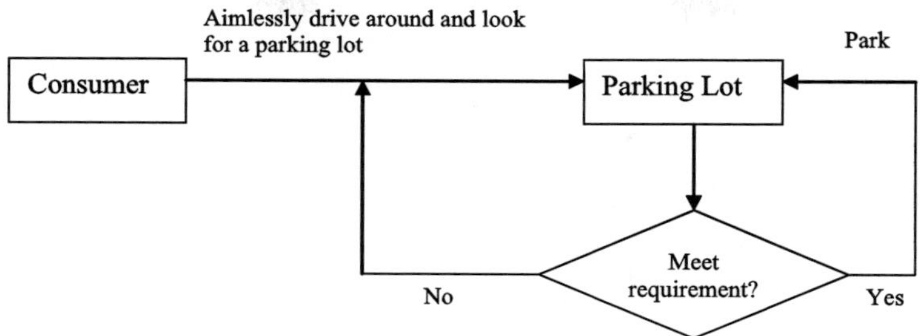

process of finding a parking lot. The application will act as an information agent by collecting and distributing critical information. It will save consumers time, money, and effort and also act as a targeted mobile marketing tool for parking lots and area businesses. The new process is illustrated in Figure 2, and it provides the following benefits:

- Consumers are well informed beforehand to make an intelligent decision about where to park. The chosen parking lot can better meet the consumer's requirements than a randomly found parking lot.
- Consumers can make the decision beforehand, thus avoiding an aimless parking lot search.

Figure 2. New parking lot search process

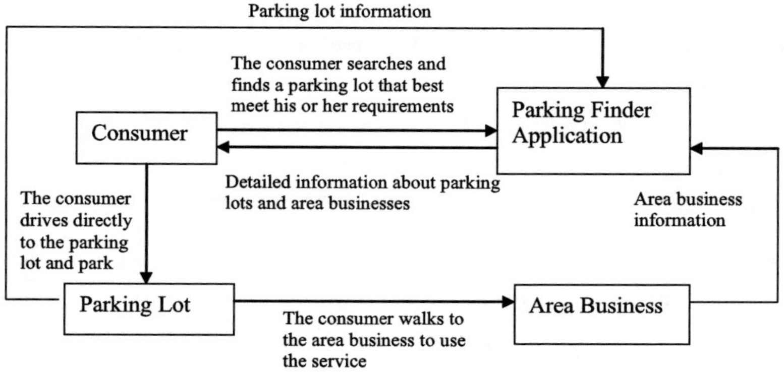

Figure 3. Site structure for the Parking Finder application

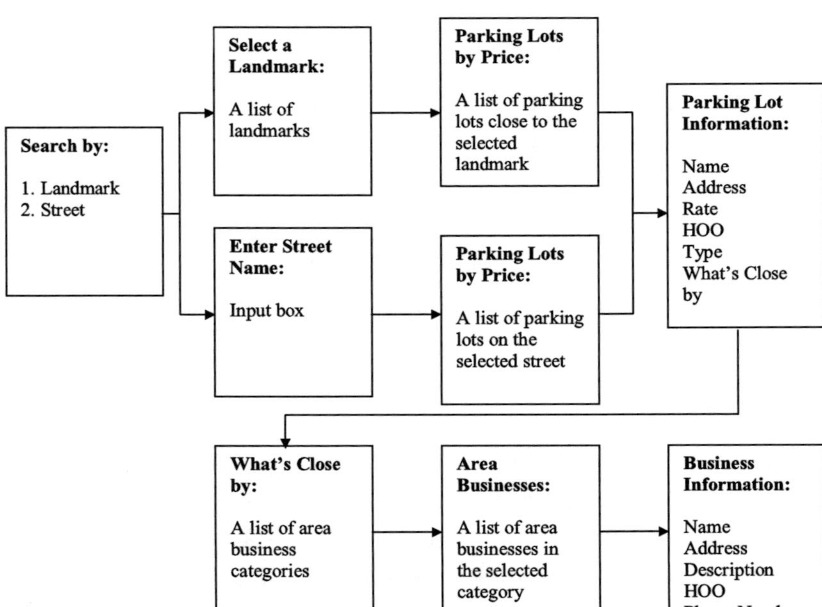

- The new business process introduces area businesses to the value chain. Relevant information can be delivered to consumers to stimulate consumption at area businesses.

WAP Site Structure

The first step in developing a WAP application is to design the site structure of the WAP site. The structure of a WAP site is referred to as a deck of cards. Each card represents a screen on the handset. Each box in Figure 3 represents a card in the deck.

Database

An MS Access database is used to supply and store data for the application. The database contains four tables: Parkinglots, Businesses, Landmarks, and Customers. The field descriptions for the tables can be found here.

Table	Field	Data Type
Parkinglots	PLID	AutoNumber
	PLName	Text
	AddNum	Number
	AddSt	Text
	Zipcode	Number
	HOO	Text
	Type	Text
	Rate	Currency
	Zonecode	Number
Landmarks	LMID	AutoNumber
	LMName	Text
	AddNum	Number
	AddSt	Text
	Zipcode	Number
	Zonecode	Number
Businesses	BID	Autonumber
	Bname	Text
	AddNum	Number
	AddSt	Text
	Zipcode	Number
	Type	Text
	Detail	Text
	HOO	Text
	Phone	Text
	Zonecode	Number
Customers	CustID	AutoNumber
	CustName	Text
	Email	Text

Building the Application

1. Select **Start | Programs | Microsoft Visual Studio .NET 2003**. This launches Visual Studio .NET 2003.
2. Select **File | New | Project** to start a new project (see Figure 4).
3. In the new project dialog, select "**Visual Basic Projects**" in the left pane as the project type and "**ASP.NET Mobile Web Application**" in the right pane as the template.
4. Replace the default project name, **MobileWebApplication1,** with **Parkingfinder** in the location textbox.
5. Click the **OK** button.

The central window in Figure 5 contains the Mobile Web Form Designer. A form represents a card in the WAP site. A wireless application can contain one or more cards. The form can be expanded vertically when more controls have

Figure 4. New project dialog

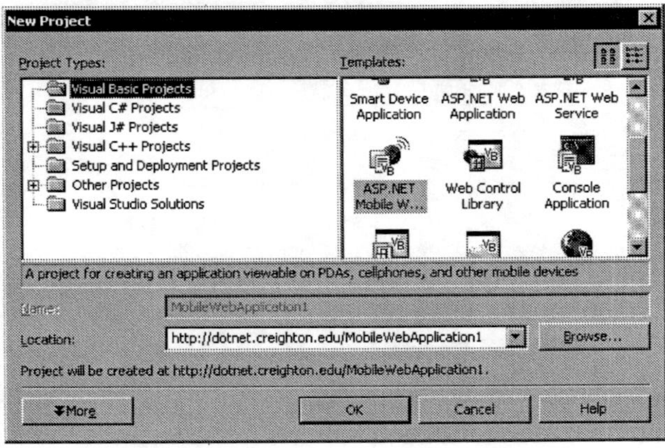

Figure 5. A new ASP .NET mobile Web application

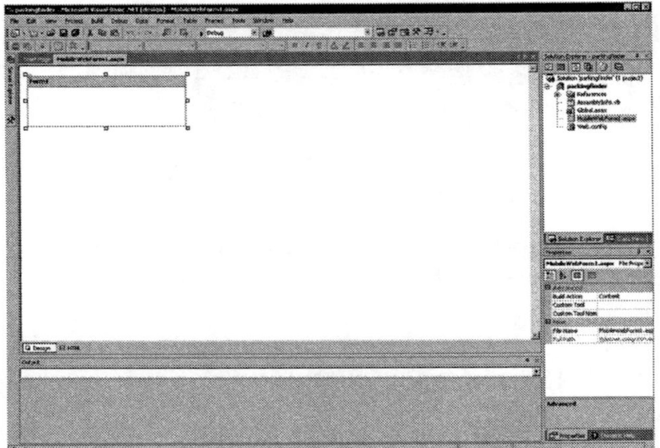

been added to the form. However, the form cannot be expanded horizontally since the width of the form is comparable to the width of the screens of most handsets. The Solution Explorer lists the components of the Parkingfinder project. The Properties Window lists the properties of the selected control.

6. Select **View | Toolbox** to display the Toolbox on the screen. The Toolbox contains a list of controls that can be used in a mobile Web application.
7. Double-click the Label control in the Toolbox. A label will appear in the form. In the Properties Window, set the **Text** property to "**Parking**

Finder". Set the **Alignment** property to **Center**. Set the **Bold** property to **True**. The form should look like Figure 6.

8. Double-click the Link control in the Toolbox to add a link in the form. Set the **Text** property to **"Search by Landmark"**. Set the **NavigateUrl** property to **"#Form2"**. This creates an internal link to another card in the same application.
9. Add another Link control in the form. Set its Text property to **"Search by Street"**, and set the **NavigateUrl** property to **"#Form3"**. Your form should look like Figure 7.
10. Select **File | Save All** to save the project.

Figure 6. Form1

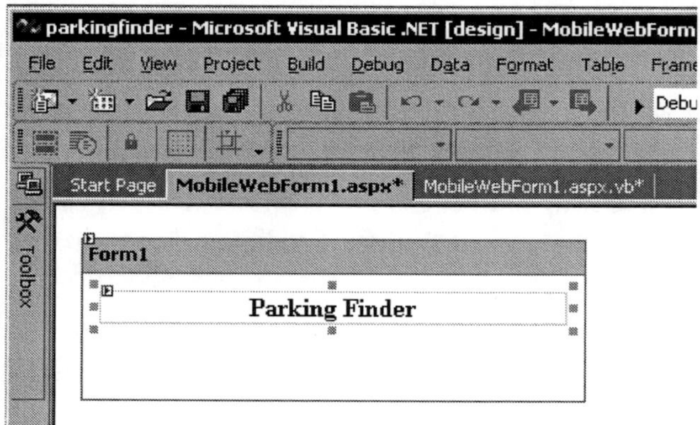

Figure 7. Form1

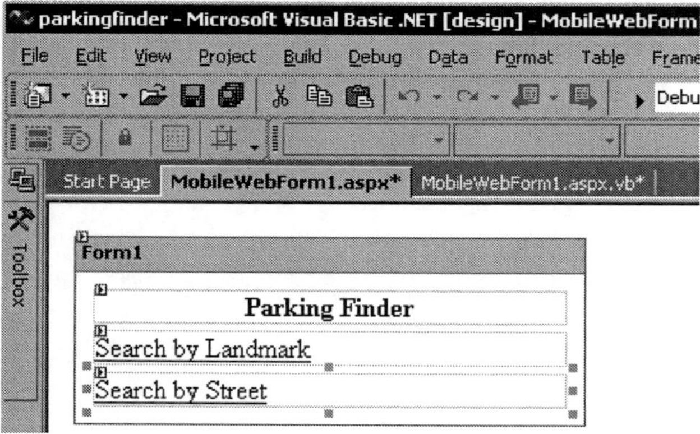

Accessing a Database

Form2 allows the user to select from a list of landmarks. The list comes from the database discussed previously. Visual Studio .NET allows developers to create database driven applications using ADO.NET (ActivX Data Objects), a tool for interacting with databases. In the following sections, you will learn the techniques to manipulate data in a database.

Step-by-Step:

1. Double-click the Form control in the Toolbox to add a new form to the application. The new form is named "**Form2**".
2. Double-click the Form control in the Toolbox to add another form called "**Form3**" to the application.
3. Double-click the Label control to add a Label in Form2. Set the **Text** property to "**Select a Landmark**:". Set the **Bold** property to **True**.
4. Double-click the Label control to add a Label in Form3. Set its **Text** property to "**Enter a Street Name:**". Set the **Bold** property to **True**.
5. Double-click the List control in the Toolbox to add a List in Form2. Set its **ID** property to "**lstLandmarks**". The list will contain the names of the landmarks to be selected. Your screen should look like Figure 8.
6. Drag a copy of the OleDbDataAdapter control from the Data tools from the Toolbox to Form2. A new component **OleDbDataAdapter1** ap-

Figure 8. Form2 and Form3

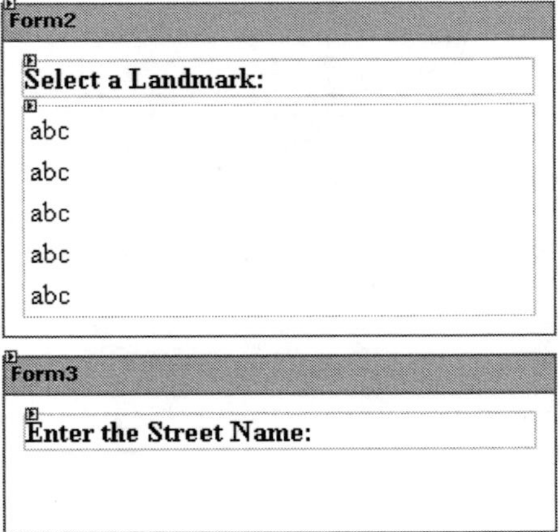

pears in the component tray at the bottom of the window. This also starts the Data Adapter Configuration Wizard. The OleDbDataAdapter serves as a bridge between a DataSet and data source for retrieving and saving data.

7. In the Data Adapter Configuration Wizard, Click **Next**.
8. Click the **New Connection** button.
9. Select the Provider tab and choose **Microsoft Jet 4.0 OLE DB Provider**. Click **Next**. The Data Link Properties dialog should appear as in Figure 9.
10. Navigate to and select **parking.mdb** in the **Select or Enter a Database Name** textbox.
11. Click the **Test Connection** button to test if the database connection is successful.
12. If the database connection is successful, click **OK**.
13. Click the **Next** button. In Choose a Query Type dialog, select the **Use SQL Statement** option. Click **Next**. Click the **Query Builder** button. The Query Builder appears as in Figure 10.
14. In the Add Table dialog, select the **Landmarks** table, click the **Add** button, and then click the **Close** button.

Figure 9. Data Link properties dialog

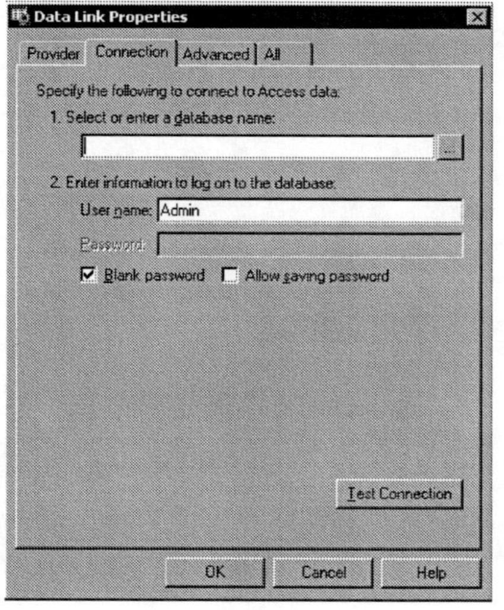

Figure 10. Query Builder

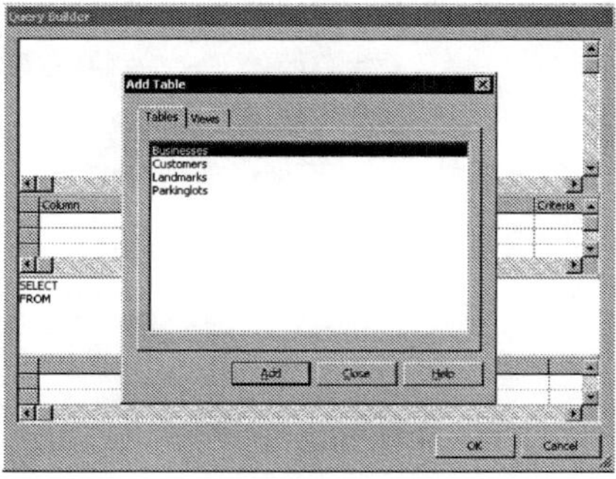

15. Select the **LMname** and **Zonecode** check boxes and set the **Sort Type** to **Ascending** for the **LMname** field. Based on your selection, the SQL command "*SELECT LMname, Zone FROM Landmarks ORDER BY LMname*" appears in the bottom window of the Query Builder (see Figure 11). Click **OK**.
16. Click the **Next** button twice.
17. Click **No** when asked if you wish to add a primary key column to the query.
18. Click the **Finish** button.
19. Click the **Don't Include Password** button.
20. Right click the **OleDbDataAdapter1** object and select **Generate Dataset** from the menu. The Generate Dataset dialog will look like Figure 12.
21. Click **OK**. A new object **Dataset11** appears in the component tray, and **DataSet1.xsd** appears in the Project Explorer.

In the next few steps, you will bind the List control in Form2 (**lstLandmarks**) to the dataset (**Dataset11**).

Figure 11. Query Builder

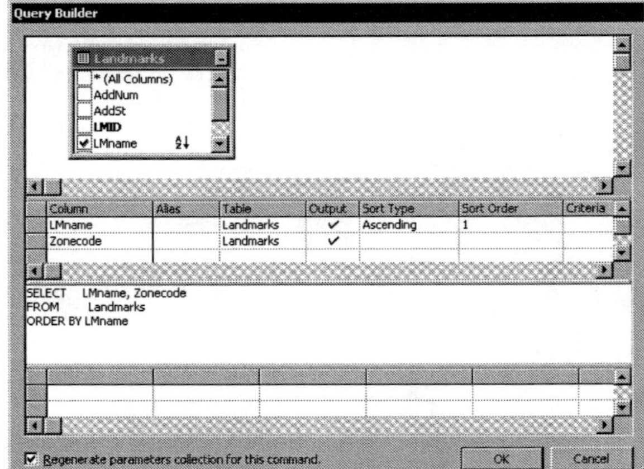

Figure 12. Generate Dataset

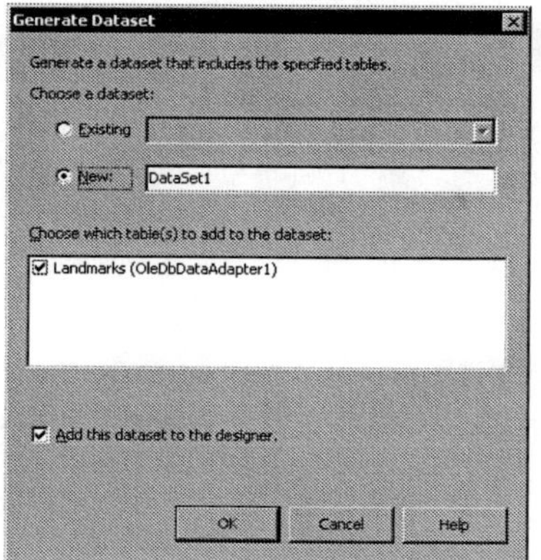

22. Select **lstLandmarks** in **Form2**. Set its properties as listed below.

Property	Setting
DataSource	DataSet11
DataMember	Landmarks
DataTextField	LMname
DataValueField	Zonecode

23. Double-click an empty area in **Form2** to switch to the Code Window.
24. Insert the highlighted statements in the **Form2_Activated** procedure.

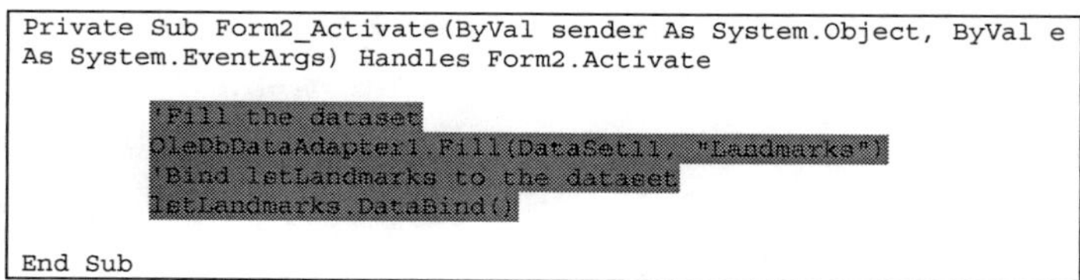

```
Private Sub Form2_Activate(ByVal sender As System.Object, ByVal e
As System.EventArgs) Handles Form2.Activate

        'Fill the dataset
        OleDbDataAdapter1.Fill(DataSet11, "Landmarks")
        'Bind lstLandmarks to the dataset
        lstLandmarks.DataBind()

End Sub
```

25. Save the project. Select **Debug | Start** to test the application.

By default, Visual Studio .NET will display the application in Internet Explorer. However, it is best to test a wireless application using a wireless device or emulator. Test the application using the Openwave SDK 6.2.2. The application should appear as in Figure 13.

Figure 13. Parking Finder displayed in Openwave SDK 6.2.2

Creating Session Variables

The user should be able to click on the name of a landmark to get a list of nearby parking lots on the handset. This requires the use of session variables. As we discussed in the previous chapter, session variables store values during a session; therefore, these variables can be accessed by any card during a session. When the session expires, session variables are deleted. To create a session variable, use the following syntax:

Session([**variable name**]) = [**value**]

Storing the Zonecode information about the selected landmark in a session variable allows subsequent cards to access this information so that they will be able to display the appropriate information. The session variable will be created when the user selects a landmark in Form2. The following steps use a session variable to pass value from one form to the next.

1. Double-click the **lstLandmark** control in **Form2** to open the Code window. Insert the highlighted statements in the **lstLandmarks_ItemCommand** procedure. The statements will be executed when an item in the list is selected by the user. After the session variable has been created, the application transfers control to **Form4**, which will contain a list of nearby parking lots.

```
Private Sub lstLandmarks_ItemCommand(ByVal sender As
System.Object, ByVal e As
System.Web.UI.MobileControls.ListCommandEventArgs) Handles
lstLandmarks.ItemCommand

        'Assign the Zonecode information of the
        'selected landmark to a session variable
        Session("currZone") = e.ListItem.Value
        'Transfer control to Form4
        ActiveForm = Form4

End Sub
```

2. Double-click the Form control in the Toolbox to add a new form, **Form4,** to the application.
3. Add a Label control to Form4. Set its **Text** property to "**Select a Parking Lot:**", and set its **Bold** property to **True**.
4. Add a List control to **Form4**. Set its **ID** property to "**lstParkinglots**".
5. Drag a copy of the OleDbDataAdapter control from the Data tools in the Toolbox to **Form4**. A new component **OleDbDataAdapter2** appears in the component tray at the bottom of the window. This also starts the Data Adapter Configuration Wizard.
6. Repeat steps 7-13 in the last section to create the database connection and start the Query Builder.
7. In the Add Table dialog, select the **Parkinglots** table, click the **Add** button, and then click the **Close** button.
8. Select the **PLID**, **PLName**, **Zonecode**, and **Rate** check boxes and set the **Sort Type** to **Ascending** for the **Rate** field. In the **Criteria** column of the **Zonecode** row, type "**=?**" and press **Enter**. Based on your selection, the SQL command "*SELECT PLId, PLname, Zonecode, Rate FROM Parkinglots WHERE (Zonecode = ?) ORDER BY Rate*" appears in the bottom window of the Query Builder (see Figure 14). The query will retrieve a list of parking lots in the area and list them in alphabetic order.
9. Click the **OK** button.
10. Click the **Next** button twice.
11. Click the **Finish** button.
12. Right click the **OleDbDataAdapter2** object and select **Generate Dataset** from the menu.

Figure 14. Query Builder

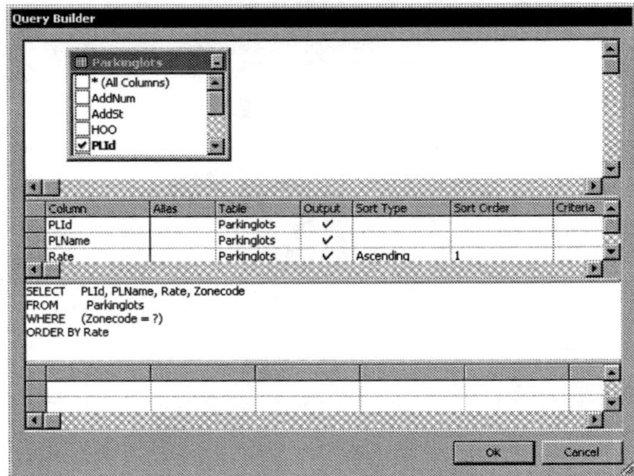

13. In the Generate Dataset dialog, choose **New** dataset and add the **Parkinglots** table to the dataset. Click **OK**. A new object **Dataset21** appears in the component tray, and **DataSet2.xsd** appears in the Project Explorer.
14. Select the **lstParkinglots** control in **Form4**. Set its properties as listed below.

Property	Setting
DataSource	DataSet21
DataMember	Parkinglots
DataTextField	PLname
DataValueField	PLID

15. Double-click on any empty space in **Form4** to open the Code Window. Insert the highlighted statements in the **Form4_Activate** procedure.

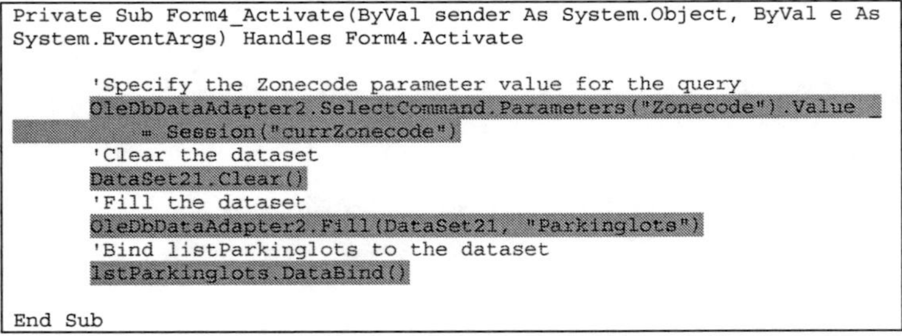

```
Private Sub Form4_Activate(ByVal sender As System.Object, ByVal e As
System.EventArgs) Handles Form4.Activate

      'Specify the Zonecode parameter value for the query
      OleDbDataAdapter2.SelectCommand.Parameters("Zonecode").Value _
          = Session("currZonecode")
      'Clear the dataset
      DataSet21.Clear()
      'Fill the dataset
      OleDbDataAdapter2.Fill(DataSet21, "Parkinglots")
      'Bind listParkinglots to the dataset
      lstParkinglots.DataBind()

End Sub
```

16. Save the project and test it using the Openwave SDK 6.2.2. Your Form4 screen should look like Figure 15.

Accessing Data from a Dataset

In this section, you will learn to extract data from a dataset by using the DataBindings property of the Label control. The next step in the project is to provide the user with a screen that contains detailed information about a selected parking lot.

1. Add a new form, **Form5**, to the project. Add the controls listed below to **Form5**. **Form 5** should look like Figure 16.

Figure 15. Form4 displayed in Openwave SDK 6.2.2

Figure 16. Form5

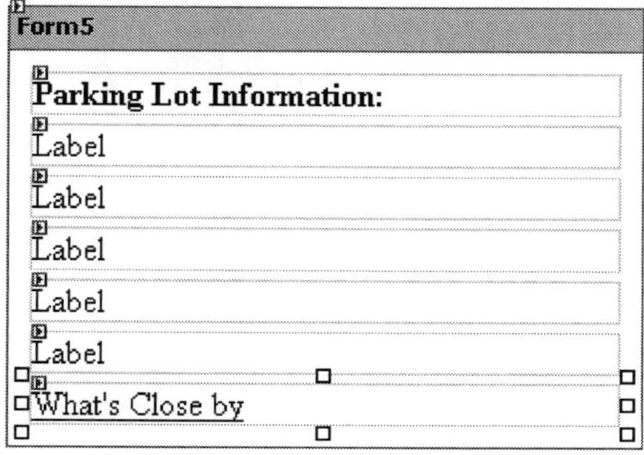

Control	Property	Value
Label	Text	Parking Lot Information:
	Bold	True
Label	ID	LblPLname
Label	ID	LblPLadd
Label	ID	LblRate
Label	ID	LblHOO
Label	ID	LblType
Link	Text	What' Close by
	NavigateUrl	#Form6

2. Double-click the **lstParkinglots** control in **Form4** to open the Code Window. Insert the highlighted statements in the **lstParkinglots_ItemCommand** procedure. These statements create a session variable to store the PLId of the selected parking lot and transfer control to **Form5**.

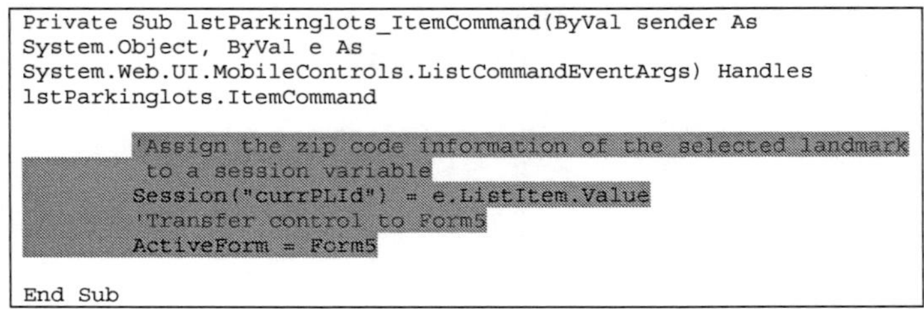

```
Private Sub lstParkinglots_ItemCommand(ByVal sender As
System.Object, ByVal e As
System.Web.UI.MobileControls.ListCommandEventArgs) Handles
lstParkinglots.ItemCommand

        'Assign the zip code information of the selected landmark
         to a session variable
        Session("currPLId") = e.ListItem.Value
        'Transfer control to Form5
        ActiveForm = Form5

End Sub
```

3. Drag an OleDbDataAdapter control from the Toolbox to **Form 5**. **OleDbDataAdapter3** will appear in the component tray. Follow the Wizard through to the Query Builder. In the Query Builder, create the following SQL statement:

SELECT AddNum, AddSt, HOO, PLId, PLName, Rate, Type, Zonecode FROM Parkinglots WHERE (PLId = ?)

4. Right-click the icon for **OleDbDataAdapter3** and select **Generate Dataset** from the menu. A new dataset, **DataSet31**, appears in the component tray, and a new component, **DataSet3.xsd**, appears in the Project Explorer.
5. Select **lblPLname** and click the ellipsis button in the **DataBindings** property in the Properties Window. The dialog in Figure 17 should appear.

Figure 17. DataBindings Dialog

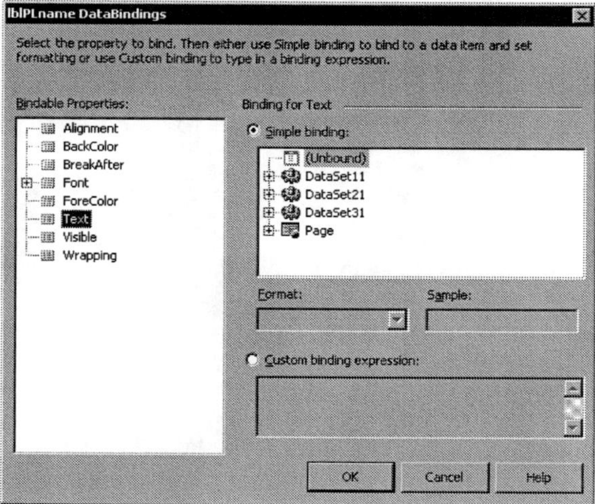

Figure 18. DataBindings dialog

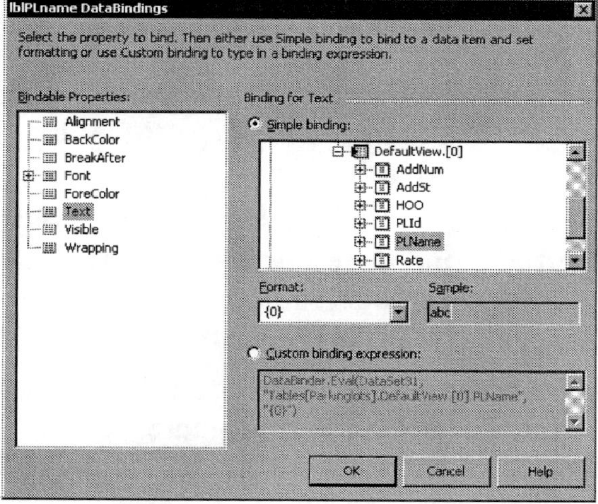

6. Keep expanding the **DataSet31** item until you get to the fields. Select the **PLName** field. Select **General – {0}** in the Format box. The dialog box should look like Figure 18.
7. Click the **OK** button.
8. Select **lblRate** and click the ellipsis button in the **DataBindings** property in the Properties Window to open the DataBindings dialog. Keep

Figure 19. Form5 displayed in Openwave SDK 6.2.2

expanding the **DataSet31** item until you get to the fields. Select the **Rate** field and **Currency – {0:C}** in the Format box. This will display the hourly rate of parking in the currency format.

9. Select **lblHOO** and click the ellipsis button in the **DataBindings** property in the Properties Window to open the DataBindings dialog. Keep expanding the **DataSet31** item until you get to the fields. Select the **HOO** field and **General – {0}** in the Format box.
10. Select **lblType** and click the ellipsis button in the **DataBindings** property in the Properties Window to open the DataBindings dialog. Keep expanding the **DataSet31** item until you get to the fields. Select the **Type** field and **General – {0}** in the Format box.
11. Double-click **Form5** to open the Code Window. Add the following statements to the **Form5_Active** procedure.

```
'Specify the PLID parameter for the query
OleDbDataAdapter3.SelectCommand.Parameters("PLId").Value _
  = Session("currPLId")
'Clear the dataset
DataSet31.Clear()
OleDbDataAdapter3.Fill(DataSet31, "Parkinglots")
```

We did not bind **lblPLadd** to any field for a reason. In the database, the building number and street name are stored separately for easy search. **LblPLadd** will join the contents of these two fields to create an address.

12. Enter the following statement to the **Form5_Active** procedure. This statement joins the **AddNum** and **AddSt** fields, and the result will be displayed in **lblPLadd**.

```
'Join the AddNum and AddSt fields together
lblPLadd.Text = String.Format("{0} {1}", _
DataSet31.Parkinglots.Rows(0).Item("AddNum"), _
DataSet31.Parkinglots.Rows(0).Item("AddSt"))
```

13. Finally, add the following statements to the Form5_Active procedure to bind the label controls to the data.

```
'Bind controls to the dataset
lblPLname.DataBind()
lblRate.DataBind()
lblHOO.DataBind()
lblType.DataBind()
```

14. Debug the application. Your screen should look something like Figure 19.

The user can also search for a nearby parking lot by typing in the name of the street of the destination. We will use a slightly different technique called data command objects for developing that portion of the application.

Data Command Objects

Data command objects can be used to retrieve information from and update information in the database. In this section, you will learn to retrieve information from the database based on a criterion by using a data command object.

Figure 20. Form3

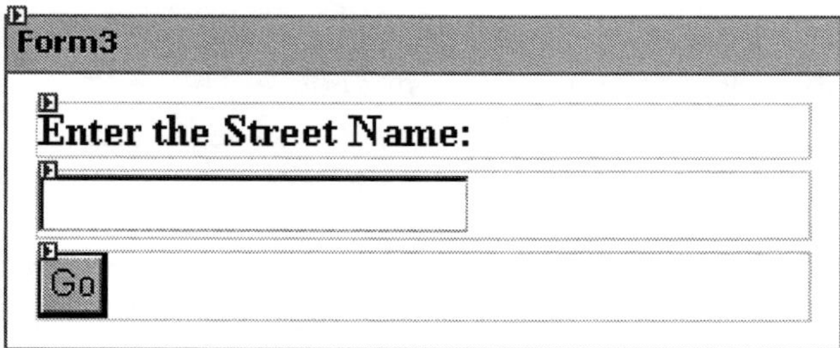

Figure 21. Form6

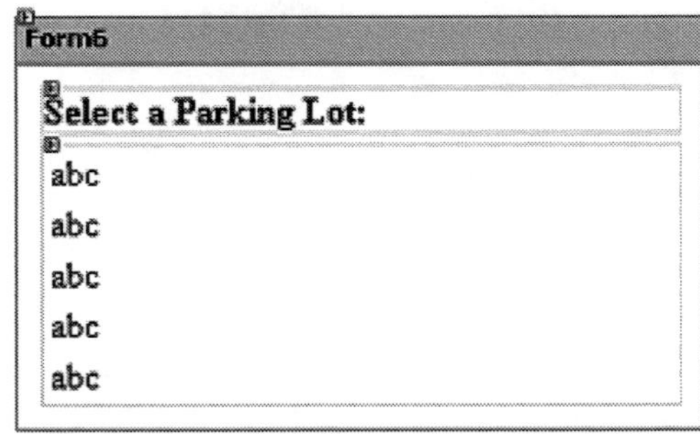

Figure 22. Query Builder

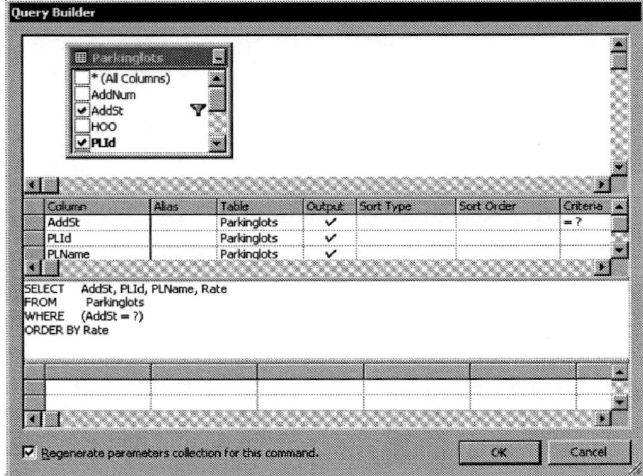

1. Add a TextBox control to **Form3**. Set its **ID** property to "**txtStreet**".
2. Add a Command control to **Form3**. Set its **ID** property to "**cmdGo**" and its Text property to "**GO**". **Form3** should look something like Figure 20.
3. Double-click **cmdGo** to open the Code Window. Enter the following statements in the **cmdGo_Click** procedure.

```
'Assign the street name to a session variable
Session("currStreet") = txtStreet.Text
'Transfer control to Form6
ActiveForm = Form6
```

The statements create a session variable to store the street name entered by the user and activate a new form, **Form6**.

4. Add a new Form, **Form6,** to the project.
5. Add a Label control to **Form6**. Set its **Text** property to "**Select a Parking Lot:**" and **Bold** property to **True**.
6. Add a List control to **Form6**. Set its **ID** property to "**lstParkinglots2**". **Form6** should look like Figure 21.
7. Drag an OleDbCommand control from the Toolbox to **Form6**. The OleDbCommand control is named **OleDbCommand1** by default. Click the down-arrow in the **Connection** property box in the Properties Window. Expand the **Existing** node and select the connection object (**OleDbConnection1**) you created earlier in this project. The connection object connects the project with its database, **parking.mdb**.
8. Select the **CommandText** property of **OleDbCommand1** in the Properties Window. Click the ellipsis button to launch the Query Builder.
9. Select the table **Parkinglots** and click the **Add** button. Click the **Close** button to close the Add Table dialog.
10. In the Query Builder, create the following SQL statement:

SELECT AddSt, PLId, PLName, Rate FROM Parkinglots WHERE (AddSt = ?)
ORDER BY Rate

Your Query Builder window should look something like Figure 22. The (AddSt = ?) portion indicates that the query will retrieve information based on the value of the street name.

11. Click the **OK** button to accept the SQL statement.
12. Click the **Yes** button in the Microsoft Development Environment dialog.

Using the Data Reader Object

The data reader object provides an easy way for a .NET application to read data from a database. However, the object cannot be used to modify data in a database. In this example, we will use the data reader object to retrieve a list of parking lots that are located on the street specified by the user.

1. Select **View | Code** to open the Code Window. Insert the following statement as the first line in the code. The statement imports the **System.Data.OleDb** namespace so that the application can use the data command and data reader objects.

```
Imports System.Data.OleDb
```

2. Select **View | Designer** to switch back to the Designer View. Double-click **Form6** to open the Code window. Enter the following statements in the **Form6_Activate** procedure.

```
'Specify the AddSt parameter for the query
OleDbCommand1.Parameters("AddSt").Value = Session("currStreet")

'Open database connection
OleDbConnection1.Open()

'Create an OleDbDataReader object and execute the SQL statement
 Dim objReader As OleDbDataReader = OleDbCommand1.ExecuteReader

'Bind lstParkinglots2 to the DataReader
lstParkinglots2.DataSource = objReader
lstParkinglots2.DataTextField = "PLname"
lstParkinglots2.DataValueField = "PLId"
lstParkinglots2.DataBind()

'Close database connection
OleDbConnection1.Close()
```

3. Select **View | Designer** to switch back to the Designer View. Double-click the **lstParkinglots2** control in **Form6** to open the Code Window. Enter the following statements to the **lstParkinglots2_ItemCommand** procedure. The statements pass the **PLId** of the selected parking lot as a session variable to **Form5**, which displays the detail information about the parking lot.

```
'Assign the zip code information of the selected landmark to a
session variable
Session("currPLId") = e.ListItem.Value
'Transfer control to Form5
ActiveForm = Form5
```

4. Save the project and debug it. Enter "Douglas" as the street name. Your screens should look something like Figure 23.

Figure 23. Figure 3 and Figure 6 displayed in Openwave SDK 6.2.2

Building the "What's Close by" Function

The next step is to develop the portion of the application that directs the user to businesses close to the selected parking lot. When the user clicks the "What's Close by" link, he or she will be presented with a list of business types. In order to avoid unnecessary key strokes, the application should only present the types of businesses that can be found near the selected parking lot. Therefore, before the list can be presented to the user, a query must be performed to find out what types of businesses exist within the zone in which the parking lot is located.

1. Select **View | Designer** to switch to the Designer View. Select the link (**"What's Close by"**) in **Form5**. Set its **Navigateurl** property to **"#Form7"**.
2. Add a new Form, **Form7**, from the Toolbox to the project. Add a Label control to **Form7**. Set the **Text** property to "**Select a Category**:" and the **Bold** property to **True**.
3. Add a List control to **Form7**. Set its **ID** property to "**lstBusCats**". Your **Form7** should look like Figure 24.
4. Double-click **Form5** to open the Code Window. Add the following statement at the end of the **Form5_Activate** procedure. This statement

Figure 24. Form7

Form7

Select a Category:

abc
abc
abc
abc
abc

ensures that the session variable "**currZonecode**" contains the **zonecode** of the selected parking lot.

```
'Assign the zonecode to a session variable
Session("currZonecode") = _
   DataSet31.Parkinglots.Rows(0).Item("Zonecode")
```

5. Select **View | Designer** to switch to the Designe View.
6. Drag an OleDbCommand control to **Form7**. The control is named **OleDbCommand2** by default. Click the down-arrow in the **Connection** property box in the Properties Window. Expand the **Existing** node and select the connection object (**OleDbConnection1**) you created earlier in this project. The connection object connects the project with its database, **parking.mdb**.
7. Select the **CommandText** property of **OleDbCommand2** in the Properties window. Click the ellipsis button to launch the Query Builder.
8. Select the table **Businesses** and click the **Add** button. Click the **Close** button to close the Add Table dialog.
9. In the Query Builder, check the checkboxes beside **Bid**, **Type**, and **Zonecode**. Right click the column header and select **Group By** from the menu. A new column, **Group By**, appears. In the **Bid** row, click the down arrow in the **Group By** column and select **Count**. In the **Alias** column of the **Bid** row, type "**NumOfBus**". In the **Criteria** column of the Zonecode row, type "=?". Your selection will generate the following SQL statement. The Query Builder should look similar to Figure 25.

Figure 25. Query Builder

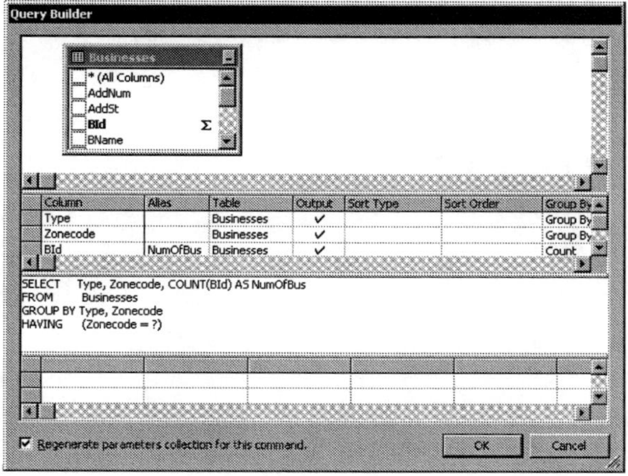

SELECT Type, Zonecode, COUNT(Bid) AS NumOfBus FROM Businesses GROUP BY type, zonecode HAVING (Zonecode = ?)

10. Click the **OK** button to accept the SQL statement.
11. Double-click **Form7** to open the Code Window. Enter the following statements in the **Form7_Activate** procedure.

```
'Specify the Zonecode parameter for the query
OleDbCommand2.Parameters("Zonecode").Value = _
   Session("currZoneCode")

'Open database connection
OleDbConnection1.Open()

'Create an OleDbDataReader object and execute the SQL statement
Dim objReader As OleDbDataReader = OleDbCommand2.ExecuteReader
```

12. Enter the following statements at the end of the **Form7_Active** procedure. The statements use a slightly different technique to read data from the database. Data are read one record at a time to ensure that only the types of businesses that are located in the zone are listed.

```
'Populate lstBusCats with data from the database
Do While objReader.Read()
   If objReader("NumOfBus") <> 0 Then
      lstBusCats.Items.Add(objReader("Type"))
   End If
Loop
```

Figure 26. Form8

13. Enter the following statement to close the database connection.

```
'Close database connection
OleDbConnection1.Close()
```

14. To display a list of businesses within the selected category, you will need to create a new form. Add a new form, **Form8**, to the project. Add a Label control to **Form8**. Set its **Text** property to "**Select a Business**:" and **Bold** property to **True**. Add a List control to **Form8**. Set its **ID** property to "**lstBusinesses**". **Form8** should look something like Figure 26.
15. **Drag an OleDbAdapter from the Toolbox to** Form8. **A new component,** OleDbAdapter4 **appears in the component tray at the bottom of the workspace. Follow the Data Adapter Wizard through to the Query Builder.**
16. In the Query Builder, Select the table **Businesses** and click the **Add** button. Click the **Close** button to close the Add Table dialog.
17. In the Query Builder, check the checkboxes beside **Bid, Bname, Type,** and **Zonecode**. In the **Criteria** column of the Zonecode row, type "=?". In the **Criteria** column of the Type row, type "?". Your selection will generate the following SQL statement. The Query Builder should look similar to Figure 27.

SELECT BName, BId, Type, Zonecode FROM Businesses WHERE (Type = ?) AND (Zonecode = ?)

Figure 27. Query Builder

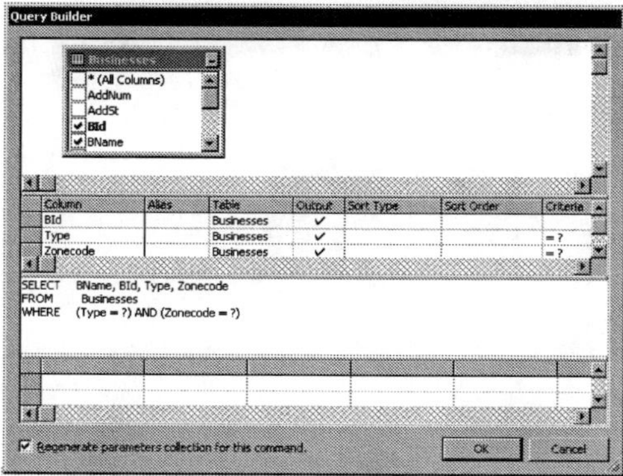

18. Click the **OK** button to accept the SQL statement.
19. Right-click the icon for **OleDbDataAdapter4** and select **Generate Dataset** from the menu. A new dataset, **DataSet41**, appears in the component tray, and a new component, **DataSet4.xsd**, appears in the Project Explorer.
20. Select **lstBusinesses** in **Form8**, set its **DataSource** property to "**DataSet41**", **DataMember** property to "**Businesses**", **DataTextField** to "**Bname**", and **DataValueField** to "**Bid**".
21. Double-click **Form8** to open the Code Window. Enter the following statements in the **Form8_Activate** procedure. These statements provide the criteria for the query and bind **lstBusinesses** to the dataset.

```
'Specify the Zonecode parameter for the query

OleDbDataAdapter4.SelectCommand.Parameters("Zonecode").Value = _
Session("currZonecode")
OleDbDataAdapter4.SelectCommand.Parameters("Type").Value = _
Session("currType")

'Clear the dataset
DataSet41.Clear()
'Fill the dataset with the query result
OleDbDataAdapter4.Fill(DataSet41, "Businesses")
'Bind lstParkinglots to the dataset
lstBusinesses.DataBind()
```

22. Save the project and test **Form7** and **Form8**. They should look like Figure 28.

Figure 28. Form7 and Form8 displayed in Openwave SDK 6.2.2

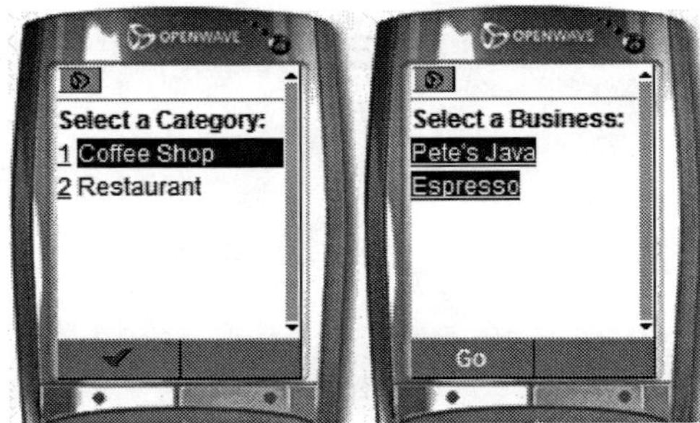

Figure 29. Form9

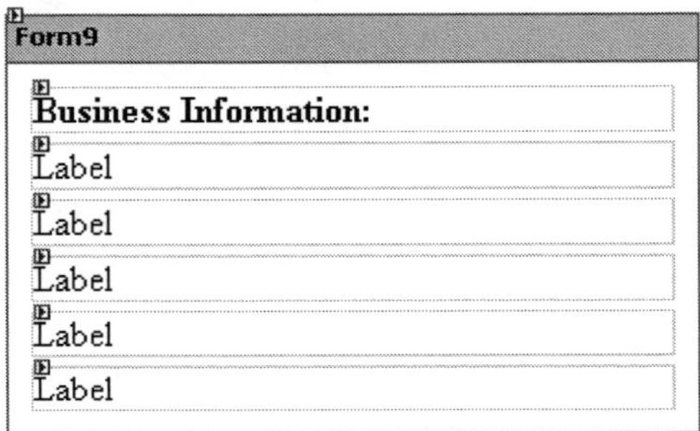

Now, you will create a new form to display detailed information about the selected business.

1. Add a new form, **Form9**, to the project. Add the controls listed below to **Form9**. **Form 9** should look like Figure 29.

Control	Property	Value
Label	Text	Business Information:
	Bold	True
Label	ID	lblBName
Label	ID	lblBAdd
Label	ID	lblBPhone
Label	ID	lblBHOO
Label	ID	lblBDetail

2. Double-click the **lstBusinesses** control in **Form8** to open the Code Window. Insert the highlighted statements in the **lstBusinesses_ItemCommand** procedure. These statements create a

session variable to store the **BId** of the selected business and transfer control to **Form9**.

```
Private Sub lstParkinglots_ItemCommand(ByVal sender As
System.Object, ByVal e As
System.Web.UI.MobileControls.ListCommandEventArgs) Handles
lstParkinglots.ItemCommand

        'Assign the zip code information of the selected landmark
         to a session variable
        Session("currBId") = e.ListItem.Value
        'Transfer control to Form5
        ActiveForm = Form9

End Sub
```

3. Drag an OleDbDataAdapter control from the Toolbox to **Form 9**. **OleDbDataAdapter5** will appear in the component tray. Follow the Wizard through to the Query Builder. In the Query Builder, create the following SQL statement:

SELECT AddNum, AddSt, BId, BName, Detail, HOO, Phone FROM Businesses WHERE (BId = ?)

4. Right-click the icon for **OleDbDataAdapter5** and select **Generate Dataset** from the menu. A new dataset, **DataSet51**, appears in the component tray, and a new component, **DataSet5.xsd**, appears in the Project Explorer.
5. Select **lblBname** and click the ellipsis button in the **DataBindings** property in the Properties Window. The DataBindings dialog in Figure 30 should appear.
6. Keep expanding the **DataSet51** item until you get to the fields. Select the **Bname** field. Select **General – {0}** in the Format box. Click the **OK** button.
7. Select **lblBphone** and click the ellipsis button in the **DataBindings** property in the Properties Window to open the DataBindings dialog. Keep expanding the **DataSet51** item until you get to the fields. Select the **Phone** field. Select **General - {0}** in the Format box. Click the **OK** button.
8. Select **lblBHOO** and click the ellipsis button in the **DataBindings** property in the Properties Window to open the DataBindings dialog.

Figure 30. DataBindings dialog

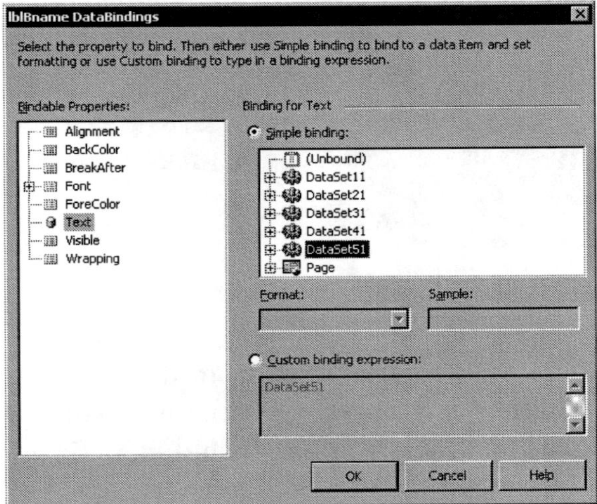

Figure 31. Form9 displayed in Openwave SDK 6.2.2

Keep expanding the **DataSet51** item until you get to the fields. Select the **HOO** field. Select **General - {0}** in the Format box. Click the **OK** button.

9. Select **lblBdetail** and click the ellipsis button in the **DataBindings** property in the Properties Window to open the DataBindings dialog. Keep expanding the **DataSet51** item until you get to the fields. Select the **Detail** field. Select **General – {0}** in the Format box. Click the **OK** button.

10. Double-click **Form9** to open the Code Window. Add the following statements to the **Form9_Active** procedure.

```
'Specify the BID parameter for the query
OleDbDataAdapter5.SelectCommand.Parameters("BId").Value = _
Session("currBId")
'Clear the dataset
DataSet51.Clear()
'Fill the dataset
OleDbDataAdapter5.Fill(DataSet51, "Businesses")

'Join the AddNum and AddSt fields together
lblBadd.Text = String.Format("{0} {1}", _
DataSet51.Businesses.Rows(0).Item("AddNum"), _
   DataSet51.Businesses.Rows(0).Item("AddSt"))

'Bind controls to the dataset
lblBname.DataBind()
lblBPhone.DataBind()
lblBHOO.DataBind()
lblBDetail.DataBind()
```

11. Save the project. Test the application. **Form9** should look like Figure 31.

Inserting Records into the Database

The previous sections discuss the techniques for retrieving data from a database. In this section, you will learn how to insert records into a database in order to entice more people to attend events and visit businesses in the downtown district. The Parking Finder will include a function for users to submit their e-mail addresses. By submitting their e-mail addresses, users will receive e-mail alerts about upcoming events and coupons for downtown businesses. The following steps create this function:

1. Select **Form1**. Add a Link control to the form. Set its **Text** property to "**Receive E-mail Alerts**" and **NavigateUrl** property to "**#Form10**".
2. Add a new form, **Form10**, to the project. Add the following controls to **Form10**. The SoftKeyLabel property dictates the caption for the softkey of the handset.

Control	Property	Value
Label	Text	To receive information and coupons for downtown events, please enter your e-mail address below:
TextBox	ID	txtEmail
Command Button	ID	cmdSubmit
	Text	Send
	SoftKeyLabel	Send

Figure 32. Form10 and Form11

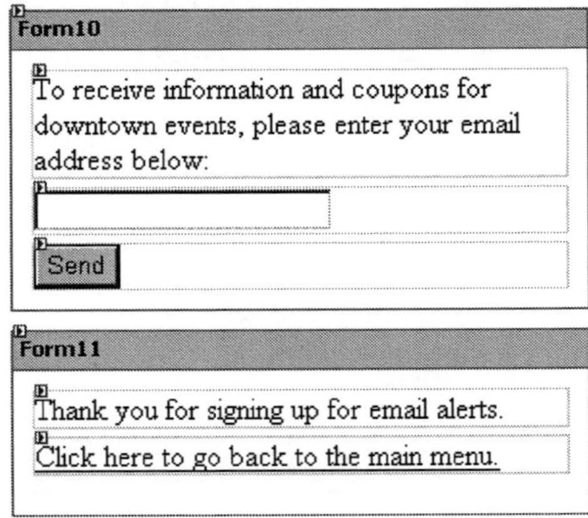

3. Add another new form, **Form11**, to the project. Add the following controls to **Form11**.

Control	Property	Value
Label	Text	Thank you for signing up for e-mail alerts.
Link	Text	Click here to go back to the main menu.
	NavigateUrl	#Form1

4. Your **Form10** and **Form11** should look like Figure 32.
5. Double-click **cmdSubmit** in **Form10** to open the Code Window. Enter the following statements in the **cmdSubmit_Click** procedure. Instead of using drag-and-drop method as you did previously, this time, you will create a new OleDbCommand object programmatically using the statements below. The new object is named **OleDbInsertCommand** as it will be used to insert records into the database.

```
'Declare a new OleDbCommand object
 Dim OleDbInsertCommand As OleDbCommand
 OleDbInsertCommand = New OleDbCommand
```

6. Enter the following statements. These statements programmatically assign values to the **CommandText** and **Connection** properties of **OleDbInsertCommand**. The **CommandText** property contains a SQL command that inserts the e-mail address input by the user into the Customers table of the database. The **Connection** property specifies that

the operation will use **OleDbConnection1**, a database connection to **parking.mdb** created earlier in the project.

```
'Specify the SQL command
OleDbInsertCommand.CommandText = _
   "INSERT INTO CUSTOMERS (Email) VALUES ('" & txtEmail.Text & _
"')"

'Specify the database connection
OleDbInsertCommand.Connection = OleDbConnection1
```

7. Enter the following statements. The **ExecuteNonQuery** method executes a SQL statement. Using this method does not require the use of a dataset. After the new record has been inserted into the database table, the user will be directed to **Form11**, which provides the user with a confirmation that the e-mail has been submitted successfully.

```
'Open the database connection
OleDbConnection1.Open()

'Execute the SQL command
OleDbInsertCommand.ExecuteNonQuery()

'Close the database connection
OleDbConnection1.Close()

'Display Form11
ActiveForm = Form11
```

8. Save the project. Test the application. Your **Form1**, **Form10** and **Form11** should look something like Figure 33.

Figure 33. Form1, Form10 and Form11 displayed in Openwave SDK 6.2.2

Summary

This chapter demonstrates how to develop a wireless application using Microsoft's integrated development environment, Visual Studio .NET. The language used in this project is ASP.NET. As the chapter has shown, Visual Studio .NET provides developers with a robust and easy-to-use development environment for creating wireless applications. It also offers extensive support for database-driven applications. This chapter discussed and demonstrated a number of techniques for interacting with database using Visual Studio .NET.

Visual Studio .NET offers many graphic objects in the Toolbox for creating the user interface for a mobile Web application. Each application can contain one or more forms. Each form represents a WML card, and a group of related forms represents a deck of WML cards that forms a WAP application.

In this chapter, you are introduced to two techniques for interacting with databases. The first technique involves the use of the OleDbAdapter and Dataset objects. The OleDbAdapter serves as a bridge between a dataset and source data. You can bind a Visual Basic control to a dataset to display the data in the dataset. The second technique uses the Data Command and Data Reader objects. The Data Command object stores and executes SQL statements while the Data Reader object provides an easy way for a .NET application to read data from a database. Besides retrieving data from a database, the Data Command object is also used to update and delete data.

Project

Create a wireless application that allows its users to locate restaurants in your city using wireless handsets. The application must have an easy-to-use interface and provide only information that are useful and can be displayed effectively on most handsets. The application should include the following features:

Find Restaurants by Name/Location/Cuisine: The application must provide convenient ways for users to find restaurants. Users can search for restaurants by their names, locations (e.g., downtown and midtown), or cuisines (e.g., continental, Italian, Chinese, etc.).

Detailed Information about Restaurants: The user will be able to access detailed information about a restaurant including its address, phone number, price range, type of cuisine, parking, and dress code. Interested users can drill down to find more information such as restaurant reviews and directions.

Online Reservation: The application will give users the option to make a reservation online using an online reservation form. A user will provide his or her name and phone number to secure the reservation. The Online Reservation option can be offered to the user when a restaurant has been selected.

Use the techniques discussed in this chapter to develop the wireless application described above.

Chapter IX

Mobile Application Development I: Developing Mobile Applications Using Microsoft Embedded Visual Tools

In this chapter, you will:

- Learn the basic techniques of developing applications using eVB
- Learn the differences between mobile and wireless applications
- Learn about eVB variable and program flow control
- Learn about eVB array
- Learn to interact with files using eVB
- Learn to use HTTP WinSock control
- Learn to develop menu-driven user interface

Introduction

Microsoft Embedded Visual Tools were designed to develop applications that run on Windows CE devices (e.g., Pocket PC and Handheld PC 2000). It is a free software product that can be downloaded at the www.microsoft.com Web site. Two programming languages are supported by Microsoft Embedded Visual Tools: Embedded Visual Basic (eVB) and Embedded Visual C++

(eVC). These two programming languages are versions of Visual Basic and Visual C++ with limited capabilities, respectively. Therefore, developers with Visual Basic or Visual C++ experience can easily leverage their existing expertise to develop mobile or wireless applications. Since many developers are familiar with Visual Basic, we will explore the techniques of using eVB to develop applications for wireless devices in this chapter.

While eVB looks very similar to Visual Basic, there are a number of significant differences between them. Some of these differences include:

1. Many VB functions are not supported by eVB.
2. eVB does not support typed variables. All variables are variants.
3. In eVB, forms can only be hidden but not unloaded. Forms will continue to occupy memory after they are hidden.

Desktop Pocket PC Emulation

In order to test your applications, you need either a Pocket PC device or Desktop Pocket PC Emulator. The emulator can be installed on your PC and simulates how your applications will function on a real device. To install the emulator, you need to download Microsoft Windows Platform SDK for Pocket PC from www.microsoft.com. Follow the instructions to install the SDK on your PC.

Mobile vs. Wireless Applications

While many people use the terms "mobile application" and "wireless application" interchangeably, there is an important distinction between these two types of applications. Wireless applications are designed to function while the client device is connected to networks (e.g., the Internet) or other devices without wires. Wireless applications often involve communicating with other devices. A mobile application, on the other hand, may involve wireless communication with networks or other devices, but it can also function without a network connection. Sometimes, we refer to a mobile application as a client or standalone application. When one is away from his or her regular computing environment (e.g., office and home), network connection may not be available. In such situations, a mobile application will allow the user to continue his or her computing activities.

eVB can be used to develop both mobile and wireless applications as we will illustrate in this chapter. We will start with a simple program to illustrate the basic techniques of using eVB.

Creating an eVB Application

Follow the steps below to create a simple eVB application:

1. Select **Start | Programs | Microsoft eMbedded Visual Tools | eMbedded Visual Basic 3.0**. This launches eVB development environment (see Figure 1).
2. In the New Project dialog, select **Window CE for the Pocket PC Project**. Click **Open**.
3. The development environment displays an empty eVB project. A default form called "**Form1**" is created (see Figure 2).

Figure 1. New project dialog

Figure 2. Creating a new project in eVB

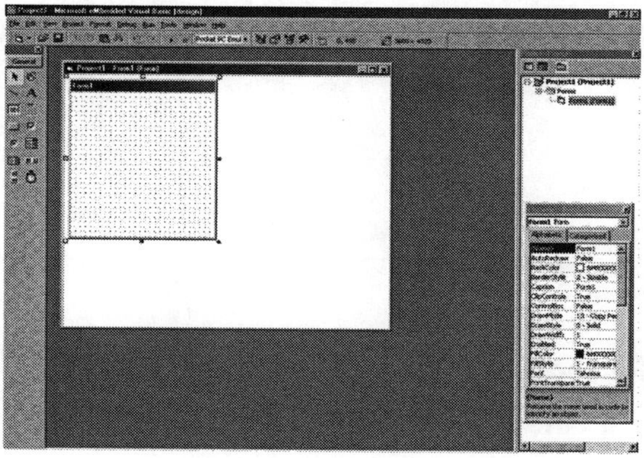

A **Form** is the work area for developing an application. In eVB, the default form size is the same as the display area of most Pocket PC devices (3600X4020). The **Toolbox** includes the standard eVB **Controls** that can be placed on the form. More controls can be added to the toolbox as needed. We will illustrate this later in this chapter. The **Project Explorer** lists the components of the current project. A user can double-click on any component to display it in the work area. The **Properties Window** lists the properties of the selected control.

4. Double-click the **Label** control in the Toolbox. A label control will appear in the form. Make sure that the label control is selected, and set the **Name** property to "**lblHello**" in the Properties Window. Set the **Left** property to **1000**, **Top** property to **1000**, **Width** property to **1500**, **Height** property to **255**, and **Caption** property to **""**. This will place an empty label control close to the center of the form.

Naming Controls

In order to make the source code of an application easy to read, most programmers follow a naming convention for the names of controls. The first three characters of the name of the control represent the type of control (e.g., lbl stands for label), and the rest of the name is a descriptive name of the control. For example, a label control that displays a hello message is named "lblHello".

Table 1. eVB controls and abbreviations

Control	Prefix	Control	Prefix
Check box	Chk	Label	lbl
Combo box	Cbo	Menu item	mnu
Command button	Cmd	Radio button	rdb
Form	Frm	Text box	txt
Image	Img		

The Table 1 contains a list of the prefixes and their corresponding controls.

5. Double-click the body of the form to open the Code Window.
6. Make sure that the object is **Form**, and set the procedure to **Load**.

EVB is an event-driven programming language. An event refers to a user action (e.g., loading a form and clicking a button). Statements will be executed when an event occurs. In this case, the code in Figure 3 will be executed when the form is loaded; therefore, the name of the event procedure is Form_Load.

7. Enter the following statements in the **Form_Load** procedure as displayed in Figure 3.

```
'Declare a string variable
Dim strYourName As String

'Accept user input
strYourName = InputBox("Please enter your name and click OK.")

'Display message
lblHello.Caption = "Hello " & strYourName & "!"
```

Figure 3. The code window

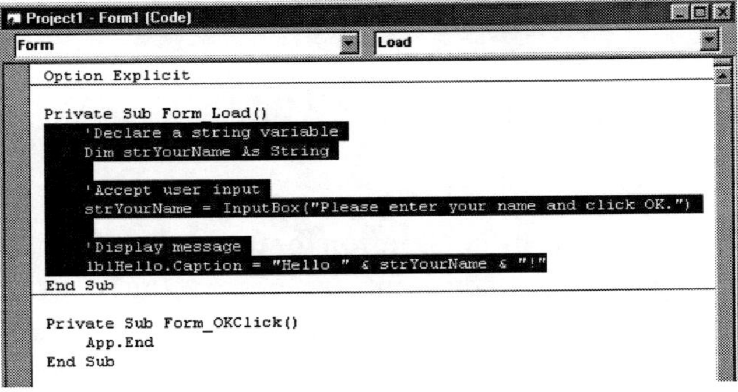

The first statement "Option Explicit" requires a variable to be declared before it can be used. A variable is a temporary location for data used in the application.

In order to improve the application's readability, a good programmer often includes comments in the program. In eVB, a comment line starts with a single quotation mark ('). Throughout the chapter, comments are provided in the code to help you understand the code better.

In eVB, a variable must be declared before it can be used. Declaring a variable allows eVB to reserve a spot in memory for it. The syntax for declaring a variable is:

```
Dim [name of the variable] {As [data type]}.
```

"Dim" stands for dimension. The Dim statement declares variables and allocates storage space. The variable declared in the procedure is only available to the statements in the procedure. EVB is a typeless programming language; therefore, the data type portion of the statement is optional. You can still declare data type for the variable, but doing so offers little value to the application.

The function InputBox() displays a dialog box that accepts user input. The user input can be assigned to a variable, in this case, strYourName. The syntax of the InputBox() function is as follows:

```
Filename = InputBox("[message]"{, "[button caption]}")
```

The [button caption] portion of the statement is optional. By default, EVB will use "OK" as the button caption.

The properties of controls can be changed during run time. In this example, the caption property of lblHello will be changed to the message "Hello [name entered by the user]!". "&" is used to connect strings together. The syntax to assign a new value to the property of an object is as follows:

```
Object.Property = [new value]
```

By default, eVB adds a Form_OKClick() procedure when a new application is created. The procedure will be executed when the "OK" button on the top right corner of a Pocket PC application is clicked. The procedure will close the program. App.End function ends the program.

8. Click **File | Save Project As** to save the project. Save the form as "**hello.ebf**" and the project as "**hello.ebp**".
9. Select **Run | Start Debug** to compile and debug the project. If you have a Pocket PC device connected, select "**Pocket PC (Default Device)**" in the Device selection box; otherwise, select "**Pocket PC Emulation**" (see Figure 4).
10. If all goes well, your application will be compiled and run as in Figure 5.

Congratulations! You just created your first eVB application.

Figure 4. Debugging the application

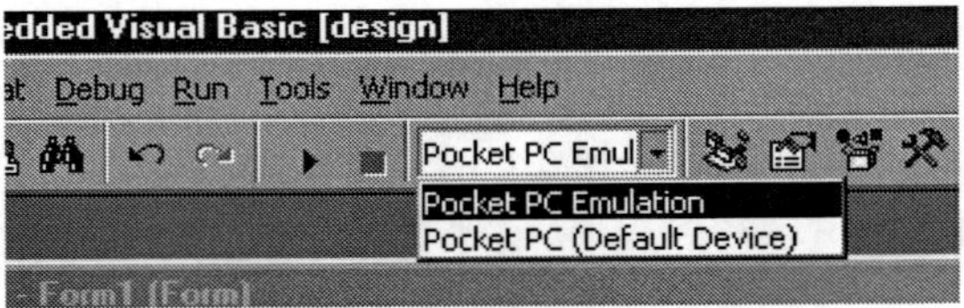

Figure 5. The Hello application

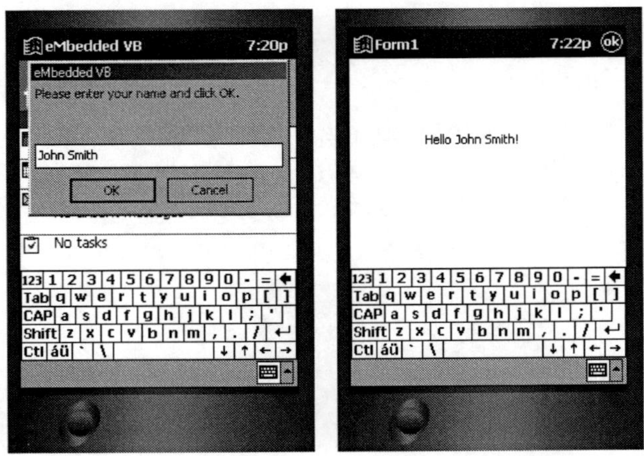

Commission Calculator 1.0

The salespeople at Wireless Solutions would like to have a commission calculator installed on their Pocket PCs. The formula the company uses to calculate sales commission is:

Sales Commission = (Sale Price * Commission Rate + (Sales Price – Dealer Cost) * 5%) * Quantity

Now, let's create a simple commission calculator for the salespeople.

1. Start eMbedded Visual Basic 3.0 and open a new project.
2. Select the form by clicking on the body of the form, and change the **Name** property to "**frmCalculator**" and the **Text** property to "**Commission Calculator 1.0**".
3. Create the following controls on the form. Your form should look like Figure 6.

Control	Name	Text / Caption
Label1	lblInstruction	Please enter the following information:
Label2	lblSalePrice	Sale Price:
Label3	lblDealerCost	Dealer Cost:
Label4	lblQuantity	Quantity:
Label5	lblCommissionRate	Commission Rate:
Text1	txtSalePrice	<delete the default text>
Text2	txtDealerCost	<delete the default text>
Text3	txtQuanity	<delete the default text>
Text4	txtCommissionRate	<delete the default text>
Command1	cmdCalculate	Calculate
Command2	cmdClear	Clear

Figure 6. Commission Calculator 1.0

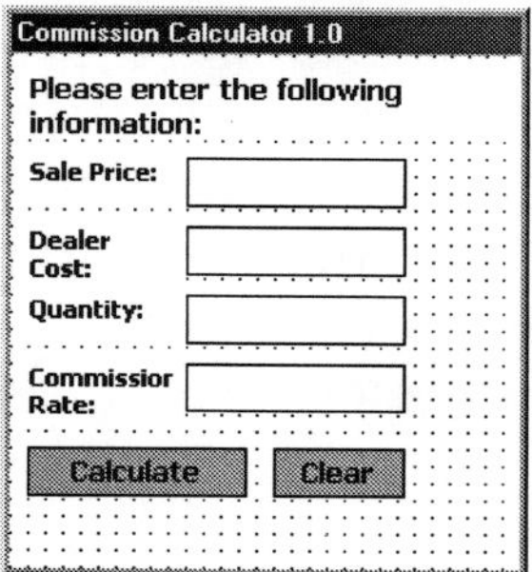

4. Double-click the **cmdCalculate** control to open the Code Window. Enter the following statements in the **cmdCalculate_Click** procedure.

```
'Declare the variables
Dim sale_price
Dim dealer_cost
Dim quantity
Dim commission_rate
Dim commission

'Initialize the variables
sale_price = txtSalePrice.Text
dealer_cost = txtDealerCost.Text
quantity = txtQuantity.Text
commission_rate = txtCommissionRate.Text

'Calculate commission
commission = (sale_price * commission_rate _
            + (sale_price - dealer_cost) * 0.05) * _
            quantity

'Display commission in a message box
MsgBox ("The commission is " & FormatCurrency(commission))
```

The MsgBox() function displays a brief message. It is often used to display an error or warning message. The FormatCurrency() function formats an expression as a currency value with a "$" sign.

5. Double-click **cmdClear** control to open the Code Window. Enter the following statements in the **cmdClear_Click** event procedure.

```
'Clear the textboxes
txtSalePrice.Text = ""
txtDealerCost.Text = ""
txtQuantity.Text = ""
txtCommissionRate.Text = ""
```

6. Save the form as **Calculator.ebf** and the project as **Calculator.efp**.
7. Select **Run | Start Debug** to compile the project. Your application should resemble Figure 7.

The commission calculator works well in most cases; however, if the salesperson forgets to enter a value or enters an invalid value (e.g., entering a letter instead of a number), a fatal error occurs. To prevent this from happening, we need to develop a mechanism to give the user a chance to correct the mistake before the error occurs. To do this, we need to check the values entered by the user before submitting the values for calculation.

Figure 7. Commission Calculator 1.0

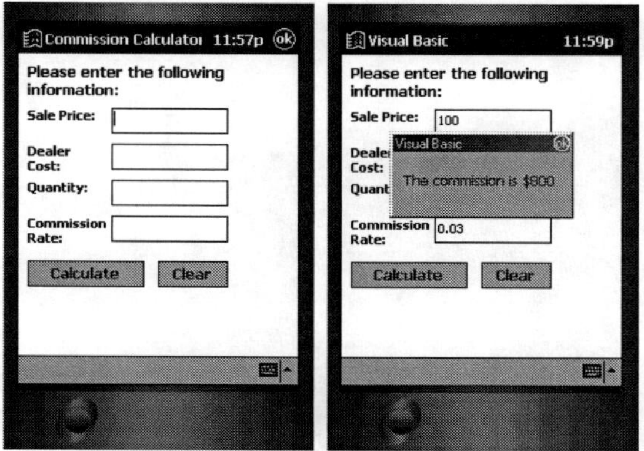

Condition Statement

If… Then … Else statement is one of the most important statements in any programming language. The statement allows the program to conditionally execute a block of statements. The condition statement contains logical expressions. For example, the condition may be "A = B". In this case, if the value of variable A is equal to the value of B, then the condition is "true", otherwise, the condition is "false". The syntax of the If … Then … Else statement is as follows:

```
If [condition] Then
            [statements]
{ElseIf [condition] Then
            [statements]}
{Else
            [statements]}
End If
```

Now, we are ready to improve the commission calculator.

1. Double-click **cmdCalculate** to open the Code Window. Add the high-lighted statements in the **cmdCalculate_Click** procedure.

```
Private Sub cmdCalculate_Click()
    'Declare the variables
    Dim sale_price
    Dim dealer_cost
    Dim quantity
    Dim commission_rate
    Dim commission

    'Check user input
    If txtSalePrice.Text = "" Then
        MsgBox ("You must enter the sale price!")
    ElseIf Not IsNumeric(txtSalePrice.Text) Then
        MsgBox ("You must enter a number for the sale price!")
    ElseIf txtDealerCost.Text = "" Then
        MsgBox ("You must enter the dealer cost!")
    ElseIf Not IsNumeric(txtDealerCost.Text) Then
        MsgBox ("You must enter a number for the dealer cost!")
    ElseIf txtQuantity.Text = "" Then
        MsgBox ("You must enter the quantity!")
    ElseIf Not IsNumeric(txtQuantity.Text) Then
        MsgBox ("You must enter a number for the quantity!")
    ElseIf txtCommissionRate.Text = "" Then
        MsgBox ("You must enter the commission rate!")
    ElseIf Not IsNumeric(txtCommissionRate.Text) Then
        MsgBox ("You must enter a number for the commission
rate!")
    Else

    'Initialize the variables
    sale_price = txtSalePrice.Text
    dealer_cost = txtDealerCost.Text
    quantity = txtQuantity.Text
    commission_rate = txtCommissionRate.Text

    'Calculate commission
    commission = (sale_price * commission_rate _
              + (sale_price - dealer_cost) * 0.05) * _
              quantity

    'Display commission in a message box
    MsgBox ("The commission is " & FormatCurrency(commission))

    End If

End Sub
```

2. Save and run the project.

Commission Calculator 2.0

The salespeople like the commission calculator we developed in the previous section, but they also pointed out that most sales involve multiple products. With the current commission calculator, the salesperson has to calculate the commission for each product separately and then add all the commissions together manually to get the total. The salespeople suggest that we improve the commission calculator by allowing them to enter multiple products for each sale.

Looping

Before we can do this, we need to introduce another important structure, looping or repetition. Looping will repeat a block of statement. There are a number of looping statements including "Do … Loop" and "For … Next".

When the number of times to repeat a block of statements is known, one can use "For …Next". The syntax of "For …Next" loop is as follows:

```
FOR [counter] = [start value] TO [end value] {STEP [step]}
    [statements]
NEXT [counter]
```

When the number of times to repeat a block of statements is unknown, one can use "Do … Loop". There are two types of "Do … Loop": "Do While …" and "Do Until …". The former repeats a block of statements while a certain condition is met while the latter repeats a block of statements until a certain condition is met. Their syntaxes are as follows:

```
DO WHILE/UNTIL [condition]
    [statements]
LOOP
or
DO
    [statements]
LOOP WHILE/UNTIL [condition]
```

Array

Another important concept that must be introduced here is the array. An array is a list of values refereed to by a variable name and a number enclosed in parentheses. Declaring an array will reserve a list of values in memory. Array is a data structure often used when you need to process a group of data with similar properties. The syntax of declaring an array is:

```
Dim Array(number) As Variant
```

To access a particular member of the array, one states the name of the array and the index. For example, productlist(0) is the first member of the array, productlist(5) refers to the sixth member of the array with the name "productlist", and so on.

Working with Multiple Forms

This project also involves multiple forms. When a new form is displayed, the current form must be hidden. You can use the following statements to accomplish these operations:

```
[form name].Hide
[form name].Show
```

The "Hide" method hides the form, and the "Show" method displays the new form. Another popular way to hide the current form is using the statement "Me.Hide". In this statement, "Me" refers to the current form.

We will need three forms in this project: commission form, data entry form, and result form. The data entry form will be displayed as long as the user still has product(s) to add.

Building the User Interface

1. Start eMbedded Visual Basic 3.0 and create a new project. Save the project as **Calculator2.efp.**
2. Change the **Name** property of the form to "**frmCommissionRate**" and **Text** property to "**Commission Calculator 2.0**".
3. Add a label, a textbox and a button. Change the properties of the controls according to the following table. Arrange the controls so that your form resembles the one in Figure 8.

Figure 8. Commission rate form

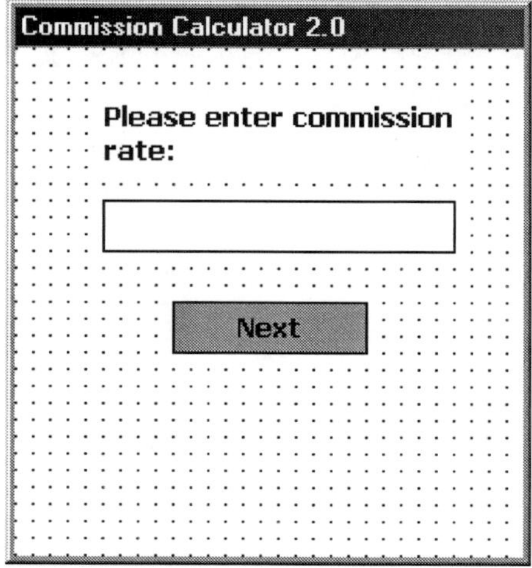

Control	Name	Text / Caption
Label1	lblInstruction	Please enter commission rate:
Text1	txtCommissionRate	<delete the default text>
Command1	cmdNext	Next

4. Select **Project | Add Form** to add a new form to the project.
5. Change the **Name** property of the form to "**frmData**" and the **Text** property to "**Commission Calculator 2.0**".
6. Add the following controls to **frmData**. Your form should resemble the form in Figure 9.

Control	Name	Text / Caption
Label1	lblProduct	Product:
Label2	lblPrice	Price:
Label3	lblCost	Cost:
Label4	lblQuanityt	Quantity:
Combo1	cboProduct	<delete the default text>
Text1	txtPrice	<delete the default text>
Text2	txtCost	<delete the default text>
Text3	txtQuantity	<delete the default text>
Command1	cmdCalculate	Calculate Commission
Command2	cmdEnterAnother	Enter Another Product

Figure 9. Data form

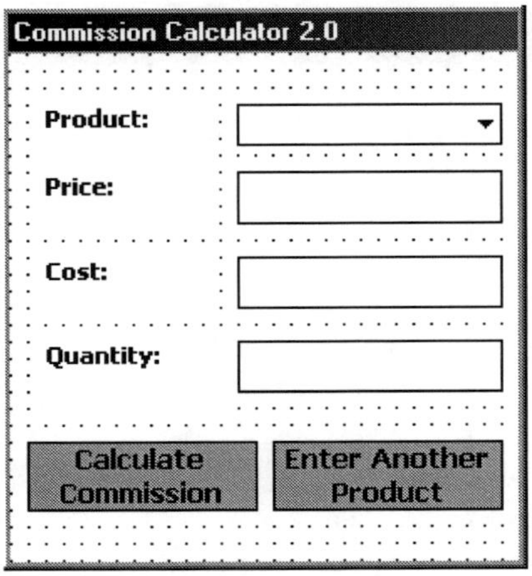

Figure 10. Result form

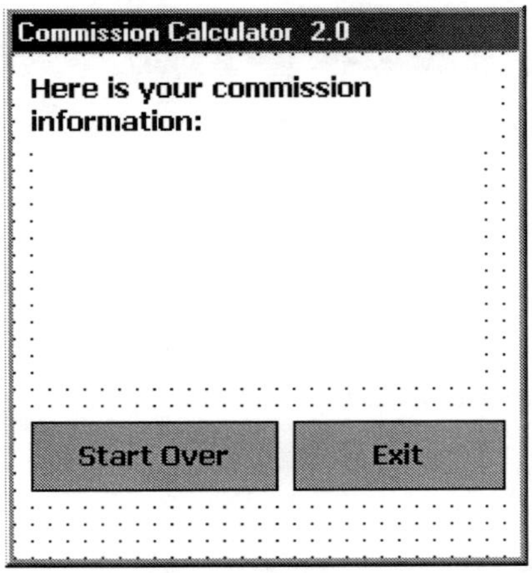

7. Select **Project | Add Form** to add a new form to the project.
8. Change the **Name** property of the form to "**frmResult**" and the **Text** property to "**Commission Calculator 2.0**".
9. Add the following controls to **frmResult**. Your form should resemble the form in Figure 10.

Control	Name	Text / Caption
Label1	lblCaption	Here is the commission information:
Label2	lblResult	<delete the default text>
Command1	cmdStartOver	Start Over
Command2	cmdExit	Exit

Programming Commission Calculator 2.0

The following pesudocode describes the basic operation of Commission Calculator 2.0.

When the user clicks the Next button in frmCommissionRate

Assign the commission rate entered by the user to a module-level variable

Hide frmCommissionRate

Show frmData

When frmData loads

Populate the ComboBox with product names

When the user clicks the Enter Another button in frmData

Assign data entered by the user to an array

Increment the index for the array by 1

Clear the form

When the user clicks the Calculate button in frmData

Calculate the commission for each product entered

Calculate the total commission

Display the result in lblResult of frmResult

Hide frmData

Show frmResult

When the user clicks the Start Over button in frmResult

Empty the array

Clear all fields in frmData

Hide frmResult

Show frmCommissionRate

When the user clicks the Exit button in frmResult

Figure 11. Adding a module to the project

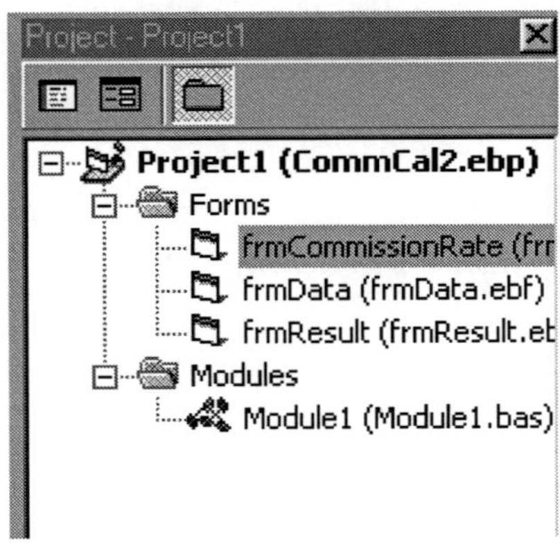

Terminate the application

1. Select **Project | Add Module**. Click **Open** in the New Module dialog. A new module will be added to your project. Your Project Window will resemble Figure 11.
2. Double-click **Module1** to open the Code Window. Type in the following statements in **Module1**. The variables defined in **Module1** are all module-level variables, which can be accessed by all objects in the application. Since most orders will have less than 20 products, it is safe to reserve space in memory for 20 values for the array. The variable I acts as the counter and the index for the array. The value 0 is assigned to I at the beginning of the program.

```
Option Explicit

'Declare module-level variables

Dim CommissionRate
Dim Product(20) As String
Dim Price(20) As Variant
Dim Cost(20) As Variant
Dim Quantity(20) As Variant
Dim I

I = 0
```

3. Double-click **cmdNext** control in **frmCommissionRate**. Type in the following statements in the **cmdNext_Click** event Code Window.

```
'Hide frmCommissionRate and show frmData

CommissionRate = txtCommissionRate.Text
Me.Hide
frmData.Show
```

When developing a mobile or wireless application, the developer should make every effort to minimize the amount of data input the user has to do as typing on wireless devices is both cumbersome and prone to errors. One way to reduce amount of data input is to use a selection box.

4. Double-click any empty space on **frmData** and type the following statements in the **Form_Load** procedure. AddItem method adds new items to the combo box.

```
'Add items to the combo box

   cboProduct.AddItem "10"" Christmas Tree"
   cboProduct.AddItem "JVC DVD Player"
```

5. Double-click **Module1** to open the Code Window. Append the following statements to the end of the code in the Code Window. Throughout the application, the fields in **frmData** will be cleared several times. To save coding time, we have created a public function called **ClearFields** in **Module1**. The function can be accessed anywhere in the application.

```
Sub ClearFields()

'Clear all text boxes

frmData.cboProduct.ListIndex = 0
frmData.txtPrice.Text = ""
frmData.txtCost.Text = ""
frmData.txtQuantity.Text = ""

End Sub
```

6. Close the Code Window and double-click **cmdEnterAnother** control to open the Code Window for **cmdEnterAnother_Click** event procedure. Enter the following statements in the procedure.

```
'Assign values to the arrays

Product(I) = cboProduct.List(cboProduct.ListIndex)
Price(I) = txtPrice.Text
Cost(I) = txtCost.Text
Quantity(I) = txtQuantity.Text

'Increment the index by 1

I = I + 1

'Call the ClearFields function

ClearFields
```

7. Close the Code Window and double-click **cmdCalculate**. Type in the following statements in the **cmdCalculate_Click** event procedure.

```
Private Sub cmdCalculate_Click()

'Declare variables

Dim counter As Integer
Dim Result As String
Dim Commission
Dim TotalCommission = 0

'Assign the last set of values to the array

Product(I) = cboProduct.List(cboProduct.ListIndex)
Price(I) = txtPrice.Text
Cost(I) = txtCost.Text
Quantity(I) = txtQuantity.Text

'Print result heading

Result = "Product Name | Commission" & Chr(13) + Chr(10) & _
"--------------------------------------" & Chr(13) + Chr(10)

'Calculate commission(s)

For counter = 0 To I
    Commission = (Price(counter) * CommissionRate + _
    (Price(counter) - Cost(counter)) * 0.05) * Quantity(counter)
    Result = Result & Product(counter) & " | " & _
    Commission & Chr(13) + Chr(10)
    TotalCommission = TotalCommission + Commission
Next
Result = Result & "Total | " & TotalCommission

'Display results in frmResult

Me.Hide
frmResult.lblResult.Caption = Result
frmResult.Show

End Sub
```

There are a number of special characters that are useful in displaying content in eVB. "Chr(13) + Chr(10)" represents the carriage return – linefeed combination.

8. Open **frmResult** and double-click **cmdStartOver** on the form to open the Code Window for **cmdStartOver_Click** event. Enter the following statements in the event.

```
'Reset values for the array

Dim counter As Integer
For counter = 0 To I
    Product(counter) = ""
    Price(counter) = ""
    Cost(counter) = ""
    Quantity(counter) = ""
Next
I = 0
Me.Hide
ClearFields
frmCommissionRate.Show
```

9. Double-click **cmdExit** to open the Code Window for **cmdExit_Click** event. Enter the following statements in the **cmdExit_Click** procedure.

```
'End the application
App.End
```

10. Debug the application and run the application. You will be allowed to enter multiple items in the commission calculator. The commission calculator will provide you with a summary of your commission information as shown in Figure 12.

Order Placement System (OPS)

The salespeople at Network Solutions travel to their clients' sites regularly and would like to have an application that allows them to record orders on the road. One requirement for the application is that data entry be easy. In order to reduce the amount of data that needs to be entered, we decide to use drop down boxes for entering customer names and product names. As the lists of customers and products change periodically, we decide to dynamically populate the two lists by reading from two text files (product.txt and customer.txt).

Figure 12. Commission Calculator 2.0

Salespeople can periodically update the product and customer lists by saving the new files on their handheld devices. Orders will be recorded in another text file (order.txt). Order.txt can be modified as needed by salespeople.

Working with Sequential Files

Accessing a file is an important operation in eVB. Since most Pocket PC devices have limited main memory and processing power, a sequential file is probably the most efficient way to store and process data as it requires little processing power. The most common operations that one can perform on a file are reading, writing and appending. In this section, we will discuss how eVB programs interact with flat files.

To interact with a file, you need to use the "Microsoft CE File System Control 3.0". This control can be added to the toolbox by selecting **Project | Components** in the menu, checking the check box beside "**Microsoft CE File System Control 3.0**", and clicking "**OK**". Before a file can be accessed, the file must be open first. The syntax for opening a file is as follows:

```
File1.Open "[path and file name]", [mode]
```

When the application finishes using the file or wants to use the file in another mode, the file should be closed. The syntax for closing a file is:

```
File1.Close
```

The mode determines how you will read or write files. The three common modes used to manipulate files are "FsModeInput" (input), "FsModeOutput" (output), and "FsModeAppend" (append).

When using "FsModeInput", you can use Input, InputB, LineInputString, and InputFields methods to read data from a file. The InputFields method reads data from a sequential file and returns a single dimension variant array. The syntax for using this method is:

```
File1.InputFields([number])
```

The number refers to the number of comma-delimited fields to read from the file. For example, File1.InputFields(50) will read the first 50 comma-delimited fields from the file and store them in an one-dimensional array.

When using the "FsModeOutput" mode, you can use LinePrint and WriteFields methods. The LinePrint method writes a single line to a sequential file. The syntax for using the LinePrint method is:

```
File1.LinePrint([output])
```

The "FsModeAppend" also allows you to use LinePrint and WriteFields methods, and its syntax is the same as that of the "FsModeOutput" mode. For example, the syntax for writing a single line to a sequential file is:

```
File1.LinePrint([output])
```

However, the difference between the "FsModeOutput" mode and "FsModeAppend" mode is that the former overwrites the content of the sequential file while the latter appends to the existing sequential file.

To illustrate the techniques for accessing a file using a pocket PC application, let us work on the following project.

Creating the Sequential Files

We will start the OPS project by creating three text files.

1. Launch File Explorer in your PocketPC or emulator. Navigate to My Documents folder.
2. Click the blank space on the screen. A shortcut menu appears.
3. Select **New Folder** to create a new folder. Name the folder "Order".
4. Click **Start | Programs**.
5. Click the PocketWord icon to launch PocketWord. PocketWord is a built-in text editor for PocketPCs.
6. Click **New** to begin a new file.
7. Type the following text in the work area. Product names are separated by ","s.

HP iPAQ H3950 Pocket PC, T-Mobile 6210 BlackBerry, Palm Tungsten C Handheld, NEC MobilePro 900, Belkin Flip Case, Socket 10/100 Ethernet CF Card, Sandisk 64MB Compact Flash Card, Viking 128MB Compact Flash Card, Motorola Talkabout T5420 Radio

8. Select **New** from the menu. You will be prompted to save the file.
9. Select **Save As....**
10. Type "**product**" for name.
11. Select "**order**" as the folder.
12. Select "**Plain Text Document (*.txt)**" for file type.
13. Click **OK**.

Repeat steps 7 through 13 to create customer.txt and order.txt. Leave order.txt blank as no order has been placed yet. Type the following text in customer.txt. Customer names are separated by ","s.

AAA Company, Corporate Design, Hansen Company

Figure 13. Entrance form with the timer control

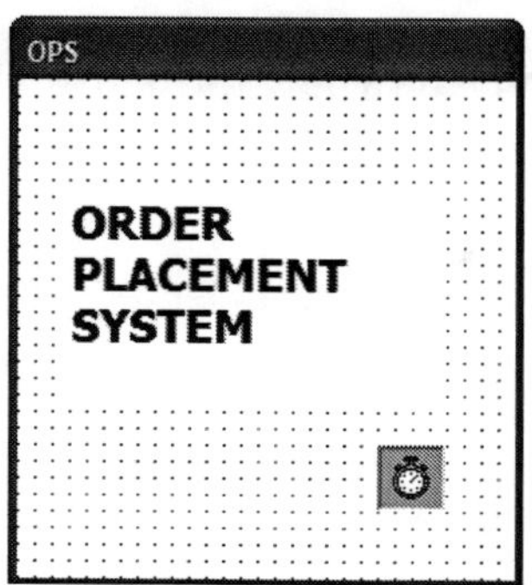

Creating an Entrance Form

1. Start eMbedded Visual Basic 3.0 and create a new project. Save the project as **Order.efp.**
2. Change the Name property of the form to **frmEntrance** and Caption property to **OPS**, which stands for Order Placement System.
3. Add a **Label** and **Timer** control. Change the properties of the controls according to the following table. Arrange the controls so that your form resembles the one in Figure 13.

Control	Name	Text / Caption
Form	FrmEntrance	OPS
Label1	Label1	Order Placement System (Tahoma, 16, bold)
Timer1	Timer1	

4. Set the **Interval** property of **Timer1** to **3000**. The Interval property of the timer control determines length of time elapses before an action is performed.
5. Double-click on Timer1 to open the Code Window. Type in the following statements in the Timer1_Timer event.

```
Private Sub Timer1_Timer()

'Automatically show frmNewOrder after 3 seconds

   frmEntrance.Hide
   frmNewOrder.Show
   Timer1.Enabled = False
End Sub
```

Creating the New Order Form

The entrance form will be hid and a new form, frmNewOrder, will appear after three seconds. Let's create frmNewOrder, in which new orders can be recorded.

1. Select **Project | Add Form** to add a new form to the project.
2. Change the **Name** property of the form to "**frmNewOrder**" and the **Text** property to "**OPS**".
3. Add the following controls to **frmNewOrder**.

Control	Name	Text / Caption
Form	FrmNewOrder	New Orders
Label1	Label1	Please fill out the form below to enter an order:
Label2	Label2	Customer:
Label3	Label3	Product:
Label4	Label4	Quantity:
Command1	cmdOrder	Save Order
Command2	cmdViewOrders	View Orders

In order to work with sequential files, a new control called File control needs to be added. The File control is not visible during run time.

4. Select **Project | Components** to open the Components dialog. Check the box beside "**Microsoft CE File System Control 3.0**". Click "**OK**". The File control appears in the toolbox.
5. Double-click the **File** control to add it to the form. Your form should resemble the form in Figure 14.

The following pseudocode describes the basic operation of the new order form.

Figure 14. New order form

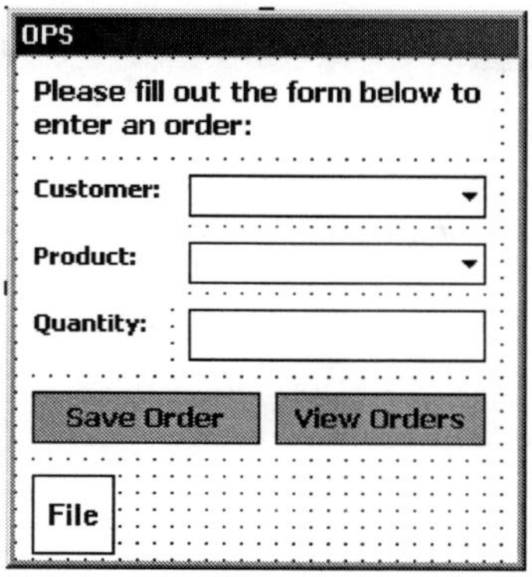

When frmNewOrder loads

Read customer.txt

Populate the Customer ComboBox

Read product.txt

Populate the Product ComboBox

When the user clicks the Save Order button

Write the order in order.txt

When the user clicks the View Orders button

Hide frmNewOrder

Read order.txt

Show frmViewOrders

When frmNewOrder is loaded, the form reads from two text files: customer.txt and product.txt. The two files will populate the two drop down lists on the form so that the user does not have to go through the cumbersome process of typing the words on a Pocket PC, and it also eliminates chance of making errors while typing.

6. Double-click any empty space in frmNewOrder to open the Code Window. Select "**Form**" as the object and "**Load**" as the procedure. Type in the following statements in the **Form_Load** procedure (see following page).

```
'Declare variables

Dim myArray As Variant
Dim myString As String
Dim I As Integer
I = 0

'Read the data in customer.txt into myArray.
'Populate cboCustomer with the data.

File1.Open "\My Documents\Order\customer.txt", fsModeInput
myArray = File1.InputFields(250)
myString = "start value"
I = 0
Do
    myString = myArray(I)
    If Len(Trim(myString)) > 0 Then
        cboCustomer.AddItem myString
    End If
    I = I + 1
Loop While myString <> ""

'Close file
File1.Close

'Read the data in product.txt into myArray.
'Populate cboProduct with the data.

File1.Open "\My Documents\Order\product.txt", fsModeInput
myArray = File1.InputFields(250)
myString = "start value"
I = 0
Do Until myString = ""
    myString = myArray(I)
    If Len(Trim(myString)) > 0 Then
        cboProduct.AddItem myString
    End If
    I = I + 1
Loop

'Close file
File1.Close

'Display the first elements of both ComboBoxes
cboCustomer.ListIndex = 0
cboProduct.ListIndex = 0
```

7. Double-click **frmNewOrder** in the Project Explorer to switch to the Design View.
8. Double-click **cmdOrder** button to open the Code Window. Type the following statements in the **cmdOrder_Click** procedure.

```
Dim a, b

'Check user input
If txtQuantity.Text = "" Then
    MsgBox ("You must enter the quantity!")
ElseIf Not IsNumeric(txtQuantity.Text) Then
    MsgBox ("You must enter a number for quantity!")
Else

'Write the order to order.txt
    File1.Open "\My Documents\Order\order.txt", fsModeAppend
    a = cboCustomer.ListIndex
    b = cboProduct.ListIndex
    File1.LinePrint (Now())
    File1.LinePrint ("Customer: " & cboCustomer.List(a))
    File1.LinePrint ("Product: " & cboProduct.List(b))
    File1.LinePrint ("Quantity: " & txtQuantity.Text)
    File1.LinePrint (" ")
    File1.Close
    MsgBox ("This order has been saved")

'Reset the order form
    cboCustomer.ListIndex = 0
    cboProduct.ListIndex = 0
    txtQuantity.Text = ""
End If
```

9. Double-click **frmNewOrder** to return to the form. Double-click **cmdViewOrders** to open the Code Window. Type in the following statements in the **cmdViewOrders_Click** procedure.

```
'Show orders

frmNewOrder.Hide
ReadFile
frmViewOrders.Show
```

The statement “ReadFile” refers to a procedure that will read from the order.txt. After reading the file, the content of the file will be displayed in the next form, frmViewOrders. Since this operation involves multiple forms, we will create a procedure in the module. Notice that we place the name of the form in front of the object and property (e.g., frmViewOrders.txtOrder.Text) to tell the compiler in which form the object is located.

10. Select **Project | Add Module**. Click **Open** in the New Module dialog box. A new module will be added to your project.
11. Double-click **Module1** to open the Code Window. Create a **ReadFile** procedure by typing in the following statements in **Module1**.

```
Public Sub ReadFile()

'A function to read order.txt

    frmViewOrders.txtOrders.Text = ""
    frmViewOrders.File1.Open "\My Documents\Order\order.txt", _
    fsModeInput
    Do While Not frmViewOrders.File1.EOF
        If frmViewOrders.txtOrders.Text = "" Then
            frmViewOrders.txtOrders.Text = _
            frmViewOrders.File1.LineInputString
        Else
            frmViewOrders.txtOrders.Text = _
            frmViewOrders.txtOrders.Text & Chr(13) + Chr(10) & _
            frmViewOrders.File1.LineInputString
        End If
    Loop
    frmViewOrders.File1.Close

End Sub
```

Create the View Orders Form

Now we are ready to create the last form in this application. The last form allows the user to review all recorded orders, make any necessary changes, save the changes to order.txt, and delete orders when they have been processed. These functions are similar to those functions found in a text editor program.

1. Select **Project | Add Form** to add a new form to the project.
2. Change the **Name** property of the form to "**frmViewOrders**" and the **Text** property to "**OPS**".
3. Add the following controls to **frmViewOrders**. Since we will be interacting with a text file, order.txt, we will need to add the **File** control to the form as well. Your form should resemble the form in Figure 15.

Control	Name	Text / Caption
Form	frmViewOrders	View Orders
Label1	Label1	The following orders have been saved:
TextBox1	txtOrders	<delete the default text>
Command1	cmdSaveChanges	Save Changes
Command2	cmdNewOrder	New Order
Command3	cmdDelete	Delete All Orders
File1	File1	

Figure 15. View orders form

Form1

The following orders have been saved:

Save Changes | New Order

Delete All Orders | File

The following pseudocode describes the basic operation of the View Orders form:

```
When frmViewOrders loads
    Set I to "0" (The changes have not been saved)
When the user clicks the Save Changes button
    Overwrite order.txt to save changes
When the user clicks the New Order button
    If I = 0
            Ask the user whether the changes need to be saved
                If Yes
                    Save changes
                    Hide frmViewOrders
                    Show frmNewOrder
                If No
                    Hide frmViewOrders
                    Show frmNewOrder
    Else
            Hide frmViewOrders
            Show frmNewOrder
When the user clicks the Delete All Orders button
    Delete all content in order.txt
    Set I to "1"
```

One important consideration in creating a text editor is that precautions must be taken incase that the user forgets to save the changes before exiting the form. In this case, we want users to be reminded to save the changes before exiting the form unless the "Save Changes" button has been clicked. In order to do that, we need to use a simple variable to record whether the changes have been saved. The variable will have the value of either 1 (Changes have been saved) or 0 (Changes have not been saved). The variable needs to be accessed by all the objects on frmViewOrders.

4. Double-click anywhere on the form to open the Code Window. Scroll up to the top of the Code Window. Insert the following statement in the next line after "Option Explicit".

```
Dim I As Integer
```

When the form is loaded, the value of "I" should be initialized to "0".

5. Select "**Form**" from the object box and "**Load**" from the procedure box to create the **Form_Load** procedure. Type in the following statement in the **Form_Load** procedure.

```
I = 0
```

As the operation of saving changes will be performed every time the user exits the form, a procedure called "SaveChanges" is created so that the procedure can be reused when needed.

6. Press "**Enter**" key to insert a new line in the Code Window. Enter the following statements. The Code Window will automatically add the dividing lines for the new procedure.

```
Sub SaveChanges()

'Save the file with changes

    File1.Open "\My Documents\Order\order.txt", fsModeOutput
    File1.LinePrint (txtOrders.Text)
    File1.Close
    MsgBox ("The changes have been saved")
    I = 1
End Sub
```

7. Switch to the form window. Double-click the "**Save Changes**" button to create the **cmdSaveChanges_Click** procedure in the Code Window. Enter the following procedure call in the procedure.

```
'Call the SaveChanges procedure
SaveChanges
```

8. Switch to the form window. Double-click the "**New Order**" button to create the **cmdNewOrder_Click** procedure in the Code Window. Enter the following statements in the procedure.

```
Dim Response As Integer
If I = 0 Then
    Response = _
    MsgBox("Do you want to save your changes?", vbYesNoCancel)

    Select Case Response

'If the user click "Yes"
        Case 6
            SaveChanges
            frmViewOrders.Hide
            frmNewOrder.Show
            I = 0

'If the user click "No"
        Case 7
            frmViewOrders.Hide
            frmNewOrder.Show
            I = 0
    End Select
Else
    frmViewOrders.Hide
    frmNewOrder.Show
    I = 0
End If
```

9. Switch to the form window. Double-click the "**Delete All Orders**" button to create the **cmdDelete_Click** procedure in the Code Window. Enter the following statements in the procedure.

```
'Delete everything from order.txt

txtOrders.Text = ""
File1.Open "\My Documents\Order\order.txt", fsModeOutput
File1.LinePrint (txtOrders.Text)
File1.Close
I = 1
```

The Order Placement System is completed. Save the project and debug the application.

Creating a WinSock Internet Connection

The salespeople like the OPS, but they also have a couple of suggestions. They would like to be able to get product specifications from the corporate server via the Internet if they can get Internet access at the client's site. They also would like to have expandable menus instead of command buttons so that there is a bigger display screen. With a bigger display screen, the user can use the internal keyboard for data entry and editing.

The WinSock control is used to provide two-way communication between a Windows CE-based device and another computer. Like file control, the WinSock control needs to be added to the standard toolbox and is invisible to the user. When using the WinSock control, you must first specify the RemoteHost name and RemotePort. The RemoteHost refers to the name of the server to connect to, and RemotePort refers to the Socket port number that the Web server uses. Common port numbers are 80 and 8080. You will then use the Connect method to create a connection to the server. The SendData method can be used to send an HTTP request through the connection. The verb "GET" is used in the HTTP request followed by the path of the resource requested.

Creating the Product Specification Form

Now let's create the product specification function. A new form needs to be created to display the product specification.

1. Select **Project | Add Form** to add a new form to the project.
2. Change the **Name** property of the form to "**frmProductSpec**" and the **Text** property to "**Product Spec**".
3. Add the following controls to **frmProductSpec**. Your form should resemble the form in Figure 16.

Control	Name	Text / Caption
Label1	Label1	Product Specification:
TextBox1	TxtProductSpec	<delete the default text>
Command1	CmdClose	Close

Figure 16. Product specification form

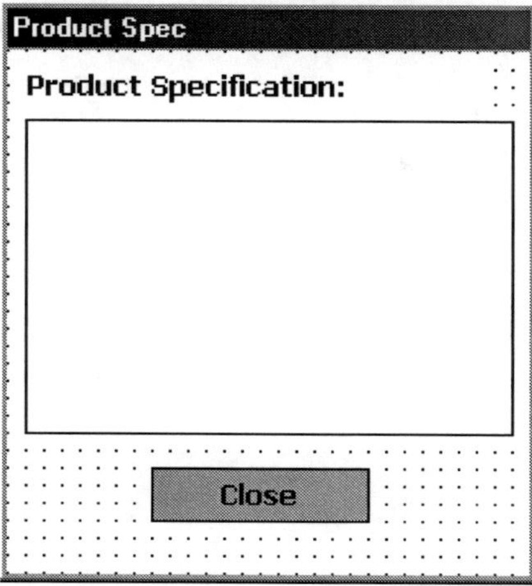

4. Double-click **cmdClose** to open the Code Window. Type in the following statements in the **cmdClose_Click** procedure. The statements will clear the textbox and hide the product specification form.

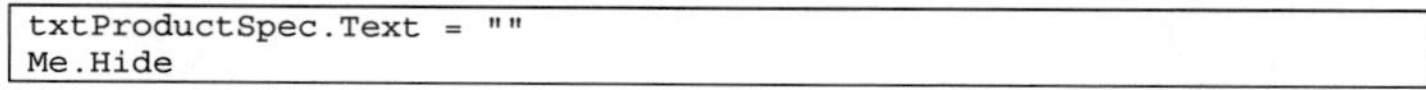

```
txtProductSpec.Text = ""
Me.Hide
```

Modifying the Order Entry Form

Now we need to add a new button and a WinSock control to the order entry form.

1. Double-click **frmNewOrder** in the Project Explorer to open the form. Add a new command button control. Change the **Name** property of the control to "**cmdGetSpec**" and the **Caption** property to "**Get Product Specifications**".
2. Select **Project | Components** to open the Components dialog. Check the box beside "**Microsoft CE WinSock Control 3.0**". Click "**OK**". The Winsock control appears in the toolbox.
3. Double-click the **WinSock** control to add it to the form. Your form should resemble the form in Figure 17.

Figure 17. New Orders form with the Winsock control

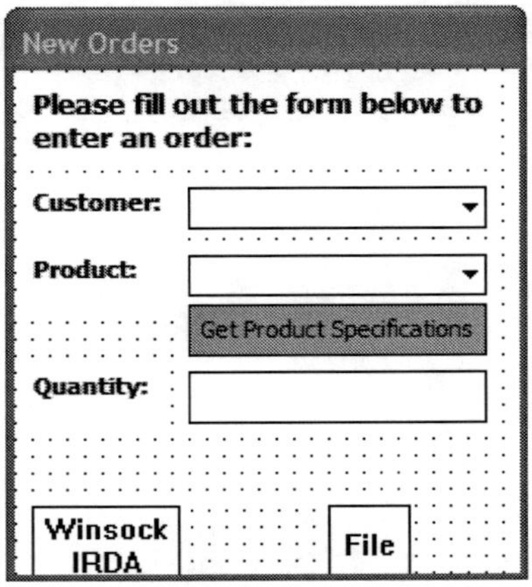

4. Double-click **cmdGetSpec** to open the Code Window. Enter the following statements in the **cmdGetSpec_Click** procedure.

```
Dim s
Dim resource As String

WinSock1.RemoteHost = "NameOfYourWebServer"
WinSock1.RemotePort = 80

WinSock1.Connect

resource = "/foldername/product" & cboProduct.ListIndex & _
    ".html"
s = "GET " & resource & vbCrLf & vbCrLf

WinSock1.SendData s

End Sub
```

5. Save and debug the project.

Creating Menus

In eVB, drop-down menus can be created programmatically using the "Microsoft CE Menubar Control 3.0". Before you can use the menubar control, you will need to add it to the standard toolbox. Following the steps below to add a Menubar control to the project.

1. Double-click **frmNewOrder** in the Project Explorer to open the form.
2. Select **Project | Components** to open the Components dialog box. Check the box beside "**Microsoft CE Menubar Control 3.0**". Click "**OK**". The Menubar control appears in the toolbox.
3. Double-click the **Menubar** control to add it to the form.

The menus will appear when the form is loaded so that the statements to create the menus will appear in Form_Load() procedure. Repeat steps 1 through 3 for frmViewOrders.

Modifying the Order Entry Form

We will replace cmdSaveOrder and cmdViewOrders with an expandable menu in the order entry form; therefore, we will delete the two command buttons. Modify frmNewOrder so that it resembles the form in Figure 18.

Modifying the View Orders Form

We will replace cmdSaveChanges, cmdNewOrder, and cmdDelete with an expandable menu in the view order form; therefore, we will delete these three command buttons. Modify your frmViewOrders so that it resembles the form in Figure 19.

Figure 18. Revised New Order form

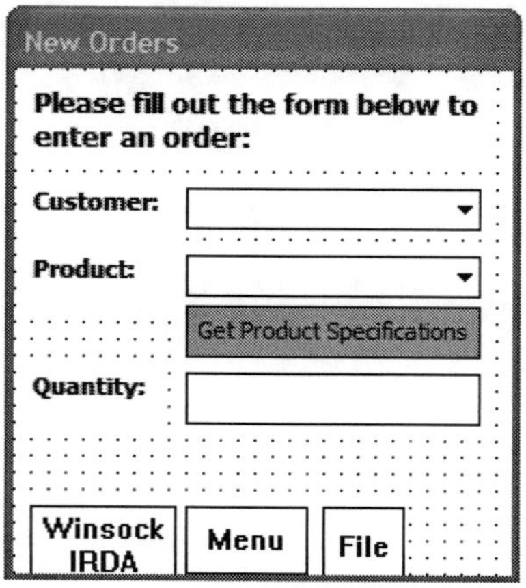

Figure 19. Revised View Orders form

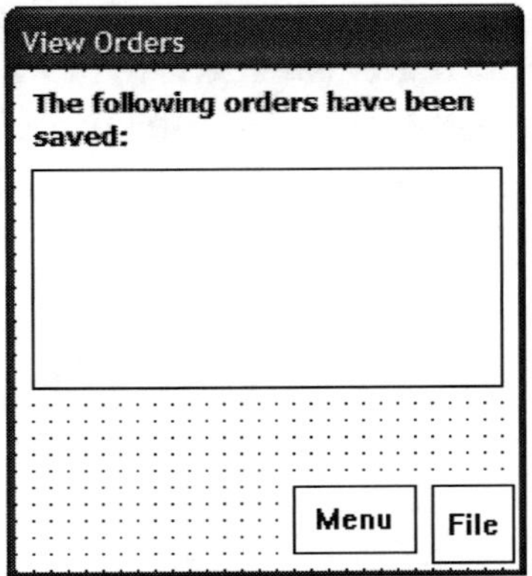

Adding Menus

In eVB, you need to add menu bars programmatically. The menu bars will be added to the application when the form loads; therefore, the statements that add menu bars will appear in Form_Load() procedure. Follow the steps below to add the menu in the New Order form.

1. Double-click **frmNewOrder** to display the form in the work area. Double-click anywhere on the form to open the Code Window. Add the highlighted statements in the **Form_Load** procedure.

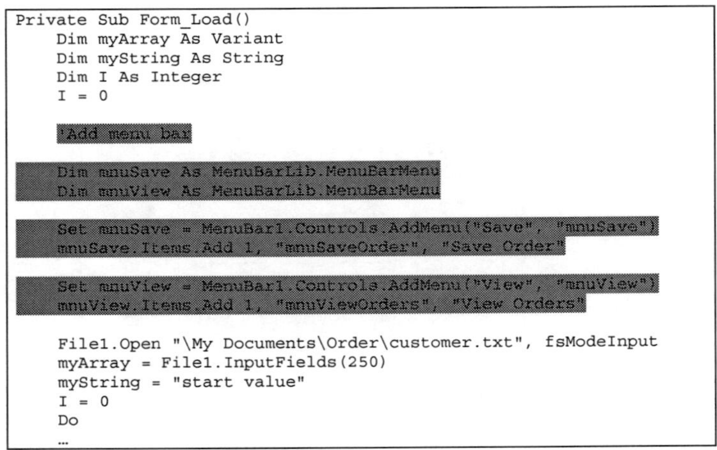

```
Private Sub Form_Load()
    Dim myArray As Variant
    Dim myString As String
    Dim I As Integer
    I = 0

    'Add menu bar

    Dim mnuSave As MenuBarLib.MenuBarMenu
    Dim mnuView As MenuBarLib.MenuBarMenu

    Set mnuSave = MenuBar1.Controls.AddMenu("Save", "mnuSave")
    mnuSave.Items.Add 1, "mnuSaveOrder", "Save Order"

    Set mnuView = MenuBar1.Controls.AddMenu("View", "mnuView")
    mnuView.Items.Add 1, "mnuViewOrders", "View Orders"

    File1.Open "\My Documents\Order\customer.txt", fsModeInput
    myArray = File1.InputFields(250)
    myString = "start value"
    I = 0
    Do
    …
```

The highlighted statements will add a menu bar to the form. Debug the project, and your new order form will resemble the one in Figure 20. As you can see, now the form has space for the internal keyboard.

Actions will be performed when the menu items are clicked. We will now assign actions to the menu items.

2. Stop debugging the project.
3. Double-click anywhere on **frmNewOrder** to open the Code Window.
4. Replace the procedure name "**cmdSaveOrder_Click()**" with "**SaveOrder()**"
5. Replace the procedure name "**cmdViewOrders_Click()**" with "**ViewOrders()**"
6. Double-click **frmNewOrder** in the project explorer to display the form in the work area.
7. Double-click **MenuBar1** to open the Code Window. Change the procedure to "**MenuClick**". This will create a new procedure called "**MenuBar1_MenuClick**".

Figure 20. New Orders form with menu

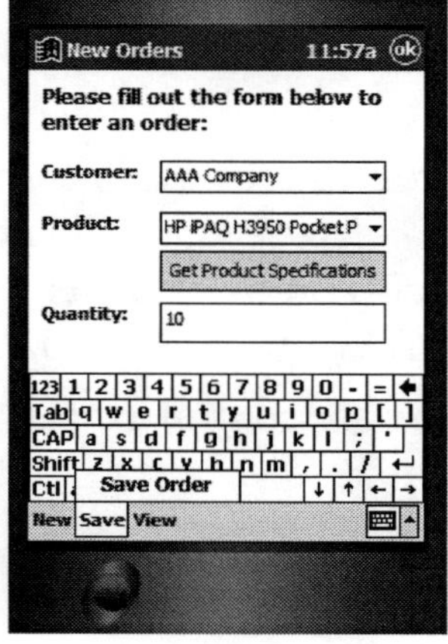

8. Enter the highlighted statements in the procedure.

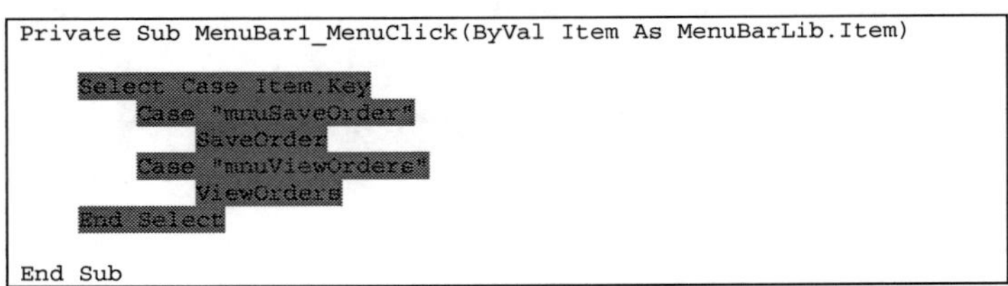

```
Private Sub MenuBar1_MenuClick(ByVal Item As MenuBarLib.Item)

    Select Case Item.Key
        Case "mnuSaveOrder"
            SaveOrder
        Case "mnuViewOrders"
            ViewOrders
    End Select

End Sub
```

9. Double-click **frmViewOrders** in the project explorer to display the form in the work area.
10. Double-click anywhere on the form to open the Code Window. Enter the highlighted statements in the **Form_Load** procedure. The statements add a menu with two separators.

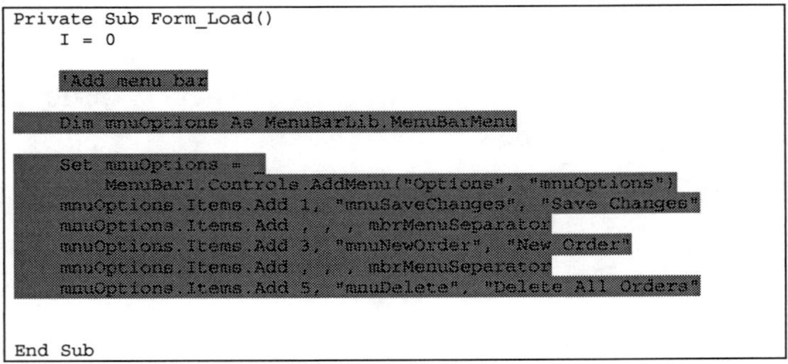

```
Private Sub Form_Load()
    I = 0

    'Add menu bar

    Dim mnuOptions As MenuBarLib.MenuBarMenu

    Set mnuOptions = _
        MenuBar1.Controls.AddMenu("Options", "mnuOptions")
    mnuOptions.Items.Add 1, "mnuSaveChanges", "Save Changes"
    mnuOptions.Items.Add , , , mbrMenuSeparator
    mnuOptions.Items.Add 3, "mnuNewOrder", "New Order"
    mnuOptions.Items.Add , , , mbrMenuSeparator
    mnuOptions.Items.Add 5, "mnuDelete", "Delete All Orders"

End Sub
```

11. Debug the program. Your view order form should resemble the one in Figure 21.
12. Stop debugging the program. Double-click **frmViewOrders** in the project explorer to display the form in the work area.
13. Double-click anywhere on the form to open the Code Window. Delete the **cmdSaveChanges_Click** procedure. Change the procedure name from "**cmdNewOrder_Click()**" to "**NewOrder**". Change the procedure name from "**cmdDelete_Click()**" to "**DeleteAll**".
14. Double-click the **Menubar** control to open the Code Window. Change the event to "**MenuClick**".

Figure 21. View Orders form with menu

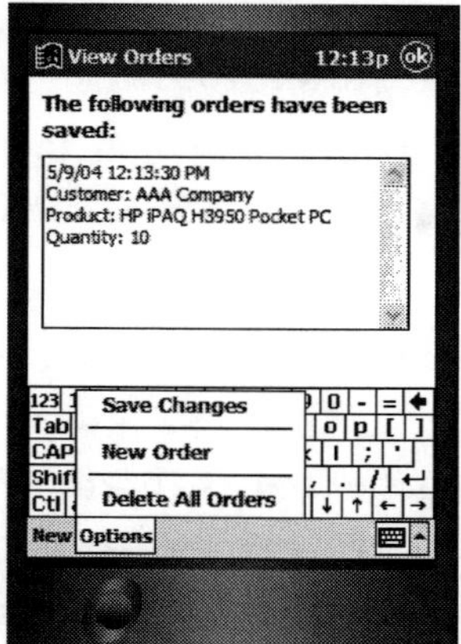

15. Enter the highlighted statements in the **MenuBar1_MenuClick** procedure.

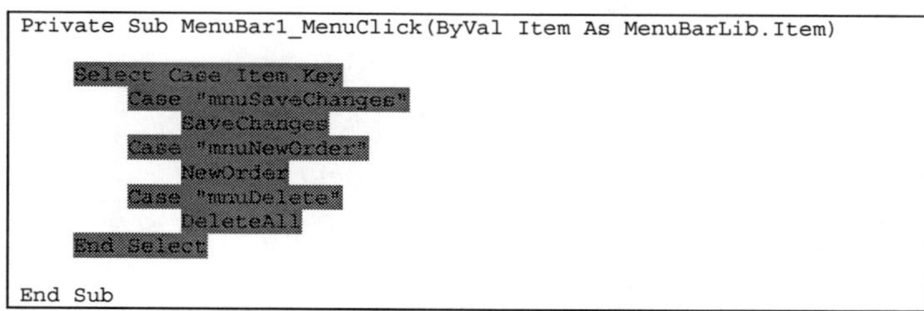

```
Private Sub MenuBar1_MenuClick(ByVal Item As MenuBarLib.Item)

    Select Case Item.Key
        Case "mnuSaveChanges"
            SaveChanges
        Case "mnuNewOrder"
            NewOrder
        Case "mnuDelete"
            DeleteAll
    End Select

End Sub
```

16. Save and debug the project.

Creating Setup Files

To easy distribute and install the application, you will need to create setup files for your application. EVB provides an Application Install Wizard that takes you through the steps for creating setup files for your application. Let's create setup files for the order placement system we created in the previous sections.

Step-by-step:

1. Select **File | Make** to create an .vb file for your project.
2. Select **Tools | Remote Tools | Application Install Wizard** from the menu bar.
3. Click "**Next**" to begin.
4. Locate the project file (order.ebp) using the **Browse** button. Click "**Next**" to continue.
5. Locate the .vb file using the **Browse** button. Click "**Next**" to continue.
6. Select an output directory for the setup files. Click "**Next**" to continue.
7. Select "**ARM 1100 (4K) v3.00**" as the CPU. This is the CPU used in the Compaq iPAQ Pocket PC. Click "**Next**" to continue.
8. Select "**Microsoft CE File Control 3.0**", "**Microsoft CE Image Control 3.0**", "**Microsoft CE WinSock Control 3.0**", and "**Microsoft PocketPC MenuBar Control 3.0**". Click "**Next**" to continue.
9. Click "**Next**" to continue.
10. Type "**OPS**" as the default Install Directory.
11. Type "**OPS**" as the application name.
12. Type " **Order Placement System**" as description.
13. Type "**Wireless Solutions**" as company name.
14. Click "**Next**" to continue.
15. Click "**Create Install**" to create the setup files.
16. Click "**Finish**" to close the Application Install Wizard.

Summary

This chapter introduces you to the techniques for developing mobile applications using Microsoft Embedded Visual Tools. Unlike wireless applications, mobile applications can function on mobile devices without a network connection. Embedded Visual Tools is a free tool designed to develop applications that run on Windows CE devices. It supports both Embedded Visual Basic (eVB) and Embedded Visual C++ (eVC).

This chapter discusses some of the most important eVB concepts including variables, control structures (e.g., choice and repetition), and arrays. You will also learn how to interact with sequential files using the File control, how to connect your applications to the Internet using the HTTP WinSock control, and how to develop menu-driven user interface for your applications. While Microsoft Embedded Visual Tools provide a free and relatively effective tool for creating mobile applications, they also have many limitations. Many of these limitations are addressed by Microsoft's latest development tool, Visual Studio .NET, which is discussed in detail in the next chapter.

Project

Create a mobile application that allows a warehouse manager to manage information about the inventory of the warehouse using a Pocket PC device. Inventory information is stored in a master file named INVENTORY.TXT. The application let the manager read from and write to the file. A menu allows the manager to access the various features of the application. The application should have the following features:

Inventory Check: This feature allows the manager to obtain a detailed list of items in the warehouse including item name, description, quantity, location, and value.

Update Inventory: This feature allows the manager to update information about an item in the inventory. The manager can update the quantity, location and value of the item.

Total Value: This feature calculates the total value of the inventory in dollar amount.

Use the techniques discussed in this chapter to develop the mobile application described above.

Chapter X

Mobile Application Development II: Developing Smart Device Applications Using Visual Studio .NET

In this chapter, you will:

- Learn how to develop smart device applications using Visual Studio .NET
- Learn to work with SQL Server CE databases
- Learn to develop user interfaces in the Design View of Visual Studio .NET
- Learn to use the SqlCeConnection, SqlCeCommand, and SqlCeDataReader objects to develop database-driven mobile applications

Introduction

In the previous chapter on mobile application development, we developed an order placement system (OPS) using Microsoft Embedded Visual Basic (EVB). Although EVB provides developers with the basic tools for developing mobile applications, it has many limitations. Microsoft Visual Studio .NET 2003 addresses these limitations by including tools for developing smart device applications. Using these tools, developers can create mobile applications for PocketPCs or other Windows CE devices with relative ease and flexibility. Similar to EVB, Visual Studio .NET uses a form-based approach to build applications and provides developers with WYSIWYG tools for user interface development, but as you will find in this chapter, it not only provides many new tools to enrich the application but also simplifies many tasks that are cumbersome in EVB (i.e., creating menus and interacting with databases). Furthermore, Visual Studio .NET allows developers to use a number of different programming languages including Visual Basic and C# to develop applications so that developers can leverage their existing programming skill sets. To illustrate how Visual Studio .NET can be deployed to develop mobile applications, we will develop an upgraded version of the OPS in this chapter. In order to provide a better comparison between Visual Studio .NET and EVB, we will use Visual Basic as the programming language in this project.

Order Placement System

There are a couple of major upgrades in the new OPS over the previous version. First, the new system will have a more usable interface, which effectively reduces key-stroke requirements and improves the intuitiveness of the application. Second, instead of interacting with files, the new system will interact with a SQL Server CE database making data storage and processing more robust. Figure 1 illustrates the structure of the new OPS. The system includes four forms: frmMenu, frmAddOrder, frmViewOrder, and frmUpdateOrder. The user should be able to traverse from form to form using the navigation aids (e.g., menus and buttons) in the application. The forms retrieves, updates, and deletes data from the SQL Server CE database, ops.sdf. The database provides local data on a mobile device so that users can

Figure 1. The structure of OPS

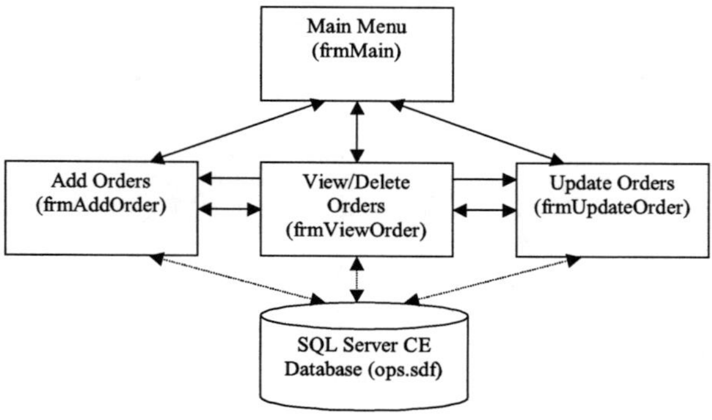

have access to data regardless of their ability to connect to a network. SQL Server CE is a relational database management system designed to perform efficient database operations on mobile devices, and it can run on any platform that Windows CE supports.

Starting a New Visual Studio .NET Smart Device Application

1. Select **Start | Programs | Microsoft Visual Studio .NET 2003** to launch the IDE.
2. Select **File | New | Project** to start a new project.
3. In the New Project dialog box, select **Visual Basic Projects** in the left pane as the project type and **Smart Device Application** in the right pane as the template (see Figure 2).
4. Replace the default project name, **SmartDeviceApplication1**, with **OPS** in the Name textbox (see Figure 2).
5. Click the **OK** button.
6. The Smart Device Application Wizard appears (see Figure 3). Select **PocketPC** as the platform and **Windows Application** as the project type.
7. Click the **OK** button.

Figure 2. New project dialog

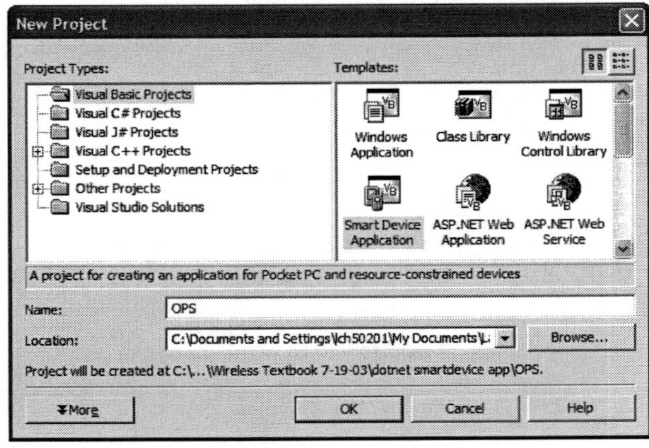

Figure 3. Smart device application wizard

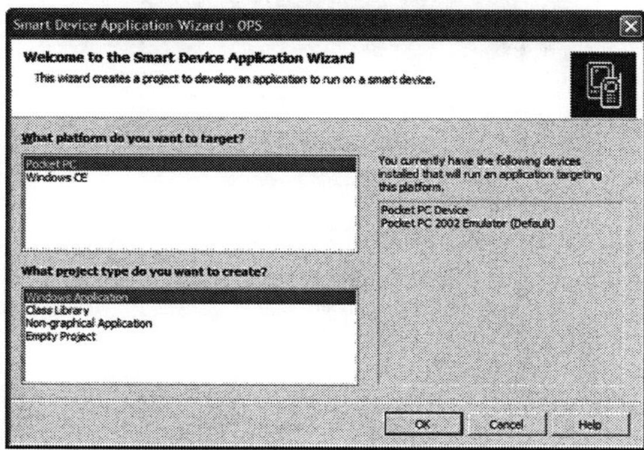

By now, you should be familiar with the development environment of Visual Studio .NET. If you are not familiar with the development environment, please refer to Chapter VIII. We also assume that you are familiar with the simple Visual Basic syntax and SQL.

Creating the Forms

1. Select **Form1**. Change its **Name** property to "**frmMain**" and **Text** property to "**OPS**" in the Properties Window.
2. Add the following controls to **frmMain**. Your **frmMain** should look something like Figure 4.

Control	Property	Value
Label	Text	Order Placement System
	Font	Size = 12; Font Style = Bold
Button	Name	CmdNewOrder
	Text	New Orders
Button	Name	CmdViewOrder
	Text	View/Delete Orders
Button	Name	cmdUpdateOrder
	Text	Update Orders

3. Double-click **cmdNewOrder** to open the Code Window. Enter the following statements in the **cmdNewOrder_Click** procedure. The first statement creates an instance of the **frmAddOrder** object, and the

Figure 4. Main menu

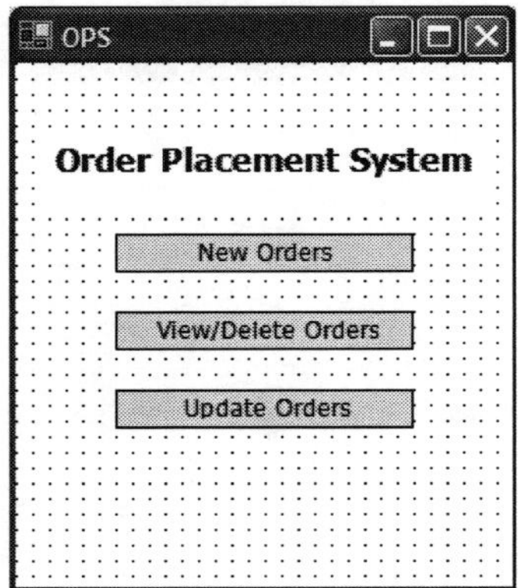

second statement uses the Show() method to display the New Orders screen.

```
'Go to frmAddOrder
Dim nextForm As New frmAddOrder
nextForm.Show()
```

4. Select **View | Designer** to return to the Design View. Double-click **cmdViewOrder** to open the Code Window. Enter the following statements in the **cmdViewOrder_Click** procedure. These statements will display the View/Delete Orders screen when the button is clicked.

```
'Go to frmViewOrder
Dim nextForm As New frmViewOrder
nextForm.Show()
```

5. Select **View | Designer** to return to the Design View. Double-click **cmdUpdateOrder** to open the Code Window. Enter the following statements in the **cmdUpdateOrder_Click** procedure. These statements will display the Update Orders screen when the button is clicked.

```
'Go to frmUpdateOrder
Dim nextForm As New frmUpdateOrder
nextForm.Show()
```

6. Select **Project | Add Window Form** to add a new form to the project.
7. Change the Name to **frmAddOrders.vb** in the Add New Item dialog. Click the **Open** button.

8. Select the form. Change its **Name** property to "**frmAddOrder**" and **Text** property to "**Add Orders**" in the Properties Window.
9. Select **Project | Add Window Form** to add a new form to the project.
10. Change the Name to **frmViewOrders.vb** in the Add New Item dialog. Click the **Open** button.
11. Select the form. Change its **Name** property to "**frmViewOrder**" and **Text** property to "**View/Delete Orders**" in the Properties Window.
12. Select **Project | Add Window Form** to add a new form to the project.
13. Change the Name to **frmUpdateOrders.vb** in the Add New Item dialog. Click the **Open** button.
14. Select the form. Change its **Name** property to "**frmUpdateOrder**" and **Text** property to "**Update Orders**" in the Properties Window.
15. Select **Debug | Start** to debug the application. Select **Pocket PC 2002 Emulator** in the Deploy dialog and click the **Deploy** button. The application will be launched in the Pocket PC Emulator as shown in Figure 5.

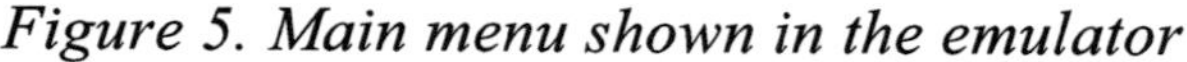

Figure 5. Main menu shown in the emulator

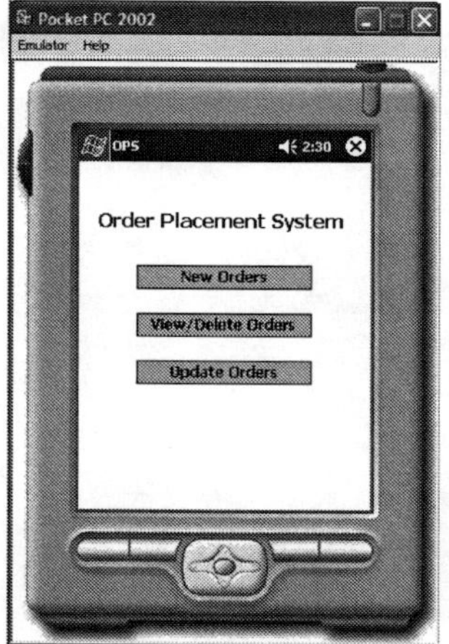

Installing the SQL Server CE Database on the Emulator

To interact with a local database, SQL Server CE and the database file both need to be installed on the emulator or the device. For this application, we are going to create the database from SQL code. When OPS is launched, the application checks to see if the database file ops.sdf exists in the My Documents folder of the device. If the database does not already exist, a new database is created.

The database for this project contains the following four tables and their attributes:

Customer (cust_id, cust_name, f_name, l_name, address, phone)

Orders (ord_id, cust_id, orderdate)

Orderline (ord_id, p_id, qty)

Product (p_id, p_desc, price)

Before the database can be used, SQL Server CE needs to be installed on the client device. The following steps install SQL Server CE and the database on the client device:

Figure 6. Add Reference dialog

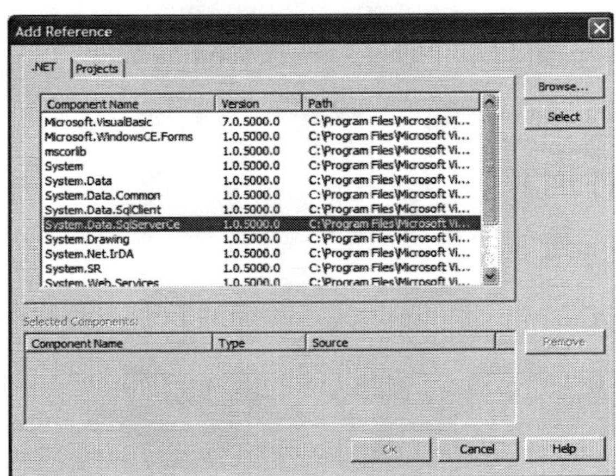

1. Select **Project | Add Reference**.
2. Select the **System.Data.SqlServerCe** component in the Add Reference dialog (see Figure 6). Click the **Select** button. Then click the **OK** button. This will install SQL Server CE when the project is deployed to the device.
3. Select **View | Designer** to open the Design View.
4. Double-click the form to open the Code Window. Enter the following statements in the **frmMain_Load** procedure. These statements first create an empty SQL Server CE database named OPS.sdf in the My Documents folder of the device using the System.Data.SqlServerCe.SqlCeEngine object. A database connection to OPS.sdf is then created. Finally, after the database connection is opened, an instance of the SqlCeCommand object called **sqlCreateTable** is created for storing and executing SQL statements. The **ssceconn.CreateCommand()** method creates and returns a SqlCeCommand object associated with the database connection, **ssceconn**.

```
'Create a new database
Dim engine As New _
   System.Data.SqlServerCe.SqlCeEngine _
   ("Data Source = \My Documents\OPS.sdf")
engine.CreateDatabase()

'Create a new database connection
Dim ssceconn As New _
   System.Data.SqlServerCe.SqlCeConnection _
   ("Data Source = \My Documents\OPS.sdf")

'Open the database connection
ssceconn.Open()

'Create an instance of SqlCeCommand
Dim sqlCreateTable As _
   System.Data.SqlServerCe.SqlCeCommand _
   = ssceconn.CreateCommand()
```

5. Enter the following statements to create the tables in the database: Customer, Orders, Product, and Orderline. When the **ExecuteNonQuery** method is invoked, the SQL statement in the **CommandText** property is executed.

```
'Create tables
sqlCreateTable.CommandText = _
   "CREATE TABLE Customer(cust_id int PRIMARY KEY, " & _
   "cust_name ntext, f_name ntext, l_name ntext, " & _
   "address ntext, phone ntext)"
sqlCreateTable.ExecuteNonQuery()

sqlCreateTable.CommandText = _
   "CREATE TABLE Orders(ord_id int Primary Key, " & _
   "cust_id int, OrderDate ntext)"
sqlCreateTable.ExecuteNonQuery()

sqlCreateTable.CommandText = _
   "CREATE TABLE Product(p_id int PRIMARY KEY, " & _
   "p_desc ntext, price money)"
sqlCreateTable.ExecuteNonQuery()

sqlCreateTable.CommandText = _
   "CREATE TABLE Orderline(ord_id int NOT NULL, " & _
   "p_id int NOT NULL, qty int)"
sqlCreateTable.ExecuteNonQuery()
```

6. Enter the following statements to enter data into the database tables. Here, you are creating another SqlCeCommand called **sqlInsertRow** to insert rows into tables.

```
'Create an instance of SqlCeCommand
Dim sqlInsertRow As _
   System.Data.SqlServerCe.SqlCeCommand = _
   ssceconn.CreateCommand()

'Insert data into tables

'Insert rows into the Orders table
sqlInsertRow.CommandText = _
   "INSERT INTO Orders(ord_id, cust_id, orderdate) " & _
   "VALUES(0, 0, '1900-01-01 00:00:00')"
sqlInsertRow.ExecuteNonQuery()

'Insert rows into the Customers table
sqlInsertRow.CommandText = _
   "INSERT INTO Customer(cust_id, cust_name, f_name, " & _
   "l_name, address, phone) VALUES(0, 'No Customer', " & _
   "NULL, NULL, NULL, NULL)"
sqlInsertRow.ExecuteNonQuery()
```

continued on following page

```
sqlInsertRow.CommandText = _
   "INSERT INTO Customer(cust_id, cust_name, f_name, " & _
   "l_name, address, phone) VALUES(1, 'AAA Company', " & _
   "'Steve', 'Parks', '4322 W.Maple St., Omaha, NE 68178', " & _
   "'(402)-555-8888')"
sqlInsertRow.ExecuteNonQuery()

sqlInsertRow.CommandText = _
   "INSERT INTO Customer(cust_id, cust_name, f_name, " & _
   "l_name, address, phone) VALUES(2, 'Corporate Design', " & _
   "'Bruce', 'Gill', '4339 S.Ernst St., Omaha, NE 68111', " & _
   "'(402)-555-2321')"
sqlInsertRow.ExecuteNonQuery()

sqlInsertRow.CommandText = _
   "INSERT INTO Customer(cust_id, cust_name, f_name, " & _
   "l_name, address, phone) VALUES(3, 'Hansen Company', " & _
   "'Jim', 'Hansen', '940 W.Dodge Rd., Omaha, NE 68134', " & _
   "'(402)-555-5923')"
sqlInsertRow.ExecuteNonQuery()

'Insert rows into the Product table
sqlInsertRow.CommandText = _
   "INSERT INTO Product(p_id, p_desc, price) VALUES(1, " & _
   "'HP iPAQ H3950 Pocket PC Handheld', 395.99)"
sqlInsertRow.ExecuteNonQuery()

sqlInsertRow.CommandText = _
   "INSERT INTO Product(p_id, p_desc, price) VALUES(2, " & _
   "'T-Mobile 6210 BlackBerry', 299.99)"
sqlInsertRow.ExecuteNonQuery()

sqlInsertRow.CommandText = _
   "INSERT INTO Product(p_id, p_desc, price) VALUES(3, " & _
   "'Palm Tungsten C Handheld', 499.99)"
sqlInsertRow.ExecuteNonQuery()

sqlInsertRow.CommandText = _
   "INSERT INTO Product(p_id, p_desc, price) VALUES(4, " & _
   "'NEC MobilePro 900', 899.99)"
sqlInsertRow.ExecuteNonQuery()

'Close the database connection
ssceconn.Close()
```

7. Finally, add the highlighted statements in the procedure to check if OPS.sdf already exists on the device.

```
If Not System.IO.File.Exists("\My Documents\OPS.sdf") Then

   'Create a new database
   Dim engine As New _
   System.Data.SqlServerCe.SqlCeEngine _
      ("Data Source = \My Documents\OPS.sdf")
   engine.CreateDatabase()

. . .

   'Close the database connection
   ssceconn.Close()

End If
```

8. Save the project. Select **Debug | Start** to launch the project in the emulator.

Figure 7. Query analyzer

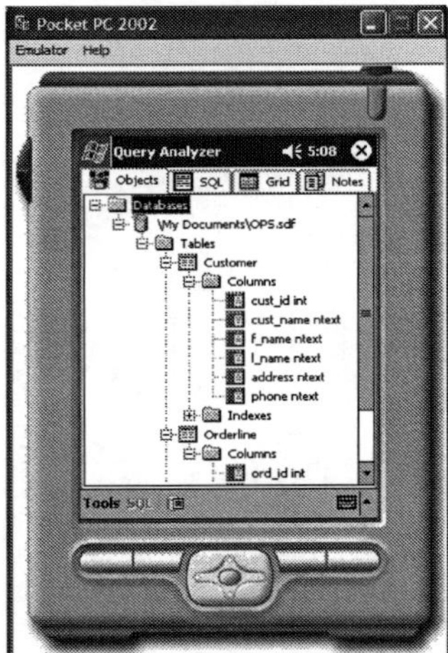

9. In the emulator, select **Start | Programs | File Explorer**. Double-click the file OPS.sdf to start the Query Analyzer. The Query Analyzer should look like Figure 7. The Query Analyzer is a graphic tool for interacting with SQL Server CE databases. It can be used to create, modify, and query databases. We will use the Query Analyzer to verify that the database tables have been created successfully.
10. Keep expanding the Databases item in the Query Analyzer until you reach the columns. Verify if all the database tables have been created successfully.
11. After verifying, click the icon at the bottom of the screen to disconnect from the database.

Creating the New Orders Form

The New Orders form allows the user to add a new order to the database. A number of requirements must be met when designing this form. First, the application must be able to generate a unique order ID for the new order. Second, the user must be able to select the customer and products for the order without extensive keyboard input in order to improve application usability and

Figure 8. New Orders form

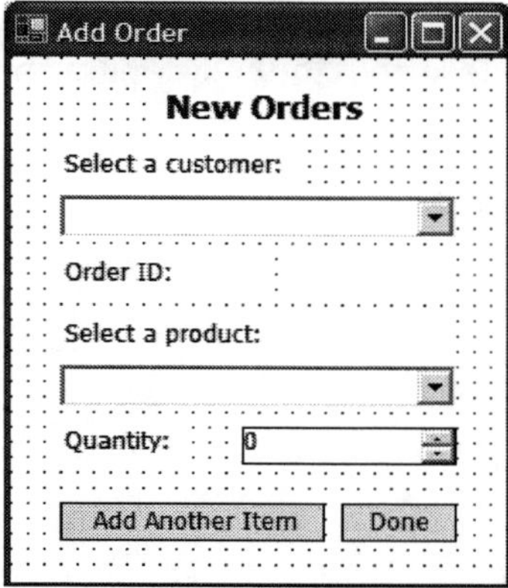

reduce error. Third, the user must be allowed to enter multiple products for the same order.

Building the User Interface

1. Add the following controls to **frmAddOrder**. Your **frmAddOrder** should look something like Figure 8.Make sure that the Enabled property for cboProduct, nudQuantity, cmdAddAnother, and cmdDone is set to False.

Control	Property	Value
Label	Text	New Orders
	Font	Size = 12; Font Style = Bold
Label	Text	Select a customer:
ComboBox	Name	cboCustomer
Label	Text	Order ID:
Label	Name	lblOrderID
	Text	Blank
Label	Text	Select a product:
ComboBox	Name	cboProduct
Label	Text	Quantity:
NumericUpDown	Name	nudQuantity
Button	Name	cmdAddAnother
	Text	Add Another Item
Button	Name	cmdDone
	Text	Done

Programming the New Orders Form

The following pseudocode describes the basic operation of the New Orders form.

When the Form loads:

Retrieve a list of customer names from the database

Populate the customer ComboBox using the list

When the user selects a customer:

Enable the product ComboBox, quantity NumericUpDown, Add Another Item button, and Done button

Retrieve the selected customer name's corresponding customer ID

Generate a unique order ID

Retrieve a list of product descriptions from the database

Populate the product ComboBox using the list

When the user clicks the Add Another Item button:

Retrieve the selected product's corresponding product ID

If it is a new order

Insert a new record in the Orders table

Insert a new record in the Orderline table

Set quantity to 0

Set neworder to False

When the user clicks the Done button:

If the quantity is not 0

Retrieve the selected product's corresponding Product ID

If it is a new order

Insert a new record in the Orders table

Insert a new record in the Orderline table

Set neworder to True

Close the form

Follow the following steps to program the New Orders form:

1. You will first need to declare a number of global variables, which are accessible from any procedures in the class. While eVB is a typeless language, Visual Basic .NET is not; therefore, you need to specify a data

type when declaring a variable. Select **View | Code** to open the Code Window. Enter the highlighted statements.

```
Public Class frmAddOrder
   Inherits System.Windows.Forms.Form

   'Declare global variables
   Dim order_id As Integer
   Dim customer_id As Integer
   Dim product_id As Integer
   Dim neworder As Boolean = True
```

2. Select **View | Designer** to return to the Design View. Double-click **frmAddOrder** to open the Code Window. Enter the following statement in the **frmAddOrder_Load** procedure.

```
'Call the GetCustomers procedure
GetCustomers()
```

3. The statement above is a procedure call, which invokes a procedure named **GetCustomers**. Enter the following statements in the Code Window. These statements creates the procedure **GetCustomers**. The procedure retrieves the customer names from the Customer table and populate the **cboCustomer** ComboBox with the customer names.

```
Sub GetCustomers()

      'Create a connection to the database
      Dim ssceconn As New _
         System.Data.SqlServerCe.SqlCeConnection _
         ("Data Source = \My Documents\OPS.sdf")

      'Open the connection to the database
      ssceconn.Open()

      'Create an instance of SqlCeCommand
      Dim cmd As System.Data.SqlServerCe.SqlCeCommand

      'Create an instance of SqlCeDataReader
      Dim dtr As System.Data.SqlServerCe.SqlCeDataReader

      'Read from the database
      cmd = New System.Data.SqlServerCe.SqlCeCommand _
      ("SELECT * FROM Customer", ssceconn)
      dtr = cmd.ExecuteReader()

      'Clear the ComboBox
      cboCustomer.Items.Clear()

      'Populate the ComboBox
      While dtr.Read()
         cboCustomer.Items.Add(dtr("cust_name"))
      End While

      'Close the DataReader
      dtr.Close()

      'Close the database connection
      ssceconn.Close()

End Sub
```

As the statements above show, reading from the database using a DataReader object requires the following steps: 1) creating a database connection; 2) create an instance of SqlCeCommand; 2) creating an instance of SqlCeDataReader; 3) using a SQL SELECT statement to retrieve data into the DataReader; 4) closing the DataReader; and 5) closing the database connection. A DataReader object allows the application to make a single pass through a set of records. Its Read() method returns the value "False" if the end of the records is reached.

4. Select **View | Designer** to switch to the Design View. Double-click **cboCustomer** to open the Code Window. Enter the following statements in the **cboCustomer_ Selected IndexChanged** procedure.

```
'Enable controls
cboProduct.Enabled = True
nudQuantity.Enabled = True
cmdAnother.Enabled = True
cmdDone.Enabled = True

'Call GetCustomerID procedure
GetCustomerID()
'Call GetOrderID procedure
GetOrderID()
'Call GetProducts procedure
GetProducts()
```

5. Enter the following statements to create the **GetCustomerID** procedure. The procedure retrieves the customer ID of the selected customer.

```
Sub GetCustomerID()

   'Create a connection to the database
   Dim ssceconn As New _
      System.Data.SqlServerCe.SqlCeConnection _
      ("Data Source = \My Documents\OPS.sdf")

   'Open the database connection
   ssceconn.Open()

   'Create an instance of SqlCeCommand
   Dim cmd As System.Data.SqlServerCe.SqlCeCommand

   'Create an instance of SqlCeDataReader
   Dim dtr As System.Data.SqlServerCe.SqlCeDataReader

   'Read from the database
   cmd = New System.Data.SqlServerCe.SqlCeCommand _
      ("SELECT cust_id FROM Customer WHERE (cust_name LIKE '" & _
      cboCustomer.Text & "')", ssceconn)
   dtr = cmd.ExecuteReader()

   dtr.Read()

   customer_id = Convert.ToInt32(dtr("cust_id"))

   'Close the DataReader
   dtr.Close()

   'Close the database connection
   ssceconn.Close()

End Sub
```

6. Enter the following statements to create the **GetOrderID** procedure. The procedure retrieves the maximum order ID in the Orders table and add one to the order ID to generate a unique order ID.

```
Sub GetOrderID()

    'Create a connection to the database
    Dim ssceconn As New _
       System.Data.SqlServerCe.SqlCeConnection _
       ("Data Source = \My Documents\OPS.sdf")

    'Open the connection to the database
    ssceconn.Open()

    'Create an instance of SqlCeCommand
    Dim cmd As System.Data.SqlServerCe.SqlCeCommand

    'Create an instance of SqlCeDataReader
    Dim dtr As System.Data.SqlServerCe.SqlCeDataReader

    'Retrieve the maximum order ID from the Orders table
    cmd = New System.Data.SqlServerCe.SqlCeCommand _
       ("SELECT Max(ord_id) as maxid FROM Orders", ssceconn)
    dtr = cmd.ExecuteReader()

    'Read the DataReader
    dtr.Read()

    'Generate a new order ID and display it
    order_id = Convert.ToInt32(dtr("maxid")) + 1
    lblOrderID.Text = Convert.ToString(order_id)

    'Close the DataReader
    dtr.Close()

    'Close the database connection
    ssceconn.Close()

End Sub
```

7. Enter the following statements to create the **GetProducts** procedure. The procedure retrieves the products from the Product table and populate the **cboProduct** ComboBox with the products.

```
Sub GetProducts()

    'Create a connection to the database
    Dim ssceconn As New _
       System.Data.SqlServerCe.SqlCeConnection _
       ("Data Source = \My Documents\OPS.sdf")

    'Open the database connection
    ssceconn.Open()

    'Create an instance of SqlCeCommand
    Dim cmd As System.Data.SqlServerCe.SqlCeCommand
```

continued on following page

```
'Create an instance of SqlCeDataReader
   Dim dtr As System.Data.SqlServerCe.SqlCeDataReader

   'Retrieve products from the Product table
   cmd = New System.Data.SqlServerCe.SqlCeCommand _
      ("SELECT * FROM Product", ssceconn)
   dtr = cmd.ExecuteReader()

   'Clear the ComboBox
   cboProduct.Items.Clear()

   'Populate the ComboBox
   While dtr.Read()
      cboProduct.Items.Add(dtr("p_desc"))
   End While

   cboProduct.SelectedIndex = 0

   'Close the DataReader
   dtr.Close()

   'Close the database connection
   ssceconn.Close()

End Sub
```

8. Select **View | Designer** to switch to the Design View. Double-click **cmdAddAnother** to open the Code Window.
9. Enter the following statement in the **cmdAddAnother_Click** procedure. The statement is a procedure call that invokes the **AddAnotherProduct** procedure.

```
'Call the AddAnotherProduct procedure
AddAnotherProduct()
```

10. Enter the following statements to create the **AddAnotherProduct** procedure. The procedure inserts a new row in the Orderline table, and if it is a new order, a new row is also inserted into the Orders table.

```
Sub AddAnotherProduct()

   'Call the GetProductID procedure
   GetProductID()

   'Create a new database connection
   Dim ssceconn As New _
      System.Data.SqlServerCe.SqlCeConnection _
      ("Data Source = \My Documents\OPS.sdf")
```

continued on following page

```
    'Open the database connection
    ssceconn.Open()

    'Create an instance of sqlCeCommand
    Dim sqlInsertRow As System.Data.SqlServerCe.SqlCeCommand = _
       ssceconn.CreateCommand()

    If neworder = True Then
       'Insert a new record in the Orders table
       'if it is a new order
       sqlInsertRow.CommandText = _
          "INSERT INTO Orders(ord_id, cust_id, OrderDate) " & _
          "VALUES(" & order_id & ", " & customer_id & "," & _
          "'" & Date.Now & "')"
       sqlInsertRow.ExecuteNonQuery()
    End If

    'Insert a new record in the Orderline table
    sqlInsertRow.CommandText = _
       "INSERT INTO Orderline(ord_id, p_id, qty) " & _
       "VALUES(" & order_id & ", " & product_id & "," & _
       nudQuantity.Value & ")"
    sqlInsertRow.ExecuteNonQuery()

    'Close the database connection
    ssceconn.Close()

    nudQuantity.Value = 0

    neworder = False

End Sub
```

11. Enter the following statements to create the **GetProductID** procedure. This procedure retrieves the product ID of the selected product.

```
Sub GetProductID()

    'Create a connection to the database
    Dim ssceconn As New _
       System.Data.SqlServerCe.SqlCeConnection _
       ("Data Source = \My Documents\OPS.sdf")

    'Open the connection to the database
    ssceconn.Open()

    'Create an instance of SqlCeCommand
    Dim cmd As System.Data.SqlServerCe.SqlCeCommand

    'Create an instance of SqlCeDataReader
    Dim dtr As System.Data.SqlServerCe.SqlCeDataReader

    'Retrieve the product ID of the selected product
    cmd = New System.Data.SqlServerCe.SqlCeCommand _
       ("SELECT p_id FROM Product WHERE (p_desc LIKE '" & _
       cboProduct.Text & "')", ssceconn)
    dtr = cmd.ExecuteReader()

    'Read from the DataReader
    dtr.Read()

    product_id = Convert.ToInt32(dtr("p_id"))

    'Close the DataReader
    dtr.Close()

    'Close the database connection
    ssceconn.Close()

End Sub
```

12. Select **View | Designer** to switch to the Design View. Double-click **cmdDone** to open the Code Window.
13. Enter the following statement in the **cmdDone_Click** procedure. The statement is a procedure call that invokes the **EnterOrder** procedure.

```
'Call the EnterOrder procedure
EnterOrder()
```

14. Enter the following statements to create the **EnterOrder** procedure. When the **Done** button is pressed, the application enters the last order item into the database if the quantity value is not 0.

```
Sub EnterOrder()

   If nudQuantity.Value <> 0 Then

      GetProductID()

      'Create a new database connection
      Dim ssceconn As New _
         System.Data.SqlServerCe.SqlCeConnection _
         ("Data Source = \My Documents\OPS.sdf")

      'Open the database connection
      ssceconn.Open()

      'Create an instance of SqlCeCommand
      Dim sqlInsertRow As System.Data.SqlServerCe.SqlCeCommand _
         = ssceconn.CreateCommand()

      If neworder = True Then
         'Insert a new record in the Orders table
         sqlInsertRow.CommandText = _
            "INSERT INTO Orders(ord_id, cust_id, OrderDate) " & _
            "VALUES(" & order_id & ", " & customer_id & "," & _
            "'" & Date.Now & "')"
         sqlInsertRow.ExecuteNonQuery()
      End If

      'Insert a new record in the Orderline table
      sqlInsertRow.CommandText = _
         "INSERT INTO Orderline(ord_id, p_id, qty) VALUES(" & _
         order_id & ", " & product_id & "," & _
         nudQuantity.Value & ")"
      sqlInsertRow.ExecuteNonQuery()

      'Close the database connection
      ssceconn.Close()

   End If

   neworder = True

   'Close the form
   Me.Close()

End Sub
```

15. Save the project and debug it. The New Orders form should look something like Figure 9.

Figure 9. New Orders form shown in the emulator

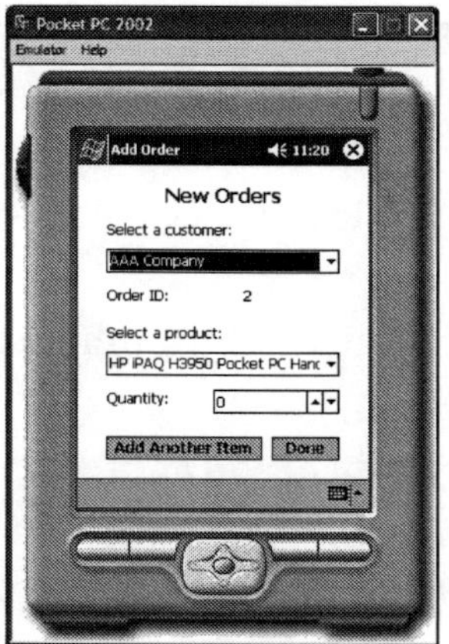

Creating View/Delete Orders Form

The View/Delete Orders form allows the user to view a single order and be able to delete the order if the user chooses to. The form will display the detailed information about the order including the customer, order date, product(s), quantity, and price.

Building the User Interface

1. Add the following controls to **frmViewOrder**.

Control	Property	Value
Label	Text	View/Delete Orders
	Font	Size = 12; Font Style = Bold
Label	Text	Select order ID:
ComboBox	Name	cboOrderID
Label	Text	Customer:
Label	Name	lblCustomer
	Text	Nothing
Label	Text	Order date:
Label	Name	lblOrderDate
	Text	Nothing
ListView	Name	lvwOrderDetail
Button	Name	cmdDelete
	Text	Delete Order
	Enabled	False
Button	Name	CmdDone
	Text	Done
	Enabled	False

2. The ListView control is used to display a list of items, in this case, a list of order lines. When it is in the Details view, it can display multiple columns for each item. Select **lvwOrderDetail**, set its **View** property to **Details**. Click the ellipsis button beside the **Columns** property to open the ColumnHeader Collection Editor.
3. Click the **Add** button to add a new column header. Set its **Text** property to **Product**.
4. Click the **Add** button again to add another column header. Set its **Text** property to **Unit Price**
5. Click the **Add** button again to add another column header. Set its **Text** property to **Quantity**.
6. Click the **OK** button. Your **frmViewOrder** should look something like Figure 10.

Programming the View/Delete Orders Form

The following pseudocode describes the basic operation of the View/Delete Orders form.

When the Form loads:

Retrieve a list of order IDs from the database

Populate the order ID ComboBox with the list

When the user selects an order ID:

Enabled the command buttons

Figure 10. View/Delete Orders form

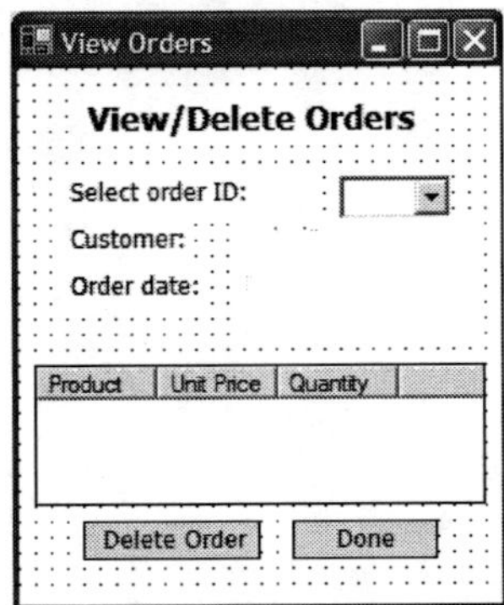

Retrieve the selected order ID's corresponding customer name and order date
Display the customer name and order date
Retrieve the order lines of the selected order
Populate the ListView with the order lines
When the user clicks the Delete Order button:
Delete the order information from the Orders and Orderline tables
Reset the screen to its original state
When the user clicks the Done button:
Close the form

Follow the following steps to program the View/Delete Orders form:

1. Double-click **frmViewOrder** to open the Code Window. Enter the following statement in the **frmViewOrder_Load** procedure. The statement calls the **GetOrderID** procedure.

```
'Call the GetOrderID procedure
GetOrderID()
```

2. Enter the following statements to create the **GetOrderID** procedure.

```
Sub GetOrderID()

   'Create a new database connection
   Dim ssceconn As New _
      System.Data.SqlServerCe.SqlCeConnection _
      ("Data Source = \My Documents\OPS.sdf")

   'Open the database connection
   ssceconn.Open()

   'Create an instance of SqlCeCommand
   Dim cmd As System.Data.SqlServerCe.SqlCeCommand

   'Create an instance of SqlCeDataReader
   Dim dtr As System.Data.SqlServerCe.SqlCeDataReader

   'Retrieve data from the Orders table
   cmd = New System.Data.SqlServerCe.SqlCeCommand _
      ("SELECT * FROM Orders", ssceconn)
   dtr = cmd.ExecuteReader()

   cboOrderID.Items.Clear()

   'Populate the Order ID ComboBox
   While dtr.Read()
      cboOrderID.Items.Add(dtr("ord_id"))
   End While

   'Close the DataReader
   dtr.Close()

   'Close the database connection
   ssceconn.Close()

End Sub
```

3. Select **View | Designer** to switch to the Design View. Double-click **cboOrderID** to open the Code Window. Enter the following statements in the **cboOrderID_SelectedIndexChanged** procedure. The last statement calls the **GetOrderDetail** procedure, which retrieves and displays order details.

```
'Enable the command buttons
cmdDelete.Enabled = True
cmdDone.Enabled = True

'Call the GetOrderDetail procedure
GetOrderDetail()
```

4. The **GetOrderDetail** procedure performs two tasks. First, it retrieves and displays the selected order ID's corresponding customer name and order date, and then it retrieves and displays the items included in the order. Enter the following code to create the first half of the **GetOrderDetail** procedure.

```
Sub GetOrderDetail()
    'Create a new database connection
    Dim ssceconn As New _
       System.Data.SqlServerCe.SqlCeConnection _
       ("Data Source = \My Documents\OPS.sdf")

    'Open the database connection
    ssceconn.Open()

    'Create an instance of SqlCeCommand
    Dim cmd As System.Data.SqlServerCe.SqlCeCommand

    'Create an instance of SqlCeDataReader
    Dim dtr As System.Data.SqlServerCe.SqlCeDataReader

    'Retrieve data from the Customer and Orders tables
    cmd = New System.Data.SqlServerCe.SqlCeCommand _
       ("SELECT customer.cust_name, orders.orderdate " & _
       "FROM customer, orders " & _
       "WHERE customer.cust_id = orders.cust_id " & _
       "AND orders.ord_id = " & cboOrderID.Text, ssceconn)
    dtr = cmd.ExecuteReader()

    'Read and display the data
    dtr.Read()
    lblCustomer.Text = dtr("cust_name")
    lblOrderDate.Text = dtr("orderdate")

    'Close the DataReader
    dtr.Close()
```

5. Since a database connection to OPS.sdf has been created and opened, the procedure can use the same database connection to perform the second task. Order details will be displayed in the ListView control. To display a list of items in the ListView control, one needs to follow these steps:

(1) create a new ListView item by declaring a new instance of ListViewItem;

(2) load subitems (attributes) into the ListView item by using the [ListView item name].SubItems.Add() method (The first column displays the Text property of the ListView item, and the subsequent columns display the SubItems);

(3) add the item to the ListView control using the [ListView control name].Items.Add([ListView item name]) method.

Enter the following statements to complete the **GetOrderDetail** procedure.

```
'Retrieve data from the Product and Orderline tables
   cmd = New System.Data.SqlServerCe.SqlCeCommand _
      ("SELECT product.p_desc, product.price, orderline.qty " & _
      "FROM product, orderline " & _
      "WHERE product.p_id = orderline.p_id " & _
      "AND orderline.ord_id = " & cboOrderID.Text, ssceconn)
   dtr = cmd.ExecuteReader()

   Dim order_detail As ListViewItem

   lvwOrderDetail.Items.Clear()

   While dtr.Read()
      'Create a new ListView item
      order_detail = New ListViewItem

      'Load the data into the item
      order_detail.Text = dtr("p_desc")

      order_detail.SubItems.Add(dtr("price").ToString)

      order_detail.SubItems.Add(dtr("qty").ToString)

      'Add the item into the LIstView control
      lvwOrderDetail.Items.Add(order_detail)

   End While

   'Close the DataReader
   dtr.Close()

   'Close the database connection
   ssceconn.Close()

End Sub
```

6. Select **View | Designer** to switch to the Design View. Double-click the Delete Order button **(cmdDelete)** to open the Code Window. Enter the following statement in the **cmdDelete_Click** procedure. The statement calls the **DeleteOrder** procedure.

```
'Call the DeleteOrder procedure
DeleteOrder()
```

7. The **DeleteOrder** procedure uses a delete SQL statement to delete the record about the order from the Orders table and the corresponding records in the Orderline table. Enter the following statements to create the **DeleteOrder** procedure.

```
Sub DeleteOrder()

   'Create a new database connection
   Dim ssceconn As New _
      System.Data.SqlServerCe.SqlCeConnection _
      ("Data Source = \My Documents\OPS.sdf")

   'Open the database connection
   ssceconn.Open()

   'Create an instance of SqlCeCommand
   Dim sqlDeleteRow As System.Data.SqlServerCe.SqlCeCommand = _
      ssceconn.CreateCommand()

   'Delete a row from the Orders table
   sqlDeleteRow.CommandText = _
      "DELETE FROM Orders WHERE ord_id = " & cboOrderID.Text
   sqlDeleteRow.ExecuteNonQuery()

   'Delete row(s) from the Orderline table
   sqlDeleteRow.CommandText = _
      "DELETE FROM orderline WHERE ord_id = " & cboOrderID.Text
   sqlDeleteRow.ExecuteNonQuery()

   'Close the database connection
   ssceconn.Close()

   'Reset the form to its original state
   GetOrderID()
   lblCustomer.Text = ""
   lblOrderDate.Text = ""
   lvwOrderDetail.Items.Clear()
   cmdDelete.Enabled = False
   cmdDone.Enabled = False

End Sub
```

8. Select **View | Designer** to switch to the Design View. Double-click the Done button to open the Code Window. Enter the following statement in the **cmdDone_Click** procedure. The statement closes the form when the user clicks the Done button.

```
'Close the form
Me.Close()
```

9. Save the project and debug it. The View/Delete Orders form should look like Figure 11.

Creating the Update Orders Form

The Update Orders form allows the user to update existing orders by adding products, deleting products, or changing quantity. The user will need to first

Figure 11. View/Delete Orders form shown in the emulator

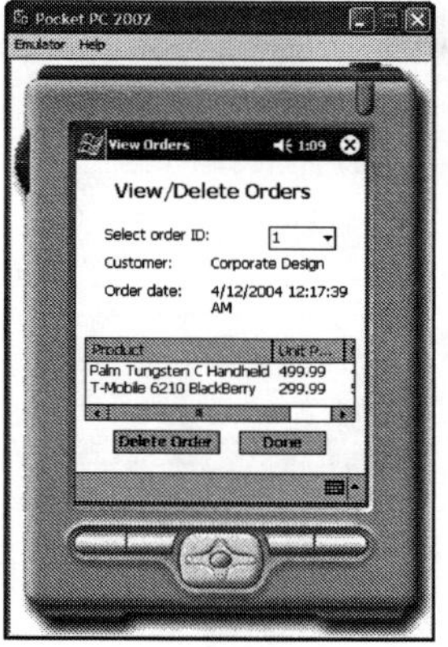

indicate whether he or she will add another product to the order or edit the quantity of a product in the order. (To delete a product from the order, the user can edit the quantity to zero). Based on the user's selection, necessary information will be provided for the user to complete the task.

Building the User Interface

1. Add the following controls to **frmUpdateOrder**. The **frmUpdateOrder** should look something like Figure 12.

Programming the Update Orders Form

The following pseudocode describes the basic operation of the View/Delete Orders form.

When the Form loads:

  Retrieve a list of order IDs from the database

  Populate the order ID ComboBox with the list

When the user selects an order ID:

  Enable the Edit and Add Item command buttons

When the user clicks the Edit command button

  Retrieve the selected order ID's corresponding product descriptions

  Populate the product ComboBox with the product descriptions

Figure 12. Update Orders form

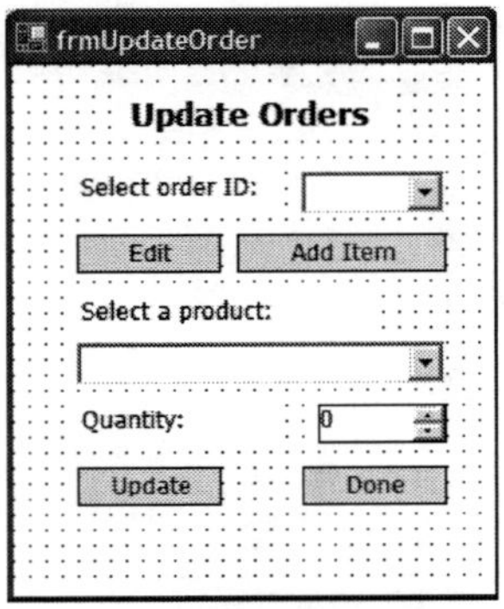

```
        Enable the product ComboBox
        Set additem to False
When the user clicks the Add Item command button
        Retrieve a list of products from the database
        Populate the product ComboBox with the list
        Enable the product ComboBox
        Set additem to True
When the user selects a product:
        Disable the Edit and Add Item command buttons
        Disable the order ID ComboBox
        Enable the quantity NumericUpDown
        Enable the Update and Done command buttons
        If additem is False
                Retrieve the selected product's corresponding quantity and product
        ID
        Else
                Retrieve the selected product's corresponding product ID

When the user clicks the Update button:
        If additem is False
                If the quantity is 0
Delete the record pertaining to the select product from the
        Orderline table
                Else
Update the record pertaining to the selected product in the
```

Orderline table

Else

Insert a new record in the Orderline table

Confirm that the order has been updated

When the user clicks the Done button:

Close the form

Follow the following steps to program the Update Orders form:

1. Double-click **frmUpdateOrder** to open the Code Window. Enter the following statement in the **frmUpdateOrder_Load** procedure. The statement calls the **GetOrderID** procedure.

```
'Call the GetOrderID procedure
GetOrderID()
```

2. Enter the following statements to create the **GetOrderID** procedure. This procedure is the same as the **GetOrderID** procedure used in the View/Delete Orders form. The procedure retrieves a list of existing orders from the database and display the list in the order ID ComboBox.

```
Sub GetOrderID()

   'Create a new database connection
   Dim ssceconn As New _
      System.Data.SqlServerCe.SqlCeConnection _
      ("Data Source = \My Documents\OPS.sdf")

   'Open the database connection
   ssceconn.Open()

   'Create an instance of SqlCeCommand
   Dim cmd As System.Data.SqlServerCe.SqlCeCommand

   'Create an instance of SqlCeDataReader
   Dim dtr As System.Data.SqlServerCe.SqlCeDataReader

   'Retrieve data from the Orders table
   cmd = New System.Data.SqlServerCe.SqlCeCommand _
      ("SELECT * FROM Orders", ssceconn)
   dtr = cmd.ExecuteReader()

   cboOrderID.Items.Clear()

   'Populate the order ID ComboBox
   While dtr.Read()
      cboOrderID.Items.Add(dtr("ord_id"))
   End While

   'Close the DataReader
   dtr.Close()

   'Close the database connection
   ssceconn.Close()

End Sub
```

3. Select **View | Designer** to switch to the Design View. Double-click the order ID ComboBox to open the Code Window. Enter the following statements in the **cboOrderID_SelectedIndexChanged** procedure.

```
'Enable the Edit and Add Item command buttons
cmdEdit.Enabled = True
cmdAddItem.Enabled = True
```

4. Select **View | Designer** to switch to the Design View. Double-click the Edit button to open the Code Window. Enter the following statements in the **cmdEdit_Click** procedure.

```
'Call the GetOrderProducts procedure
GetOrderProducts()

'Enable the product ComboBox
cboProduct.Enabled = True

additem = False
```

5. Enter the following statements to create the **GetOrderProducts** procedure. The procedure retrieves a list of products found in the selected order.

```
Sub GetOrderProducts()

    'Create a new database connection
    Dim ssceconn As New _
       System.Data.SqlServerCe.SqlCeConnection _
       ("Data Source = \My Documents\OPS.sdf")

    'Open the database connection
    ssceconn.Open()

    'Create an instance of SqlCeCommand
    Dim cmd As System.Data.SqlServerCe.SqlCeCommand

    'Create an instance of SqlCeDataReader
    Dim dtr As System.Data.SqlServerCe.SqlCeDataReader

    'Retrieve the products found in the selected order
    cmd = New System.Data.SqlServerCe.SqlCeCommand _
       ("SELECT product.p_desc FROM product, orderline " & _
       "WHERE product.p_id = orderline.p_id " & _
       "AND orderline.ord_id = " & cboOrderID.Text, ssceconn)
    dtr = cmd.ExecuteReader()

    cboProduct.Items.Clear()

    'Populate the product ComboBox
    While dtr.Read()
       cboProduct.Items.Add(dtr("p_desc"))
    End While

    'Close the DataReader
    dtr.Close()

    'Close the database connection
    ssceconn.Close()

End Sub
```

6. Select **View | Designer** to switch to the Design View. Double-click the Add Item button to open the Code Window. Enter the following statements in the **cmdAddItem_Click** procedure. The procedure call calls the **GetProduct** procedure. Notice that **GetProduct** procedure is different from the **GetOrderProduct** procedure in the previous step. Instead of retrieving the products found in the selected order, **GetProduct** procedure simply retrieves a list of products from the Product table.

```
'Call the GetProduct procedure
GetProduct()

'Enable the product ComboBox
cboProduct.Enabled = True

additem = True
```

7. Enter the following statements to create the **GetProduct** procedure.

```
Sub GetProduct()

   'Create a new database connection
   Dim ssceconn As New _
      System.Data.SqlServerCe.SqlCeConnection _
      ("Data Source = \My Documents\OPS.sdf")

   'Open the database connection
   ssceconn.Open()

   'Create an instance of SqlCeCommand
   Dim cmd As System.Data.SqlServerCe.SqlCeCommand

   'Create an instance of SqlCeDataReader
   Dim dtr As System.Data.SqlServerCe.SqlCeDataReader

   'Retrieve data from the Product table
   cmd = New System.Data.SqlServerCe.SqlCeCommand _
      ("SELECT * FROM Product", ssceconn)
   dtr = cmd.ExecuteReader()

   cboProduct.Items.Clear()

   'Populate the product ComboBox
   While dtr.Read()
      cboProduct.Items.Add(dtr("p_desc"))
   End While

   'Close the DataReader
   dtr.Close()

   'Close the database connection
   ssceconn.Close()

End Sub
```

8. Select **View | Designer** to switch to the Design View. Double-click **cboProduct** to open the Code Window. Enter the following statements in the **cboProduct_SelectedIndexChanged** procedure.

```
'Enable the controls
cmdEdit.Enabled = False
cmdAddItem.Enabled = False
cboOrderID.Enabled = False
nudQuantity.Enabled = True
cmdUpdate.Enabled = True
cmdDone.Enabled = True

If additem = False Then

   'Call GetQuantity procedure
   GetQuantity()
   'Call GetProductID procedure
   GetProductID()

Else

   'Call GetProductID procedure
   GetProductID()

End If
```

9. Enter the following statements to create the **GetQuantity** procedure. The procedure retrieves the quantity of the product from the Orderline table and display the quantity in **nudQuantity**.

```
Sub GetQuantity()

   'Create a new database connection
   Dim ssceconn As New _
      System.Data.SqlServerCe.SqlCeConnection _
      ("Data Source = \My Documents\OPS.sdf")

   'Open the database connection
   ssceconn.Open()

   'Create an instance of SqlCeCommand
   Dim cmd As System.Data.SqlServerCe.SqlCeCommand

   'Create an instance of SqlCeDataReader
   Dim dtr As System.Data.SqlServerCe.SqlCeDataReader

   'Retrieve the quantity from the Orderline table
   cmd = New System.Data.SqlServerCe.SqlCeCommand _
      ("SELECT orderline.qty FROM product, orderline " & _
      "WHERE product.p_id = orderline.p_id " & _
      "AND orderline.ord_id = " & cboOrderID.Text & _
      " AND p_desc LIKE '" & cboProduct.Text & "'", ssceconn)
   dtr = cmd.ExecuteReader()

   'Display the quantity in nudQuantity
   dtr.Read()
   nudQuantity.Value = dtr("qty")

   'Close the DataReader
   dtr.Close()

   'Close the database connection
   ssceconn.Close()

End Sub
```

10. Enter the following statements to create the **GetProductID** procedure.

```
Sub GetProductID()

    'Create a new database connection
    Dim ssceconn As New _
       System.Data.SqlServerCe.SqlCeConnection _
       ("Data Source = \My Documents\OPS.sdf")

    'Open the database connection
    ssceconn.Open()

    'Create an instance of SqlCeCommand
    Dim cmd As System.Data.SqlServerCe.SqlCeCommand

    'Create an instance of SqlCeDataReader
    Dim dtr As System.Data.SqlServerCe.SqlCeDataReader

    'Retrieve the product ID from the Product table
    cmd = New System.Data.SqlServerCe.SqlCeCommand _
       ("SELECT p_id FROM Product WHERE " & _
       "(p_desc LIKE '" & cboProduct.Text & "')", ssceconn)
    dtr = cmd.ExecuteReader()

    dtr.Read()
    product_id = Convert.ToInt32(dtr("p_id"))

    'Close the DataReader
    dtr.Close()

    'Close the database connection
    ssceconn.Close()

End Sub
```

11. Select **View | Designer** to switch to the Design View. Double-click the Update button to open the Code Window. Enter the following statement in the **cmdUpdate_Click** procedure. The statement calls the **UpdateItem** procedure.

```
'Call the UpdateItem procedure
UpdateItem()
```

12. Enter the following statements to create the **UpdateItem** procedure.

```
Sub UpdateItem()

    'Create a new database connection
    Dim ssceconn As New _
       System.Data.SqlServerCe.SqlCeConnection _
       ("Data Source = \My Documents\OPS.sdf")

    'Open the database connection
    ssceconn.Open()
```

continued on following page

```
If additem = False Then

      If nudQuantity.Value = 0 Then

         Dim sqlDeleteRow As _
            System.Data.SqlServerCe.SqlCeCommand = _
            ssceconn.CreateCommand()

         'Delete the item if the quantity is 0
         sqlDeleteRow.CommandText = _
            "Delete FROM orderline WHERE ord_id = " & _
            cboOrderID.Text & " AND p_id = " & product_id
         sqlDeleteRow.ExecuteNonQuery()

      Else

         Dim sqlUpdateRow As _
            System.Data.SqlServerCe.SqlCeCommand = _
            ssceconn.CreateCommand()

         'Update the item in the Orderline table
         sqlUpdateRow.CommandText = _
            "UPDATE orderline SET qty = " & _
            nudQuantity.Value & " WHERE ord_id = " & _
            cboOrderID.Text & " AND p_id = " & product_id
            sqlUpdateRow.ExecuteNonQuery()

      End If

   Else

      Dim sqlInsertRow As _
         System.Data.SqlServerCe.SqlCeCommand = _
         ssceconn.CreateCommand()

      'Insert the item in the Orderline table
      sqlInsertRow.CommandText = _
         "INSERT INTO orderline(ord_id, p_id, qty) " & _
         "VALUES (" & cboOrderID.Text & ", " & _
         product_id & ", " & nudQuantity.Value & ")"
      sqlInsertRow.ExecuteNonQuery()

   End If

   'Confirm that the item has been updated
   MsgBox("The item has been updated.")

   'Close the database connection
   ssceconn.Close()

End Sub
```

13. Select **View | Designer** to switch to the Design View. Double-click the Done button to open the Code Window. Enter the following statement in the **cmdDone_Click** procedure.

```
'Close the form
Me.Close()
```

14. Save the project and debug it. The Update Orders screen should look similar to Figure 13.

Adding Menus

Menus are important components in Windows programs. Creating menus using Visual Studio .NET is a much more straight-forward process than using Embedded Visual Basic.

1. Switch to the Design View of the New Orders form. Double-click the MainMenu control in the Toolbox to add a MainMenu control to the project. The icon for the MainMenu control appears in the component tray instead of the form. A box that reads "Type Here" appears at the bottom of the form.
2. Click the "Type Here" box, type "Options" and press the Enter key. Set the **Name** property of the menu item to **mnuOptions**.
3. Type "New Orders" in the box above the Options menu. Set the **Name** property of the menu item to **mnuNewOrder**.
4. Type "View/Delete Orders" in the box below the New Orders menu item. Set the **Name** property of the menu item to **mnuViewOrders**.
5. Type "Update Orders" in the box below the View/Delete Orders menu item. Set the **Name** property of the menu item to **mnuUpdateOrders**. The New Orders form should look something like Figure 14.
6. The menu items need to be programmed in order to work. Double-click the New Orders menu items to open the Code Window. Enter the following statements in the **mnuNewOrders_Click** procedure. The statements show the New Orders form and close the current form.

```
Dim nextForm As New frmAddOrder
nextForm.Show()
Me.Close()
```

7. Select View | Designer to switch to the Design View. Double-click the View/Delete Orders menu item to open the Code Window. Enter the following statements in the **mnuViewOrders_Click** procedure.

```
Dim nextForm As New frmViewOrder
nextForm.Show()
Me.Close()
```

8. Select View | Designer to switch to the Design View. Double-click the Update Orders menu item to open the Code Window. Enter the following statements in the **mnuUpdateOrders_Click** procedure.

```
Dim nextForm As New frmUpdateOrder
nextForm.Show()
Me.Close()
```

9. Repeat these steps for the View/Delete Orders and Update Orders forms.
10. Save the project and debug it. The New Orders form should look like Figure 15.

Summary

This chapter discusses the techniques for developing mobile applications using Visual Studio .NET. Visual Studio .NET offers many improvements over EBV tools discussed in the previous chapter. Mobile application are developed in

Figure 13. Update Orders form shown in the emulator

Visual Studio .NET using the Smart Device Application tools. As a result, the application's interface is richer, and the development of the application is simplified. Visual Studio .NET is quickly becoming a popular development tool for all types of business applications including mobile and wireless applications.

SQL Server CE is designed to perform database operations on mobile devices, and it can run on any platform that Winodws CE supports. This chapter discusses how to install SQL Server CE databases on a client device and how to use the Query Analyzer, a tool for interacting with SQL Server CE databases.

In this chapter, you are also introduced to the techniques for developing database-driven mobile applications. SqlCeconnection, SqlCeCommand, and SqlCeDataReader objects are the essential tools for an application to interact with a SQL Server CE databases. The SqlCeConnection object establishes a connection to the database, the SqlCeCommand object executes SQL commands through that connection to retrieve, insert, delete, or update data, and the SqlCeDataReader object creates a local copy of the data returned to be used by the application.

Project

According to the 1997 U.S. Census, there were nearly 657,000 construction establishments in a number of market segments, including residential and

Figure 14. New Orders form with menus

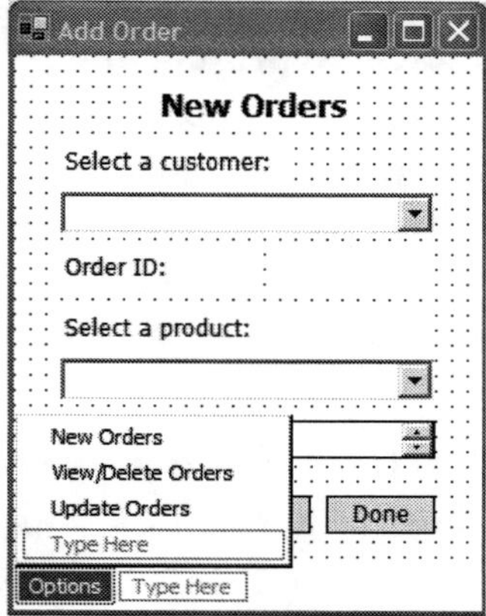

Figure 15. New Orders form with menus shown in the emulator

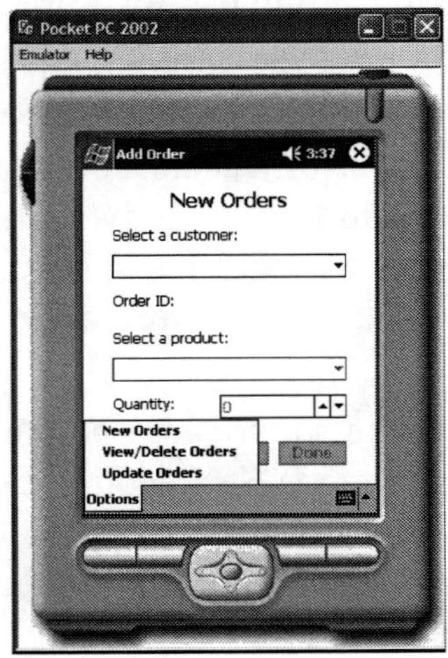

nonresidential construction. There were nearly 5.7 million total employees in construction. Construction delays are often caused by untimely or erroneous information. Field construction managers often do not have access to the information they need when they need it. Your team is commissioned to design a mobile solution that will help solve the problem. The mobile solution will allow field managers to access mission-critical data from their PocketPC devices. The data on the device is synchronized with the company database every morning to ensure that the data is up-to-date. The mobile application should include the following features:

Project Manager: Project Manager allows users to locate a project either by project number or keywords. Project Manager also provides summary information about a selected project and its jobs. By clicking on the description of a job, a form should appear that displays information regarding the current phase of the construction job, such as the current subcontractors on-site and the tasks they're performing. The user should be able to edit the current phase, status, priority, and job history of a selected job. The user should also be able to submit a new job related to the project.

Contractors: The Contractors function allows users to locate a contractor and all the current jobs that are associated with that contractor. Contact information of the contractor should be displayed. When the user click on the description of a job, the job form will be displayed.

Material Order Form (MOF): The MOF allows users to authorize material purchases. The user will specify the type and quantity of the material to be ordered. The user will also choose the project that the material is ordered for from a dropdown list of existing projects.

Use the techniques discussed in this chapter to develop a mobile application using the Smart Device Application Tools of Visual Studio .NET.

Glossary

1G – Developed in the 70s and 80s, the first generation (1G) wireless communications technology refers to the analog cellular technology. Popular 1G technology includes AMPS.

2G – The second generation (2G) wireless communications technology refers to the digital cellular technology. Popular 2G technology includes CDMA and GSM.

2.5G – Extension of existing 2G cellular network protocols to provide additional features such as packet-switching and enhanced data rates. Popular 2.5G technology includes GPRS and EDGE.

3G – The next generation of wireless communications technology that supports high-speed, high-bandwidth wireless services for advanced applications. Popular 3G technology includes W-CDMA and CDMA 2000 3x.

ADO.NET – ActiveX Data Objects for .NET. A set of data access technologies included in the .NET Framework class libraries.

Advanced Mobile Phone Service (AMPS) – A 1G standard analog mobile phone service network which operates in the 800-900MHz frequency band. It is used mainly in the US, Latin America, Australia, New Zealand, parts of Russia, and Asia-Pacific.

ASP.NET – The latest version of Microsoft's Active Server Pages technology that is designed to build server-based Web applications. It is different from its predecessor in two major ways: it supports code written in compiled language like C++, Visual Basic, and C#, and, it separates the code from the content allowing WYSIWYG editing of Web pages.

Bluetooth – A short-range radio technology aimed at simplifying wireless communications between devices and the Internet. Bluetooth's founding members include Ericsson, IBM, Intel, Nokia, and Toshiba.

Card – Key component in a WML document. In WML, documents are composed of decks of cards.

Cascading Style Sheet (CSS) – Term used to reference a number of different means of applying a style sheet to a document. Style sheets can be used inline, embedded, or linked. XHMTL Basic only supports linked style sheets.

Code Division Multiple Access (CDMA) – A technique of multiplexing, which allows multiple frequencies to be used simultaneously. It is the name of a 2G mobile phone service standard mainly used in the US.

ColdFusion Markup Language (CFML) – ColdFusion tags used to build dynamic or database-driven Web pages.

Cookie – A small file containing information stored on a client computer by a server that can be retrieved by the server later.

Deck – Body of a WML document composed of one or more cards.

Dialogs Library – WMLScript Standard Library that provides functions for communication with the user from within a WMLScript program.

Float Library – WMLScript Standard Library that contains functions for manipulation and conversion of floating-point numbers.

Form variable – A variable whose value is passed to the subsequent Web page via a form.

General Packet Radio Service (GPRS) – A 2.5G packet-switching technology for GSM networks that supports flexible data transmission rate typically up to 20 or 30 Kbps as well as continuous connection to the wireless network.

Global Positioning Systems (GPS) – A satellite-based navigation system that allows users to determine their exact geographic position.

Global System for Mobile Communications (GSM) – A 2G standard for digital cellular communications. It has become the most widely used mobile system in the world.

Hyperlink – Reference used to links cards or decks in WML. Links can also address an external function or location in another file.

Location Based Service (LBS) – New and improved services enabled by a range of positioning techniques.

Mobile application – An application designed for mobile devices. Unlike a wireless application, a mobile application can function without a network connection.

Mobile business (m-business) – Content delivery (notification and reporting) and transactions (purchasing and data entry) on mobile devices.

Open Database Connectivity (ODBC) – A Microsoft standard for accessing different database systems in a Windows environment.

Personal Digital Assistant (PDA) – A small handheld computer for managing personal information. Most PDAs require the use of a stylus.

Radio Frequency Identification (RFID) – A type of electronic identification that transmits radio frequency signals to an RFID receiver. It is an alternative to bar coding.

SDK – software development kit – Programming package that contains tools that aid the programmer in developing applications in a particular language.

Session variable – A variable whose value exists for the duration of a session.

Shopping cart application – A program that allows customers to order from an online catalog or virtual store.

Style Sheet – A methods by which a text file can be used as a template for formatting of a Web page. Elements such as background color, hyperlink color, margin control, typeface, text, and placement of objects on a page can be included in a style sheet.

Splash Screen – A common initial screen that provides a welcome or graphic when the program is first executed. Splash screens can often be turned off after early use of the program.

SQL Server CE – Microsoft's relational database management system (RDBMS) for PDAs and small devices.

String Library – WMLScript Standard Library containing functions that provide support for manipulation and conversion of character strings.

Structured Query Language (SQL) – A language used by relational database to query, update, and manage data.

URL Library – WMLScript Standard Library that supports URL manipulation and verification.

URL variable – A variable whose value is passed to the subsequent Web page as part of the URL.

.wbmp – Extension of graphic files supported by WML.

WAP – Wireless Application Protocol – Stacked protocol designed for use with mobile wireless application development and for the deployment of data services.

Wideband Code Division Multiple Access (WCDMA) – A 3G technology for wideband digital radio communications of Internet, multimedia, video, and other capacity-demanding applications.

Wi-Fi – Short for wireless fidelity, Wi-Fi is a wireless network protocol that uses unregulated spectrum for establishing a network connection in a local area network environment. It refers to any type of IEEE802.11 network, including 802.11b, 802.11a, and 802.11g.

Windows CE – A version of Windows designed to run on PDAs or other small devices.

Wireless application – An application designed to function when the client device is connected to networks (e.g., the Internet) or other devices wirelessly.

Wireless Application Layer (WAE) – Highest layer in WAP where the applications are executed. Major area of interest to application developers.

Wireless Datagram Protocol (WDP) – Similar to UPD in the Internet Protocol (IP). Used for interfacing wireless networks among a variety of different carrier technologies.

Wireless Session Protocol (WSP) – Supports interchange of content between wireless device and application server in a client/server model.

Wireless Transaction Protocol (WTP) – Provides methods for transactions. Certain methods provide more reliability than others.

Wireless Transport Layer (WTL) – Responsible for isolating the upper layers of WAP from the physical network. Used to detect and correct errors. Uses the Wireless Datagram Protocol.

Wireless Transport Layer Security (WTLS) – Optional layers used to support authentication, privacy, and secure connections.

WMLBrowser Library – WMLScript Standard Library containing functions that aid in the controlling of the WML browser. Used to acquire and assign values to variables in a WML document and for returning control to a WML document.

WMLScript – Scripting language that can be used in conjunction with document written in WML.

WMLScript Standard Libraries – A set of six collections of functions that are supported by WMLScript. These libraries of routines are: Lang, Float, String, URL, WMLBrowser, and Dialogs.

About the Authors

Lei-da Chen, Ph.D. is an associate professor of information systems and technology in the College of Business Administration of Creighton University. Dr. Chen received his Ph.D. in management information systems from The University of Memphis. His research and consulting interests include electronic commerce, mobile e-commerce, Web-based systems development, data warehousing and mining, and diffusion of information technology in organizations. Dr. Chen has published more than 40 professional articles in refereed journals and national and international conference proceedings. His research has appeared in *Information & Management, ACM SIGMIS Data Base, International Journal of Mobile Commerce, Communications of AIS, Journal of Management Systems, Information Systems Management, Logistics Information Management, Information Resources Management Journal, Journal of Computer Information Systems, Electronic Markets,* and *Journal of Education for MIS.* In 2001, Dr. Chen was recognized as one of the most published e-commerce researchers by the *International Journal of Electronic Commerce.* Dr. Chen is on the review board for a number of professional journals and is listed in the Who's Who in Information Technology.

Gordon W. Skelton, Ph.D. is an associate professor of computer engineering and telecommunications in the School of Engineering, College of Science, Technology and Engineering at Jackson State University. Prior to joining Jackson State, Dr. Skelton was an adjunct professor with the University of

Mississippi's Jackson Engineering Graduate Program in computer engineering and telecommunications. Prior to accepting his current position at Jackson, Dr Skelton was employed as vice president for information services with Mississippi Valley Title Insurance Company in Jackson, MS. He received his M.S. in computer science from the University of Southern Mississippi and his Ph.D. in computer science from the University of South Africa. He has published and lectured on the subject of wireless application development and software quality. His current research interests are directed towards wireless application development, mobile computing, software quality assurance, embedded application development, and wireless sensor networks. Dr. Skelton is an IEEE Certified Software Development Professional and an ASQ Software Quality Engineer. Dr. Skelton is listed in the Who's Who in Science and Engineering.

Index

Symbols

<anchor> 46

 40
<CFELSE> 147
<CFIF> 147
<do> 53
<input> 58
<optgroup> 62
<option onpick> 60
<option> 60
<p> 40
<setvar> 56
[SQL statement] 142
1G 15
2.5G 14
3G 14

A

access control 82
advanced mobile phone systems (AMPS) 15
analog cellular networks 14
application framework 141
application level security 155
ASP .NET 194
assignment 68

B

Bluetooth 14
break and continue statements 75
business-to-business (B2B) 3
business-to-consumer (B2C) 3
business-to-employee (B2E) 3

C

card 37
cascading style sheets (CSS) 130
CDMA2000 14
cell 51
cellular digital packet data (CDPD) 14
CFAPPLICATION 173
CFCOL 151
CFCOOKIE 159
CFFORM 157
CFINPUT 157
CFLOCK 174
CFLOOP 143
CFMAIL 162
CFML 136
CFOUTPUT 142
CFPARAM 160
CFQUERY 142
CFSELECT 157
CFSET 160
CFTABLE 151

CFTRANSACTION 177
code division multiple access (cdma) 14
comments 67
condition statement 237
conditional operator 72
connection-oriented service 26
connectionless service 26
consumer-to-consumer (C2C) 3
cookie 159
cycle time 5

D

data types 66
database 138
database-driven mobile applications 270
dataset objects 193
decision-making 73
deck 37
DELETE 164
dialogs library 88
digital cellular networks 14
Dim 233
Do … Loop 239
document type definition (DTD) 37

E

e-mail 162
emulators 29
enhanced data rates for GSM evolution (EDGE) 14
eVC 229
event-driven programming language 232
events 53
ExecuteNonQuery 278
extern 67
external file specification 82

F

float library 98
flow control 66
For … Next 239
form variable 144

G

general packet radio service (GPRS) 14
global issues 18
global positioning systems (GPS) 10
global systems for mobile communications (GSM) 14
globalization of m-business 18

H

HTML 139
HTML/WML generator 140
hypertext reference 44

I

IEEE802.11a 13
IEEE802.11b 13
If … Then … Else statement 237
If statements 73
images 52
impact/value framework 4
indirect Events 54
information float 5
information transparency 9
infrared 14
input statement 59
InputBox() 233
INSERT 164
iteration 74

K

killer applications 18

L

Lang Library 91
line-of-sight infrared 14
looping 239

M

m-marketing 10
meta-information 83
microbrowser 28

Microsoft CE File System Control 3.0 248
Microsoft CE Menubar Control 3.0 263
Microsoft Jet 4.0 OLE DB Provider 201
miniaturization of mobile devices 18
mobile application 229
mobile business (m-business) 1
module-level variables 244
MsgBox() 236

N

Nokia Mobile Internet Toolkit, 4.0 22

O

ODBC 140
OleDbDataAdapter 193
OleDbDataCommand 193
OleDbDataReader objects 193
Open Mobile Alliance (OMA) 23
Openwave SDK 6.2.2 22
operator 70
Orthogonal Frequency Division Multiplexing 14

P

personal communications system (PCS) 14
pesudocode 243
Pocket PCs 5
point-of-sale (POS) 6
pragmas 82
pseudocode 282

Q

query builder 202

R

radio frequency (RF) 14
radio frequency identification (RFID) 9
return statement 81

S

sales force automation system (SAS) 137
satellites 14
server-side technology 139
service quality 6
session variables 172, 204
shopping cart 171
soft key 186
software development kits (SDKs) 37
spread spectrum technology 14
SQL 273
SQL Server CE 271
SqlCeDataReader 270
sqlCreateTable 277
sqlInsertRow 278
String Library 101
System.Data.SqlServerCe 277

T

tables 48
text editor 140
time division multiple access (TDMA) 14
timer events 54
transaction-oriented tasks 138
typeof operator 72

U

Universal Product Code (UPC) 9
UPDATE 164
URL Library 112
URL variable 144

V

value proposition 2
value-added services 8
variables 56
Visual Basic 273
Visual Studio .NET 193, 270

W

W-CDMA 14
WAP Forum Ltd. 23

WAP gateway 28
while statement 74
Wi-Fi (e.g., IEEE802.11b) 13
wireless application 136
wireless application protocol (WAP) 22, 139
wireless e-commerce 1
wireless local area networks (WLANs) 13
wireless personal area networks (WPANs) 13
wireless technology adoption 18
wireless telephony applications interface (WTAI) 189
wreless wide area networks (WWANs) 13
wmbp 52
WMLBrowser Library 112
WMLScript 65
WMLScript functions 66
World Wide Web Consortium (W3C) 119
WYSIWYG 194

X

XHTML 119
XHTML basic 120
XML 37
XML header 37